THE STORY OF AN INDIAN UPLAND

THE TRIAL OF LUCK DURING THE SOHRAE

Frontispiece
(see page 256)

THE STORY OF AN INDIAN UPLAND

BY

F. B. BRADLEY-BIRT

B. A., I. C. S.

Late Scholar of Brasenose College, Oxford, Fellow of the Royal Geographical Society Corresponding Fellow of the Geographical Society of Lisbon, Author of 'Chota Nagpore: A Little-known Province of the Empire'

With 20 Illustrations and A Map

And an Introduction
By

The Hon. H. H. Risley

C.S.I., C.I.E. I.C.S.

Home Secretary to the Government of India

GYAN

Published by

GYAN

Gyan Publishing House
5, Ansari Road
Daryaganj, New Delhi-110002
Phone: 011-47034999, 9811692060
E-mail: books@gyanbooks.com

Distribution Network
gyanbooks.com
India, USA, Canada, UK, Australia, France

ISBN : 978-81-212-4063-5 (PB)
First Published, London, 1905

2nd Impression 2020

Printed at: Gyan Press, Delhi.

The Story of An Indian Upland
Author: F. B. Bradley-Birt

THE STORY
OF
AN INDIAN UPLAND

BY

F. B. BRADLEY-BIRT

B.A., I.C.S.

LATE SCHOLAR OF BRASENOSE COLLEGE OXFORD

FELLOW OF THE ROYAL GEOGRAPHICAL SOCIETY

CORRESPONDING FELLOW OF THE GEOGRAPHICAL SOCIETY OF LISBON

AUTHOR OF 'CHOTA NAGPORE: A LITTLE-KNOWN PROVINCE OF THE EMPIRE'

WITH 20 ILLUSTRATIONS AND A MAP

AND AN INTRODUCTION

BY

THE HON. H. H. RISLEY

C.S.I., C.I.E., I.C.S.

HOME SECRETARY TO THE GOVERNMENT OF INDIA

LONDON

SMITH, ELDER, & CO., 15 WATERLOO PLACE

1905

AS A SMALL TOKEN

OF AFFECTION AND GRATITUDE

FOR MUCH KINDLY HELP AND ENCOURAGEMENT

THIS BOOK

WAS ORIGINALLY DEDICATED TO

THE LATE LORD NORTHBROOK

IT IS NOW ONLY GIVEN TO ME TO INSCRIBE IT

TO HIS MEMORY

PREFACE

These pages, written for the most part in camp among the Santals on the borders of the Santal Parganas, make no claim to give an exhaustive account of the Santals and the Paharias, and of the country they have made their own. In the attempt to present only so much concerning this little-known part of our Indian Empire as may be of interest to the general reader, to whom the Blue Book and the official report make no appeal, much that is of interest solely to the ethnologist and the specialist has been necessarily omitted. But if the following pages in some measure faithfully portray this interesting land and its peoples, as they have been and as they are to-day, they will have fulfilled their mission. The lack of interest shown by the average Englishman at home in India and Indian affairs, long proverbial, is now happily becoming a thing of the past, and the kind reception accorded to 'Chota Nagpore, a Little-known Province of the Empire,' leads me to hope that a similar interest may be evinced in 'The Story of an Indian Upland.'

To Sir William Ward my thanks are due for the photograph of the Hon. John Petty Ward, and to the Rev. Dr. Campbell of Pokhuria, who so constantly placed his great knowledge of the Santals at my disposal. I find it hard to acknowledge adequately the debt I owe to the late Sir William Hunter, my first guide into the fascinating land of Indian history and ethnology, and to the Hon. Mr. Risley, who, in spite of his heavy official duties, has so generously given me his help.

Gobindpur, Manbhum,
Chota Nagpore: *October* 29, 1904.

INTRODUCTION

We are sometimes told by the omniscient journalist that the Indian civilian of to-day has lost interest in the country and the people, and devotes his scanty leisure to counting the days till he can retire on pension. It needs only a book like this to demonstrate the futility of the charge. For the various observations recorded so pleasantly by Mr. Bradley-Birt are the common heritage of his brother officers all over India. A long series of monographs, gazetteers, district histories, settlement reports, and the like bears unmistakable testimony to the same sympathy with the people, the same spirit of research, the same capacity for appreciating the picturesque aspects of an Indian landscape, that have inspired this fascinating book. Of the value of the subject-matter of this half-forgotten literature so good a judge as Sir Henry Maine wrote many years ago in terms of the highest approval; and now that India promises to play a larger part on the stage of international politics, Mr. Bradley-Birt's most readable sketch of the history, the scenery, and the inhabitants of a single Indian district may lead the politician, or even the general reader, in England to seek for fuller knowledge of the bewildering miscellany of countries, races, religions, and languages that makes up the Indian Empire. He will find that knowledge where our foreign critics now seek it in the official writings to which I have referred.

Concerning the merits of the peculiar system of administration that was introduced into the Santal Parganas after the Rebellion of 1856, there is room for some difference of opinion. Old Santal officers have assured me with pride that 'the writ of the High Court did not run in the Parganas,' as if this negative blessing were of itself sufficient for the well-being of a patriarchal Arcadia where people did what they were told, and it would have been bad manners to appeal. One of my friends indeed went so far as to mature a scheme for the better government of India, the leading feature in which was the division of the entire country into districts of a thousand square miles (after the pattern of a Santal sub-district) each under the absolute sway of a single Englishman, who was never to be transferred and never to get an increase of pay. On idealists of this type argument was wasted; one could only take refuge in guarded allusions to Utopia and Comte's 'Politique.' On the west of the Barakar River we of Chutia Nagpur, with plenty of Santals and other wild people of our own to look after, did not think so highly of the methods of the Parganas. We settled our tribal rent questions—some of them very big ones—without any special law; and on one notable occasion, when the Santals had been inflamed to the point of overt rebellion by a miracle-working devotee, we quieted them down by a sort of Socratic dialogue tempered by whisky and cigars, while their brethren in the Parganas only a few miles away were burning bungalows and cutcherries, and generally making themselves unpleasant, and two regiments of the Indian Army were marching around to keep the peace.

It would be waste of space to pursue the comparison further. Both systems—theirs and ours—were the outcome of similar conditions. Both represented the revolt of the official conscience against the *laisser faire* style of administration which the Permanent Settlement, as originally interpreted, imposed upon Bengal. Each was brought about by a peasants' war, and each serves to demonstrate the incurable defects of a system which expects a British officer to administer a district efficiently without a field survey, without a record of the cultivators' rights, and without a village agency to keep the record up to date. Had these things existed neither the Bhumij Rebellion of 1833 nor the Santal Rebellion of 1856 would ever have taken place. The district officers would have known what was going on, and in matters of this kind knowledge is the one thing essential.

H. H. RISLEY.

CONTENTS

CHAPTER		PAGE
I.	A LAND OF LEGEND AND MYSTERY	1
II.	EARLY DAYS IN THE RAJMAHAL HILLS	23
III.	THE COMING OF THE BRITISH	50
IV.	AUGUSTUS CLEVELAND	78
V.	THE DAMAN-I-KOH	118
VI.	THE COMING OF THE SANTALS	138
VII.	THE SANTAL REBELLION	159
VIII.	THE SANTAL PARGANAS OF TO-DAY	207
IX.	THE YEARLY ROUND IN SAGARBHANGA	240
X.	LIFE IN A PAHARIA VILLAGE	287
XI.	DEOGHAR, THE HOLY CITY	311
	APPENDICES	
	I. AUGUSTUS CLEVELAND	341
	II. THE SANTAL SEPTS AND SUBSEPTS	343
	INDEX	347

ILLUSTRATIONS

THE TRIAL OF LUCK DURING THE SOHRAE . . .	*Frontispiece*
A FERRY ON THE BARAKAR RIVER	*To face p.* 12
IN THE HEART OF THE DAMAN-I-KOH	„ 40
A TYPICAL SCENE IN THE RAJMAHAL HILLS . .	„ 58
A PRIMITIVE MODE OF IRRIGATION	„ 76
PLOUGHING	„ 76
A GROUP OF PAHARIA WOMEN	„ 98
PORTRAIT OF THE HONOURABLE JOHN PETTY WARD	„ 120
THE DAMUDA: THE SACRED RIVER OF THE SANTALS	„ 132
A SANTAL YOUTH FULLY EQUIPPED FOR THE DANCE	„ 142
THE OJHA	„ 164
A GROUP OF SANTAL MANJHIS	„ 180
GOFUR KHAN, AN OLD SEPOY OF THE 41ST HINDUSTANI REGIMENT	„ 194
AN OJHA DIVINING BY MEANS OF SAL LEAVES . .	„ 222
A SAGAR	„ 244
A SACRIFICE IN THE SACRED GROVE	„ 258
A SANTAL SHOOTING	„ 274
MUSICIANS BEING REFRESHED WITH LIQUOR DURING THE PROGRESS OF A FESTIVAL . .	„ 276
THE BATHING-GHAT BY THE SIVAGUNGA AT DEOGHAR	„ 314
PRIEST ABOUT TO SACRIFICE TO MAHADEO . . .	„ 322
THE HIGH PRIEST OF DEOGHAR	„ 336
MAP OF SANTAL PARGANAS	„ 354

THE

STORY OF AN INDIAN UPLAND

CHAPTER I

A LAND OF LEGEND AND MYSTERY

It is a fascinating land of legend and mystery, this strip of country in Central Bengal now designated by the picturesque name of the Santal Parganas. Set apart from the rest of the province, with its own laws and its own peoples, its rugged range of hills, where a race of hillmen has doggedly held possession, as they believe, since time began, stands like a barrier to turn the Ganges from its course. Bordering on Chota Nagpore it has many of the physical characteristics of that picturesque land. Like an arm thrown out from the plateau of the neighbouring province, this narrow tract of hill and jungle sinks in a series of rocky tree-clad heights and soft undulating slopes till it meets the plains below or ends abruptly where the mighty river, forcing its way round the foot of the hills, has formed for it a broad but restless and capricious boundary. The Ganges, ever fickle in its course, seeking to widen yet more its three-mile breadth of bed, slowly but surely washes away the bank by which it flows.

Here Bengal, Behar, and Chota Nagpore meet. Thrust in between them like a wedge is this debatable ground, a tangled mass of hill and jungle peopled by uncouth aboriginal races, standing like the furthest outpost of barbarism to face the highest civilisation that Hindu and Musulman successively planted at its gates. Its primitiveness untouched by the stir of passing events, it has looked down with unresponsive gaze upon all that was best and highest and furthest advanced in the India of the day. It is the most interesting spot in all Bengal. Round the ruined cities that lie scattered at the foot of the hills gather memories of mighty empires long since passed away that rose and fell with typical Eastern suddenness, each bearing within itself from its foundation the seeds of incipient decay. But twenty miles, as the crow flies, from its borders stand the cities of Gaur and Pandua, magnificent even in decay and mindful of the pomp and glory that once was theirs: while but little further away lies Murshedabad, which faring better at the hands of Fate still retains a living memory of its pride of place and power in the days of the Musulman empire. Here were fought out the great issues between Hindu and Musulman, Moghul and Pathan, emperor and rebellious viceroy—issues that transferred from one allegiance to another, as by a stroke of the pen, vast territories, careless under whom they fell, since the oppressor must needs be. Scene after scene as in a panorama passed in these cities of the plains, yet upon the rugged tract that frowned upon them from across the Ganges they made not even the most fleeting of impressions. There no change of vital importance ever came. In the first century of their existence this land and its original inhabitants could scarcely have been more primitive than they are to-day.

Yet within it is a land of sharp and vivid contrasts. Five and a half thousand square miles in extent, it lies between the Vindhyan Hills and the great plain that stretches all over Northern India to the foot of the Himalayas. Midway between the two it partakes something of the nature of them both. Within its limits in striking contrast are three distinct types of country, each fashioning its own history and influencing for all time the races which have made of it their home. From the Ganges on the north for a hundred miles to the south, it is a land of hill and jungle. Save for the valley of

Barhait, there is no wide stretch of level country anywhere. On all sides rise precipitous tree-clad hills with bold irregular escarpments, huge gneiss rocks, moss-grown, piled carelessly one above another. To the south this rugged range sinks gradually to meet the plains. To the north the Ganges cuts it abruptly in full height, bringing it up sharply face to face with the ricefields of Bengal that lie in all their fertile luxuriance upon its northern bank. It is the meeting-place of the old and the new, the river circling round the foot of the hills, as if to cut them off from the progress that has marked the more accessible lands that lie beyond. Steep, rocky, and inaccessible, clothed in a dense shrub jungle, the passing of the centuries has left but little mark on the Rajmahal Hills. They stand almost as wild and untouched to-day as when the earliest of the hillmen who still people them first came in the long-forgotten past and took possession.

The second stretch of country, almost equal in extent, presents a far different aspect. Here Nature has adopted a milder mood. It is a land full of gentle undulations, a rolling country of long sweeping slopes which the cultivator has eagerly seized upon, and whereon he has found his labour well repaid. In the hollows, where the ridges dip, is abundance of rich alluvial soil retaining the moisture poured down from the heights long after the rains have ceased, and returning to the cultivator a hundredfold for all the labour he expends. But the higher ridges, sterile gravel or dry stiff clay, that rise above the fertile hollows lie still uncultivated, affording but little encouragement even to the unexacting demands of the poorest villager. Here and there rough patches of jungle survive in all their rugged primitiveness. A group of rocks, huge and ungainly, piled high on one another as Nature in volcanic mood cast them up, breaks the gentle slope of cultivated land, or a thick patch of jungle rises high above the surrounding level, covering a range of hills in miniature on whose rocky slopes nothing less hardy than the ubiquitous sal tree or a mass of shrubs has survived the struggle for existence. Close below, in sharp contrast to their barrenness, lie the smiling ricefields in the hollows, a carpet of brilliant green when the rice is young, or a waving sea of golden corn when the days draw near to harvest. It is here that the Santal within recent times has made his home, joyfully settling to the work of intake and slowly reclaiming step by step the fertile lands that had so long awaited the touch of his awakening hand.

The third stretch of country draws still nearer to the plains. This might almost be the flat alluvial rice-land of Bengal. Some six hundred and fifty square miles in extent, it runs a narrow strip along the eastern border of the Parganas for a hundred and seventy miles, the railway taking advantage of its level unbroken surface to thread its way round the impassable hill and jungle of the uplands. Here towards the south, with no natural boundary to sever them, the Santal Parganas join the neighbouring districts of Murshedabad and Birbhum, merging imperceptibly in the great unbroken plain that stretches away over Lower Bengal. To the west, in Deoghar, there is the same descent, nothing here again but a political boundary, set by the hand of man, separating it from the province of Behar, to which by Nature it belongs. But it lacks the inherent fertility of the rich alluvial strips on the eastern boundary. Swept by the westerly winds at the foot of the hills, its soil is dry and sandy, resembling in its rapid drainage the lowlands of Chota Nagpore, which it in part adjoins.

Not only has Nature made this district a land of contrast—the meeting-place of hill and plain—but the various races that have peopled it have still further accentuated its diversity of character. Here the influence of geographical conditions on the history of a district is vividly presented. Nature seems to have fashioned this land as the meeting-place of all the races, furnishing to each in its time of need the succour and resources that it most required. In this small strip of country many antagonistic peoples differing from one another in origin, thought, and speech, have found the home best suited to their capabilities and to their mode of life. Upon each race, as it has made a portion of the soil its own, the physical characteristics of the land have exercised their subtle influence, whether the newcomer has toiled and ploughed and planted or rested content with what Nature in her luxuriance has provided.

Among the first in the land of whom record remains were the Paharias, of Dravidian stock, the wildest and most backward of all the aboriginal tribes in Bengal. Whence they came and what events led to their coming no man knows. Buried in the long-forgotten past their early doings can only be surmised. In all probability they were in the advance guard of the great race movement that finally found its home in the neighbouring uplands, and urged onward by the stronger and more energetic tribes that followed in their rear they found themselves at last in the Rajmahal Hills—to them a veritable *cul-de-sac* shut in by the Ganges and the plains beyond, which were already peopled by a civilised and hostile race. Here they were at bay. Advance or retreat was impossible. But, fortunately for them, these hills provided all that they desired for their subsistence, and here they made their home. Nature seemed to have adapted herself to all their needs. Drawing them into her mountain fastnesses, well-nigh inaccessible and impregnable against attack, she furnished them a safe retreat against their foes. They found the jungles on the slopes of the hills well stocked with game and herbs and fruits—all that their simple habits led them to demand of life. If need came they could sweep down upon the peaceful homesteads of the plains and carry off the harvests that a more industrious people had sown and reaped. The very position and luxuriance of the Rajmahal Hills encouraged them in idleness and depredations. There was little need for labour where Nature supplied so much, while no better home for banditti could well have been designed than the rocky heights that overlooked the plains, yet defied the lowlander by their strength and inaccessibility. In the Rajmahal Hills the original stock of the Paharias has ever since held possession, exclusive and jealous of all outside interference, clinging to their rocky homes with all the passionate devotion of a hill people. Successfully they have resisted every effort to dislodge them, forcing special terms even from the all-conquering British Raj, and to-day they still survive among their ancestral hills, tamed indeed to an unwonted law and order, but in possession still.

In the 'Skirts of the Hills' dwell the Santals. Here, again, Nature seems to have stepped in to provide for a people in need a home and the means of subsistence best suited to the manner of men they were. At the foot of the hills had lain, undisturbed for centuries, a fertile land waiting only the touch of the plough to yield a grateful and abundant return. Augustus Cleveland in the latter part of the eighteenth century, intent on his measures to turn the wild Paharias into contented and law-abiding subjects of the British Raj, had offered them, rent free, this unappropriated land, hoping to draw them from their lawless life among the hills and induce them to learn the arts of civilisation and peace. But submitting to many of his directions, as they had done, owing to the confidence he had inspired, they nevertheless on this point made a firm stand. Always suspicious of men of another race, they utterly refused to descend and mingle with them on the lowland slopes. Even when government drew a ring of pillars round the 'Skirts of the Hills' three hundred miles in circumference, declaring that no foreigner, as zemindar, should ever pass within to trouble them, they still demurred. Their deep attachment to the hills that had so long provided them a safe retreat held them back, and to a people who knew little of the arts of cultivation the fertile lands spread out before them offered no temptation. Nature had already furnished them with the most fitting home that she could devise, and they refused to leave it at man's bidding. So the great stone pillars continued to look upon a deserted land, and for a time it seemed that they had been built in vain. But it was only for a time. The wisdom of Nature in withholding the Paharias was soon made manifest. There was another race, stronger and more vigorous, with a passion for cultivation, which, rapidly multiplying and urged on like the Paharias by the great race movements in its rear, was urgently in need of a home in the general settling down of conditions under British rule. It seemed as if Nature had reserved this land from all time for the Santals in their hour of need, and no race could have been more fit and worthy so great an inheritance. Repeatedly driven out of the lands they had made their own by the oppression of Hindu and Musulman, zemindar and moneylender, they hailed the Daman-i-koh as a veritable Promised Land, where the oppressor might not come. The untouched, unbroken nature of the soil appealed to them with special force. Deep down in the very fibre of their being lay a passionate devotion to the land. The joy of intake, the enthusiasm of reclaiming the jungle, the strenuous labour of turning the virgin soil, and the joy of harvest—these have been theirs from the beginning. Once admitted within the pillars that marked the Daman-i-koh, they rapidly overran the land, transforming it from a mass of tangled jungle into a smiling stretch of fertile fields and prosperous homesteads. The grateful soil awoke at last beneath the touch of the hand for which it had so long waited, and the Santal had found at last the home which he had travelled so far and suffered so many vicissitudes to gain.

It is on the outskirts of this upland district, where it merges with the plains, that the diverse character of its inhabitants is nearest to seek. Here dwell the Katauri, a branch of the original Paharia stock, who, scorning their aboriginal descent, have long since embraced Hinduism and sought inclusion within its ranks. Centuries of contact with a higher civilisation than their own account for the numerous other semi-Hinduised tribes in these outlying portions of the Santal Parganas. Without the advantages of the Santals and Paharias, who have secured a land of their own apart, they have been forced into close connection with the Hindus, a far more intelligent and highly civilised race. Looked down upon by them with the utmost contempt, placed even below their lowest and most menial castes, they have sought inclusion in the Hindu system as their only hope of emancipation from their degraded position. Though never formally acknowledged, some have won their way to wealth and influence. The Bhuiyas, a great Dravidian tribe, have long since counted themselves Hindus, and number among them many important rajas, chiefs, and zemindars, who, regardless of their nigritic features, proudly classify themselves as Rajputs, claiming solar descent. They are a typical product of the land they occupy, the meeting-place of the races, aboriginal and Hindu, the weaker giving way before the stronger, imitating its customs and religion and seeking inclusion within its ranks. Merging in Bengal, Chota Nagpore, and Behar to the east, the south, and the west, these semi-Hinduised tribes form, as it were, a ring fence round three sides of the Santal Parganas, hemming in the aborigines, with whom they scorn connection, and upon whom the mighty force of Hinduism has even now made but little mark.

Mingling in this outer circle and congregating in the larger towns is an increasing contingent of Hindus of pure stock and a remnant of Musulmans —all that is left of the once all-conquering race near the site of their former triumphs. Round Deoghar, the sacred city, where conditions closely approximate to Behar, which it adjoins, most of the Hindu section are to be found, while the Musulmans still

A FERRY ON THE BARAKAR RIVER, WHICH SEPARATES THE SANTAL PARGANAS FROM CHOTA NAGPORE

linger on the banks of the Ganges in the neighbourhood of their once imperial city of Rajmahal.

Before the coming of the British all that concerned this heterogeneous district is shrouded in legend and myth. The Musulman chroniclers are far too busy with court intrigues and palace revolutions to have much space to spare for the subject peoples at their gates, while the Hindu records that survive concern themselves chiefly with the pedigrees of local potentates and a bare record of great events that happened in their day. For the most part tradition is the only guide, and tradition handed down orally among an ignorant and illiterate people can scarce have come whole and unpolluted through countless generations. Tradition in the East is own sister to Rumour, who was ever a lying jade, yet she is often all that offers to guide inquiry into the past, and must needs be taken on trust, checked and tempered always in the fierce light of the few historical facts that remain. For centuries this land and the contending races who had made of it their battlefield had gone without a written history, with scarce a record even in the annals of their conquerors, to show what manner of things had befallen them, and what they had accomplished during all the years of turmoil and unrest. Then suddenly in the sixth decade of the eighteenth century the darkness that surrounds them lifts. There came a race of men, methodical, given to much writing of many reports, with a passion for probing beneath the surface of things, and eager to gather information on every point that concerned the people and the district. The light of investigation and inquiry was turned in full force upon the jumble of legend and myth, mystery and tradition, that none had attempted to disentangle hitherto. From the first moment of his coming the British official busied himself with voluminous piles of correspondence, records, and reports, throwing light upon the dark pages of Indian history, upon the manners and customs of the people, their institutions and beliefs, and revealing unconsciously here and there by a graphic touch or an ingenuous phrase what manner of man he himself was.

It is a fascinating pursuit to probe among these records of the past in many a dim and dusty record-room with shelves piled ceiling-high, only too often in careless disorder and disarray. Year after year they have lain, undisturbed, awaiting the touch that should rouse their slumbering memories and for a brief space win them back to life. Worm-eaten, yellow with age, and fast falling into decay, their very touch awakes in one on whom the glamour of research into the past has fallen the knowledge of much treasure within that they alone can yield, and, as one reverently turns the crumbling pages and scans the fading ink, pictures of the long-forgotten past arise instinct with life, breathing the passions of strong men, the trivial jealousies of a passing day, or the deep pathos of a suffering and afflicted people. The words written in the heat of passion—often the words of a great man, yet so many and so contentious over so trivial a matter—here live side by side with the weighty and well-considered administration report, the sympathetic and touching account of a famine-stricken people, or the record of a case revealing at once the ignorance, the superstition, the ingrained lawlessness, and yet the very humanity of some backward native race.

The first pioneers of British rule were men of whom the Empire may well be proud. These records reveal them strong, quick to grapple with sudden and unforeseen events, fair and impartial in the administration of justice, and combining in themselves the multifarious offices of judge, soldier, lawgiver, and collector of the revenue. They were many-sided men who responded ably to the call to evolve order out of chaos, and to inspire a people who had hitherto known no restraint, save such as their own crude tribal customs and primitive institutions had taught them, with a respect for the first principles of law and justice. Here the records reveal them, fighting with strenuous mental and physical exertion the deadly ravages of plague and famine; personally moving among the people to relieve their suffering and distress: busy settling the tenure of the land—that most fruitful source of Indian trouble—carefully inquiring into custom and tradition that no injustice might be done, or again moving through the district bringing to justice the evil-doer and spreading peace and order through the land. In those early days, when all was new and the links in the chain of the complicated system of British government had not yet been completely forged, immense power of necessity remained in the hands of the local authority, and the personality of the man was given full scope. The need of the strong man was great, and it was well that England could produce such men as Augustus Cleveland to represent her in this out-of-the-way corner of the world, to inaugurate the reign of law and order, and to initiate a wild and backward people into the arts of civilisation and peace.

If the records did not sometimes disclose more ignoble and less lofty sentiments and ambitions, they would be no true records of human life and character. One can smile in the calm light of a hundred years later at the petty jealousies and official bickerings that loomed so large in their day and found an outlet in so many folios of correspondence. Wedged in between matters of graver import are pages of dispute between the civilian Collector of Bhagalpur and the Colonel in command of the neighbouring military station at Monghyr. Their powers, ill defined and often overlapping, were a source of constant friction. The Colonel writes that all within certain limits is under his sole jurisdiction. The Collector with veiled threats forcibly protests. The Colonel sets up a market within his limits compelling all who pass down the Ganges to land their merchandise there, thus preventing them from reaching Bhagalpur, whose market consequently suffers. The Collector sarcastically congratulates him on the successful character of his military undertaking against the peaceful traders, ending again with dark hints of vengeance and stigmatising his enemy as little better than a brigand stopping and disorganising the trade and commerce of the Ganges. The Colonel replies that he has every bit as much right to trade as a civilian, and threatens darkly in return that if he is transferred from his station through the Collector's agency the Collector shall not long remain at Bhagalpur. So the dispute drags on, to be succeeded by others no less spiteful and undignified even down to our own day. Yet one cannot but gratefully acknowledge that the later the date of the dispute the less acrimonious is the correspondence and the greater the self-restraint exhibited. Extensive powers and a consequent undue sense of their own importance doubtless increased the impatience of opposition and gave play to the natural freedom of language of the first officials. They were men upon whom lay great responsibilities, and who lived at high pressure, with none of the latter-day inventions to make life bearable in the worst of climates. Their little pedantries, their jealousies, their official bickerings, may well be looked on with a tolerant eye or gratefully forgotten in the memories of the great and strenuous part they played in the building of the Empire.

This brief glance at the district and the many races who each in its own way have helped to make it what it is to-day may well lead one to a question of the future. Great movements have been at work in the centuries that have passed shaping and moulding the destinies of this land and people. Many of these forces have worked out their destiny and are at rest. Others still move on to their appointed end, some openly that all men may see, others hidden deep down in the heart of a strange and mystic people who between the stranger and their own intimate thoughts have ever drawn the veil of secrecy. The great race movements on the old tribal scale have perforce ceased. The land has been long since settled. Each race, from choice or necessity, has fixed its home where it now holds possession, and none but extraordinary forces, as yet unforeseen, are likely to disturb the present distribution of the many races that now lie broadcast over the Santal Parganas. For the Paharias and even for the Santals it is difficult to conceive a future dissociated from the past. As it was in the beginning, and still is, it is impossible to believe that it will not always be until the end. The Paharias to-day cling as faithfully to their secluded hills as they have done through all the centuries that have gone by. They are as violently opposed to outside interference and as suspicious of all beyond their ken now as they have ever been; and if a future remains for them, differing in the smallest degree from their past, it is far to seek. But that they will ever be ousted from the hills they have so long held, who shall say? The words of a great Welsh prince, spoken with a sublime aspiration for his own wild hill country and his own nationality of Wales, may not unfittingly be uttered of the Rajmahal Hills and the people who have clung to them with such passionate devotion. 'Nor deem I,' their chronicler may say with confidence, 'that other race or other tongue will answer for this corner of the world before the Judge of all at the last day than this people and this tongue of the Paharias.'

Among the Santals there is greater possibility of change. A strong tendency to embrace Hinduism, with all its customs and beliefs and its rigid caste system, has been evident among almost all the aboriginal tribes who have come into close and constant contact with the higher civilisation. Looked upon with scorn and contempt, they have seen that their only chance of emancipation lay in inclusion within the fold of Hinduism itself. Even among the Santals, one of the most exclusive of all the aboriginal tribes, the influence of Hinduism can be observed in their adoption of Hindu festivals and customs, though they still regard the Brahmin and his faith with all their old animosity. But a crowd of smaller tribes, such as the Bhuiya, the Bagdi, and the Chamar, have long since disclaimed their aboriginal origin and made every effort to obtain recognition as Hindu castes. Among these, Christianity has made no progress. It is only among those who have not yet come under the spell of Hinduism, among the Santals and Paharias, that missionary efforts have met with success. But hopeful as the progress of Christianity is even among them, it has exercised as yet no influence beyond a certain radius from the mission stations, and it is even now of too recent a growth in their midst to influence whole races, as Hinduism has done, and is still doing, to embrace its tenets and beliefs. Everything to-day points to Hinduism—even the Hinduism that has lost its first faith and is fighting its own battle of doubt and scepticism—as the absorbing force of the future among the aborigines of Bengal.

In the direction of increased material prosperity there is as little prospect of advance. An agricultural people with the fewest possible wants, they are content with the produce of their fields, having no thought beyond the primitive manner of life that they have always known. For industry and commerce, trade and manufacture, they have the smallest aptitude; and though Sahebgunj, in the north, on the Ganges, is a busy mart, it is not from the Santal Parganas that it draws the bulk of its merchandise. With no higher standard of existence before them towards which to attain, they are blissfully content with conditions as they are, living with careless lightheartedness from hand to mouth and utterly unmindful of the days to come. All the passion of their nature seems to have expended itself in devotion to the soil, and with that they are satisfied. They ask only that they may be left in undisturbed possession, and that their ancient rights and customs may be respected and their rents not unduly enhanced. Beyond this they are content. No restless ambition inspires them with the hope of better things, and the yearly round of festival and labour is sufficient to supply their limited intelligence with all the food for thought which it is capable of assimilating. The future promises them no change from the manner of life that has passed changeless through the centuries, and were it possible for their nature to take so much as a single thought for the morrow, that is the one and only promise that they themselves would ask of it.

CHAPTER II

EARLY DAYS IN THE RAJMAHAL HILLS

ROUND the beginning of things in this land of hill and jungle hangs a veil of impenetrable mystery. To a people ignorant of written records, and with no calendar save the moon and the changing seasons, time is vague and memory fails of all except the oral traditions of their race faithfully handed down from generation to generation, but varying of necessity from frequent repetition through long periods of time. Fragments of their history only remain buried in the records of more civilised races with whom they have come in contact. To piece together these fragments with the help of legend and tradition, and to bridge the long gaps where all is silent, is the most that modern inquiry can hope to do, striving always to raise probability to the region of historical certainty and fact.

Back to the days of the ancient Greek geographers, across forgotten centuries, must one go for the first known mention of this land and people. On the outskirts of the country rises the great hill

Mandar, once used by the gods—so runs the native legend—as the Churn of the Ocean, when as yet there was no dry land save this solitary hill whereon they reigned. To the foot of the hill came the far-travelled Greeks, and of Mount Maleus, as they named it, they have left the earliest record. But upon men who had seen the wonders of the East this rude rough mass of earth thrown up out of the plains would have made little impression save for one miraculous attribute ascribed to it by local legend. For half the year, they repeat the fable, it cast its shadow to the north, for the other half to the south, and a phenomenon so portentous made Mount Maleus worthy of a place in their annals. The Malli and Sauri, wild aboriginal tribes, they add, lived at its feet, east of the Prasii of Patna, and hemmed in by the mighty Ganges, where it abruptly turns its course from east to south. And to-day the Malli still retain possession untouched by the vicissitudes that have overwhelmed the neighbouring provinces in the centuries that have elapsed since the Greek geographers made this first brief record of their existence. The miraculous shadow of Mount Maleus has long since ceased to fall in the light of modern days, but the Mals still live and worship at its feet.

Thus the Mals or the Sauri—known by the

general name of Paharias to-day—an aboriginal race of Dravidian stock—were the first of whom any knowledge survives to people this district of such strangely united component parts. But whence they came or what course of events led them to make their home in the Rajmahal Hills even tradition fails to relate. With many of the aboriginal races, by carefully combining legend and history, it is possible to gauge, with probability of correctness, something of these earlier days. But with the Paharias the question of whence they come is one of peculiar difficulty. Unlike the majority of Kolarian and Dravidian tribes, they have preserved no vague traditions of their earlier wanderings, and such legends as they have throw no light on any time more distant than their sojourn in the Rajmahal Hills. Content to accept their present condition and their present home, their passionate attachment to the hilly tract of country they have made their own leads them to believe that it was here the race first sprang into being.

The gods created seven brothers—so runs the legend of their genesis—and sent them down from heaven to the Rajmahal Hills, thence to people the earth. The Paharias' outlook on life is limited, and their imagination runs to little beyond the common daily round varied by much conviviality and feasting. Consequently the first act that they ascribe to the seven brothers after the gods had breathed into them the breath of life is typically characteristic of the race. They prepared a great feast. Of every available thing in the jungle that it was good for man to eat they prepared it, for it was decreed that each brother in his turn should make choice therefrom of the thing that pleased him best. While as yet the feast was being made ready they arranged their plans. Each brother, beginning with the eldest, having made his choice, should straightway set out to seek for himself a new home apart in the land that he might find most suited to his needs. But when the time came and the feast was spread the eldest brother had fallen sick. So to the second brother fell the privilege of first choice. Hesitating in the face of so vast a spread from which he could take but one thing, he finally decided in favour of the vegetables because of their variety. These being better cultivated in the plains, he left his native hills and setting out went into a far country. From him is descended the Hindu race. The third brother loved meat, and took flesh of all kinds except pork and that of wild animals. He went still further afield, and reaching the great north-west became the ancestor of the Musulmans. The fourth brother also took flesh, and from him sprang the Kharwars. The fifth brother took the hog's flesh that the others had despised, and the Kiratis are his descendants. The sixth brother took rice and the flesh of wild animals, and he became the ancestor of the great and widespread Kolarian race. The youngest brother took food of all kinds from that which remained of the feast, and being of a roving disposition he travelled far and was heard of no more. But when the English came from a far-off land it was at once concluded that they who had no caste prejudices in the matter of food must be the descendants of this one of the seven brothers who had taken food of all kinds, and had for so long a time disappeared from sight. Consequently the Paharias received the English in no unfriendly spirit, assigning them a place within their own family.

It is from the eldest of the seven brothers that the Paharias trace their descent. He having fallen sick during the preparation of the feast had been unable to come forward to claim his share. His brothers, taking pity on his helplessness, as they passed away from the feast gave him each a portion of the viands they had chosen. So he ate food of all kinds, clean and unclean, and became an outcast, and being unable, on account of his sickness, to travel far made his permanent home on his native hills. Living there dependent for their subsistence on the fruits and herbs and beasts of the jungle, his descendants became wild hillmen, freebooters, and dacoits, sweeping down when need pressed on the peaceful inhabitants of the plains at their feet to carry off their flocks and herds and the produce of their carefully nurtured fields. Then, forgetful of the centuries that have intervened, the Paharias bring the legend to an abrupt conclusion. There came at last, they say, a Saheb whose name they still remember and revere—' Chilmili '—whose wise enlightened rule and broad sympathy first taught them to become the peaceable citizens of the great White Raj that they remain to-day.

Such is all the legend that the Paharias tell of the early days of their race—a legend with obvious additions of a recent date. But its value lies in the indication it gives of the various peoples with whom at different times they have evidently come in contact. From their mention of Hindus, Musulmans, Kharwars, Kiratis, and Kols in the legend it is clear that these are the tribes best known to them, though it is a singular fact that none of them can in any way be regarded as closely connected with their own race. Strangely enough, on the other hand, the Oraons, who form numerically the strongest Dravidian tribe in Bengal, and are undoubtedly their cognates, find no place in the vague Paharia legend of the distribution of the race. The Paharias, in fact, have little or no knowledge of the Oraons and claim no kinship with them. But, singular as this ignorance of their cognates is, it is not without a parallel among other aboriginal tribes of the neighbouring districts. When once a race has split into two distinct parts, cut off from each other by geographical or other distinctions, there is a remarkable tendency for each to disclaim all connection with the other, or even, as among the Kherrias of Ranchi and Manbhum, to regard each other with bitter hostility and contempt. The reason is often natural and not far to seek. One division of the race, thrown by its geographical position into closer contact with a higher civilisation than its own, gradually adopts its customs and beliefs, seeking a place in its caste system, and ignoring its own aboriginal origin. As a consequence this advanced guard soon disclaims all connection with the more conservative members of its tribe, these latter in their turn pouring equal contempt upon their brethren who have swerved from the ancient faiths. This same division is seen among the Paharias themselves, both the Sauria Maler and the Mal Paharia disclaiming all connection with each other, in spite of the very obvious traits that mark them unmistakably as kindred of one race. But between the Paharias and the Oraons there appears to be no reason for such disclaimer of kinship, while of the kinship itself there can be no doubt. Isolated geographically as the Paharias now are, a comparison of their language, physical characteristics, manners, and customs leaves no doubt that they and the Oraons are closely related. In fact the latter, whose traditions are far more definite and ambitious, fully admit the connection, and account for the separation of the Paharias from the parent stock and their establishment in the Rajmahal Hills. In the days of their prosperity, say the Oraons, they lived in Rohtas and its neighbouring hills, free and untroubled from without. But here in later times they found themselves in the line of march of the vast onrush of the all-conquering Musulman armies, and undisciplined and half-armed they were swept before them like chaff before the wind. The years in Rohtas had been years of plenty, and the race had increased there and multiplied exceedingly. Migration on the old lines in one vast family with their flocks and their herds and all that they possessed was no longer possible. So in the flight from Rohtas the tribe split into two divisions. Their chief himself, at the head of one party, turned towards the north, and finally settled in the Rajmahal Hills; while the other division, under the younger brother of the chief—and this must have been by far the larger party of the two—wandered off towards the south-east, and, pushing its way along the valley of the Son, entered Palamau, finally moving on by the Koel River until it reached the central tableland of Chota Nagpore, which is the home of the Oraons to-day. Some such division doubtless accounts for the presence of the Paharias in the Rajmahal Hills. But beyond these vague traditions and surmises their earliest history is buried in the long-forgotten past, and being a primitive people, leaving little trace to mark their resting-places, the path they trod towards their present home has been long since obliterated in the rush of hurrying feet of greater and more civilised races who have followed in their wake.

The same veil of mystery that hangs over their first coming to the land hides also all that concerned them down to comparatively recent times. Scarce a glimpse is to be obtained of them save in the annals of the Moghul conquerors, whose armies, continually moving up and down between Bengal and the great headquarter cities of the north-west, must needs pass them by. The hills that the Paharias had made their own stood right in the line of march. The great rivers in those days were almost the only highways of communication. Such roads as there were—and they were few until the Musulman produced his triumphs of engineering skill—followed of necessity the great watercourses of the plains. For more than half the year the land was dry and tanks and wells were few. A never-failing supply of water—that greatest of the eastern traveller's needs—was only to be had from the rivers, and all who went on foot must perforce keep them well in view. It was thus that the Ganges, flowing through the heart of Northern India, drew to itself all the life and movement of the day. This way came a stream of constant traffic: the trader, hurrying on with his costly bales of merchandise to find a ready market in the princely cities of Musulman or Hindu: the moneylender, eager to pursue his trade among the simple people who dwelt on the outskirts of the empire, an easy prey to his superior craft and cunning: the pilgrim and never-absent mendicant, wandering on with fervid enthusiasm or urged by ambition and the lust of place and power to the holy cities of their creed: the adventurer, descending on the rich rice plains of Bengal, where might was right and the greatest fortune awaited the least scrupulous: or the great armies of the north, following close on each other's heels as empires rose and fell and the need for their services never wavered. All these passed along the one great highway of Upper India, making the Ganges throughout its course a busy scene of continual life and enterprise.

Right in the direct line of this stream of traffic stood the home of the Mals, an isolated stretch of tangled hill and jungle offering an impenetrable barrier to all who would pass that way. Even the mighty river, sweeping on with all its strength, must needs turn aside from its course towards the sea. Keeping perforce straight on due east, it is not till the hills are passed that it can pursue again the even tenor of its way. Skirting the foot of the hills it suddenly turns well-nigh due south, forming a perfect natural boundary between them and the plains. Like the river, all those who journeyed that way must needs go by the foot of the hills ; and so it came to pass that the Paharias, the most uncivilised of all the aboriginal tribes, looked down from their rocky barrier on the chief highway of civilisation in Northern India.

To a wild race of hillmen, freebooters by instinct and profession, the Rajmahal Hills seemed designed by Nature herself for their habitation. Ensconced in their haunts far up beyond almost inaccessible jungle, they were safe from pursuit ; and confident in their unapproachable retreat they looked upon the stream of passers-by along the Ganges as their legitimate prey. A group of traders on their way from the north to the new fields of promised harvest in Bengal; a company of moneylenders pressing forward to the same goal, many travelling together for protection, but still a feeble body for resistance; or an army with its vast horde of followers encamped by night upon the river's bank—all these the Paharias watched unseen from the rocky slopes of the hills, waiting only for the moment to sweep down and take them unawares. For the hillmen these were the days of plenty. Riches lay at their feet for the taking, in greater abundance even than they could desire, and commit what crimes they might upon the passer-by, there was none to call them to account. The trader and the traveller, knowing by rumour and experience the savagery of this wild tribe, thankfully escaped with their lives in their hands, while the armies that were continually hurrying by were too intent upon the object of their march to turn aside for profitless retaliation, even had not the density of the jungle from which the banditti came warned them that punishment and subjugation would be no easy task.

Yet upon the Paharias this constant contact with a higher civilisation than their own produced no visible effect. Though from their high vantage-ground they saw the passing of all that India could boast in the way of trade and commerce, it inspired them with no answering spirit of emulation. Their rugged hills and dense jungle were unproductive of aught that they could sell or barter with the passing traders, and the rich plunder that they carried home of all the best that the artificers of the day could produce failed to awake their imagination or lead them to demand a higher standard of domestic life. Eager only to rob and plunder the passer-by and the dweller in the plains, the Paharias desired no further intercourse with the 'foreigner.' Ignorant and superstitious, they shrank from all personal contact with men of another race, content with the rough conditions of life in their isolated fastnesses and jealous of the freedom from restraint and the perfect independence that was theirs.

It was thus that wave after wave of conquest swept by and left them alone untouched. Close at their feet, not twenty miles away across the Ganges, rose the splendid city of Gaur, for long the capital of the Hindu kings of Bengal. Magnificently built, its ruins still remain, humbled by decay but evidence sufficient to show with what pride it must once have raised its head. Yet of the men who fashioned and devised it little memory else survives. Only the ruined temples and palaces tell of the former greatness of their power and civilisation, and of the sway they once held over the surrounding plains. But though this strip of country that the Paharias had made their home lay so near across the Ganges, it offered few attractions to the Hindu kings. Forest-clad, uncultivated, and inaccessible, they were content to leave it in the undisturbed possession of the hillmen, and not all the depredations of the latter were sufficient to rouse them to undertake its subjugation. Yet to the very foot of the hills the Hindu empire reached, hemming them in to the north and east and west, the great cities of Gaur and Deoghar standing like the advance watchguards of civilisation against this last retreat of barbarism. It seemed only a question of time before the Mals either by invasion or the arts of peace must be absorbed within this higher civilisation than their own. But the decree of Fate was otherwise. Above and beyond the great empire at their feet the wild hillmen preserved their independence, undisturbed by its strife, its splendour, or its power, destined as they were to see its greatness crumble in the dust before their eyes.

From the first, to those who had eyes to see, the Hindu kingdom showed within itself the signs of incipient decay. Based upon pride, greed, and the lust of power, it relied not upon loyalty but upon violence and force. Selfishness and corruption, unrelieved by one spark of patriotism, sapped its strength like the subtle advance of some insidious disease. Already in 1203 the first Moghul armies, advancing from the north, swept all before them. Passing through the Teliagharia Pass they halted within sight of Gaur. The far-famed Hindu capital, fallen from its high estate, was ill equipped to meet the storm. Lakshman Sen, king of Bengal, had reached the patriarchal age of four-score years, and physical infirmity had long since weakened his grasp of power and let loose the ever-ready spirit of intrigue. Barely escaping with his life before the victorious Musulman armies, he resigned his crown without a struggle, ending his days in peace—so tradition records—among the priests of the Temple of Jagannath at Puri by the sea. All Bengal lay at the feet of the Musulmans, and, choosing the vanquished city of Gaur, on account of its central position, they made it the capital of their new dominions. Thus a second empire built up its power in the plains that lay at the foot of the Rajmahal Hills. Once again the wild hill race that peopled them were brought face to face with an outpost of a greater organisation and a higher civilisation than India had yet known.

It was a wonderful drama that was played out at their very gates. With marvellous rapidity the conquered Hindu capital was transformed into a Musulman city. Mosques and palaces, designed with all the skill and cunning the most experienced architects of the Moghul Empire could devise, grew up on the ruins of the decaying city, enveloping and obliterating the traces of its Hindu origin. Life and activity once more reigned in its busy streets, and the countless domes and minarets and the constant call to prayer, ringing far out across the plain, bore witness to the enthusiasm of its builders' faith. So for a hundred years the city in its new garb grew and prospered.

Then, the first brief glamour of its youth gone by, the second act in the drama opened. Fakiruddin, the Musulman viceroy, favoured by the troubles that had grown thick round the central authority, threw off the yoke of the empire and founded for himself an independent kingdom in Bengal—a kingdom destined to defy the empire for over two hundred years. Eager to break with all imperial traditions, he deserted Gaur, carrying the seat of government across the Mahananda. Once again Gaur suffered eclipse, its departed glory transferred to the new capital at Pandua that rose almost within its sight. Thus sprang into being an independent Musulman kingdom, with its seat of government at the very foot of the Rajmahal Hills. It was the greatest menace that had yet threatened the independence of the hillmen. Here was no longer an outlying province awaiting its orders from a far-off power, but a free and separate kingdom, acknowledging no authority but its own. And almost at the heart of this new kingdom, freebooters and disturbers of the peace, lived the Paharias. This time escape from the hand of the conqueror seemed wellnigh impossible. Yet, even as the Hindu kingdom had passed away, the Musulman was destined to follow in its wake and leave this wild hill tribe, whom Fate seemed to have exerted herself to preserve, in undisturbed possession of their hills.

For more than two hundred years the successors of Fakiruddin maintained their independent rule. During all that time the highlanders proved a constant source of trouble, sweeping down upon the dwellers of the plains and carrying off their flocks and herds and harvests. Yet even in the first days of its strength the central power had other ambitions than the subjugation of a petty band of freebooters, forage, rob, and murder as they might. It was no task at which to set the turbulent Musulman soldiery. The Rajmahal Hills promised little hope of booty—only the certainty of an arduous campaign—and thus two hundred years of Musulman supremacy passed and left them even as they were.

Then came the third and final act in the drama. Gaur, deserted through the whim of a king, had been once more restored to its former place as the

Musulman capital. Throughout its history it had met with extraordinary vicissitudes even for an eastern city. For centuries it had suffered grievous things at the hands of its conquerors, its rulers, and the discontented soldiery, but the end was at hand. Towards the middle of the sixteenth century it became evident that the days of independent Musulman rule were numbered. The conquering race, concerned only with the doings of kings and courts and busy with intrigues and palace revolutions, paid but little heed to the vast undercurrents that were slowly but surely sapping its strength. Its dominion, based solely on the right of conquest and the power of the sword, awoke no loyalty in the subject people. It was the rule of the few, strong in their superior wealth and civilisation, imposed upon the many, weak by reason of their lack of cohesion and political organisation. But upon the vast dominions under their control they exercised the smallest permanent influence. Palace revolutions succeeded one another with startling rapidity almost unknown to the mass of the people. The oppressor must needs be, and the exchange of one for another was but a difference of degree. Yet beneath the politics of courts great forces were at work. An undercurrent of life and movement among the people at large, unaffected by the doings of courts, was slowly but surely changing the face of

IN THE HEART OF THE DAMAN-I-KOH

Bengal and presenting many a problem that it was left to a greater than the Musulman empire to solve. It was a time of great unrest, of wholesale immigration and local incursion of race upon race, great movements destined in the gradual settlement of succeeding centuries to mark the face of the land for all time. The Santals, the advance guard of the Kolarians, a huge wandering tribe, had reached beyond the southern limits of the empire to the borders of the land which now bears their name. Still eager to press forward on the march, they proved a thorn in the side of every race with whom they came in contact, robbing and plundering, when need arose, with all the impartiality of the Paharias themselves. Almost side by side with them, the Bhuiyas, of Dravidian stock, pushing up likewise from the south, were founding their petty sovereignties of Lachmipur and Passi, driving back even the Paharias from South Deoghar, and settling there as Ghatwals, while others of their race spread out on either side through Birbhum and Kharakpur. Behind these, again, still further to the south, lay the multitude of aboriginal tribes which had found the homes of their desire in the tableland of Chota Nagpore. Great race movements such as these were subtly at work during the last days of independent Musulman rule, changing the face of the land and pressing ominously on the outskirts of the empire. Beset from without, the Musulman dominion was torn by internal strife, and the court at Gaur had little leisure to deal with problems that still as yet only loomed afar off in the more distant portions of its great possessions.

Moreover, as the successors of Fakiruddin were losing their grasp on Bengal, the imperial house at Delhi was rapidly gaining strength. A new spirit had breathed the breath of life into the long-decayed empire, and in the mind of Akbar the Great the dream of a mighty imperial Musulman dominion had sprung to life. Rapidly, with characteristic eastern suddenness, the new power rose, its conquering armies carrying all before them to the furthest limits of Hindustan. Once more destruction threatened the proud city of Gaur. It was in the days of Daud Khan, the last Afghan ruler in Bengal, that the end came. Akbar's general, Man-im-Khan, led the invading forces from the north, and Daud Khan's reliance on two hundred years of freedom from imperial interference was rudely shaken as he saw his capital quickly fall into the enemy's hands.

But the end of the fated city came not by the hand of man. War, oppression, and treachery—these things Gaur had time and again survived; it was reserved for the mysterious plague and pestilence, that the hand of man could not stay, to lay the proud city at last even with the dust. The days of Gaur's prosperity had already waned, and it was not the same city—the terrestrial paradise—that it once had been in the heyday of its strength. Even now it was falling once more into decay, and the Ganges, fickle and unstable, had ceased to flow beneath its walls, as if deserting it before the end came. Low-lying marsh lands now separated it from the river that had once lapped the steps of its mosques and palaces, and already the pestilence that was so soon to accomplish its final ruin had begun its deadly work. Yet, decayed from its former splendour as the city was, its central position in Bengal appealed to the conqueror Man-im-Khan, and in spite of its growing unhealthiness he determined to retain it as his capital. But the fate of Gaur was sealed.

It was a dramatic ending to the greatness of the city that had weathered so many vicissitudes—an ending that stands out in terrible relief even in the annals of Hindu and Musulman India, where plague, pestilence and famine, battle, murder and sudden death, are writ large on every page. Man-im-Khan, flushed with victory and busy with designs for the rebuilding of the city, had encamped with his entire host within its walls. But scarcely were they quartered on the sorely stricken capital when the rainy season was upon them, and the general unhealthiness that had succeeded the withdrawal of the Ganges, and had since been sapping the city's supremacy as surely as the political disorders of the last days of independent rule, broke out into a mysterious pestilence that defied all human skill and knowledge. The city once seized by this mysterious disease, hope fled and the end was soon. Men died by hundreds in the streets, overtaken as they went about their daily tasks with that awful suddenness that paralyses the native mind with fear. As the pestilence increased the wildest panic spread quickly through the city. No man felt that he was safe from its deadly touch. The merchant ceased to buy and sell, and the moneylender forgot for once to press his claims; merchandise lay unheeded in the deserted shops, and no man stayed to take of aught that he possessed, fleeing with his life in his hand before the scourge of death. Only the old and the mothers with their babes, too weak to flee, cowered behind closed doors, preferring to meet even the slow pangs of starvation rather than to venture into the streets, where the dead lay unburied in their thousands—Hindu and Musulman side by side, high and low alike, where they had fallen, all their racial distinctions, so carefully preserved in life, lost for ever in the embrace of death. It was a city of the dying and the dead. Even the highlanders who had ventured close beneath its walls, surprised at the unwonted silence and absence of all sign of life, fled back within the safety of their hills appalled at the calamity that had overtaken the great city which had so long stood to them as the embodiment of strength and power. Before, in days gone by, they had watched the temporary eclipse of the greatness of Gaur. But that was by the hand of man. This was the hand of God, and all men recognised that it was the end. Death did not spare the conqueror, and Man-im-Khan, struck down in the midst of his plans to restore the pride and glory of the old imperial city, perished in its ruin. Those who survived fled far from the scene of desolation and made no return even to secure the treasures they had left behind them in their flight. Henceforth the name of Gaur drops out of the Musulman chronicles. Tradition and its ruins, desecrated by time and many generations, are all that testify to what its glory must once have been.

It was this destruction of Gaur that brought the imperial government yet another step nearer to the strongholds of the Paharias in the Rajmahal Hills. To another of Akbar's generals, Man Singh, fell the final conquest of Bengal and the choice of a new viceregal capital. The very name of Gaur still made men shudder. It was under the curse of God, and there could be no question of again restoring the fortunes of the city that, absolutely deserted by every living thing, was rapidly crumbling to decay. But the desirability of its site that had so often before saved it from destruction was not to be denied. Like all his predecessors, Man Singh was loth to move his capital far from so central and convenient a situation, right on the line of communication with Delhi and the far eastern limits of the empire. The new capital must of necessity be on the banks of the Ganges and not far from the famous Teliagharia Pass, through which all hope of aid by road must come in time of need. Agmahal, a place as yet of no importance, fulfilled all these conditions. Fifteen miles from Gaur as the crow flies, it was on the other side of the river, and placed on higher ground it afforded hope of a healthier climate than that which had overwhelmed the deserted city. It was, too, nearer the Teliagharia Pass, almost at the very entrance, and the headquarters of the Musulman viceroyalty established there, control over the lines of communication would be doubly secured. So in 1592 Agmahal—its name changed by Man Singh to Rajmahal—became the capital of Bengal.

As suddenly as Gaur had fallen, a great city rose into being on this new site, literally at the foot of the hills that still gave shelter to the wild uncivilised aborigines whom all the great changes and events that had passed before their eyes had left untouched. Here at last the seat of government was within their very gates. All the power and wealth and civilisation of the empire were centred in Rajmahal, and emanating thence spread far and wide across Bengal, Behar, and Orissa. It seemed as if at last the days even of the Paharias were numbered. Right above the imperial city in their mountain fastnesses, it seemed impossible that they would be allowed to maintain their independence undisturbed. But again, as by a miracle, they escaped. Though for over a century and a half—with the exception of the years when the capital was transferred to Dacca to cope with the growing Portuguese power—Rajmahal remained the centre of the Moghul dynasty in Bengal, the mysterious hand of Fate decreed that it should leave behind no trace of its existence upon the hillmen and their hills that almost overhung its gates.

Round Rajmahal were enacted many of the closing scenes in the great drama of the fall of the Moghul empire. Internal dissensions and disorder, frequent precursors of the fall of many an eastern empire, had long been rife in Bengal. Surajah Dowlah, viceroy of ill renown, after his brief success and the awful night of the Black Hole that finally settled the fate of Musulman rule in Bengal, fled from the storm that he had raised, only to be overtaken and betrayed by a fakir within sight of Rajmahal as he was hurrying on to Patna. Not far away at Murshedabad he met with the fate, though in less horrible form, that he had so often designed for others. Yet the Nawab Mir Kasim, heedless of the onrush of events, was building for himself in Rajmahal a palace of luxury and pleasure, the Nageswarbagh, on a stretch of high ground behind the city that commanded magnificent views over the great lake, the hills beyond, and the fertile plains and valleys at its feet. But even as he put the finishing touches to the walls the enemy was at his gates. Roused at last, he sallied forth with what strength lay at his command, and found the opposing force at Udhanala, scarce six miles away. It was a body of English troops under Major Adams, and the Nawab Mir Kasim, despairing of success, fled back to Rajmahal, and on thence for safety to Behar almost before the battle had begun. The long years of Moghul power in Rajmahal had reached their end. The small body of troops that had put its last independent Musulman ruler to flight was but the advance guard of a new empire whose foundations had even now been laid at Plassy—an empire that was destined at last to reduce the hitherto untamed Paharias to law and order—an empire based, not, as those that had preceded it, on ambition, greed, and intolerance, but on the broad principles of humanity, right, and justice—an empire that has not yet passed away.

The small hill tract encircled by the Ganges that had weathered so many storms and seen mighty empires rise and fall beyond its gates had reached at last the dawn of its existence as the British province of to-day.

CHAPTER III

THE COMING OF THE BRITISH

A NEW day was dawning for Bengal. The small mercantile community that one hundred and fifty years before had set out for the East—not in the spirit of Greek, Afghan, or Moghul, fired by the lust of conquest, but as the pioneers of trade and commerce—had been forced slowly but surely by the pressure of circumstances into the adoption of a new attitude, much against its will. The vicissitudes of Fort William had taught the advance guard of British enterprise that there could be no stability for the peaceful pursuits of the trader so long as the land remained a prey to disorder and misrule, and while the most solemn treaties and binding obligations failed to meet with the strict observance that Western ideas demanded. Entrenched within their small encampment on the banks of the Hooghly, the earliest settlers may well have looked out with misgiving over the vast unknown stretch of country that lay beyond, with its multitude of warlike races and all the outward symbols and traditions of imperial splendour. They had come as traders pure and simple, and though after-events proved them to be no less able as statesmen and administrators, they shrank from the embarrassments of political relations with the neighbouring chiefs. Upon the work of conquest which it was soon evident that those relations would entail, they showed unfeigned reluctance to enter, and it was not until their very existence even as a mercantile community was at stake that they were induced to take a wider outlook. Though the foundations of the British Empire in India were laid on trade and commerce, conquest and political supremacy followed of necessity in their wake.

In the middle of the eighteenth century events moved fast. Even the reluctant Company was forced at last to recognise that commercial enterprises among a less favoured people entailed responsibilities, and that the collection of the revenue from large dominions could no longer be dissociated from political relations. The first essential to the growth of industry is the security of property, and this was a desideratum that had never as yet been obtained under native rule. The state of confusion and disorder that reigned in Bengal as the eighteenth century advanced is almost impossible to exaggerate. The Musulman power that had maintained its hold over the lower provinces for more than five centuries was rapidly falling into a decay from which there was to be no awakening. Attacked not only by internal corruption and dissension, its very existence had been recently threatened by the Mahratta invasion of 1741. Even the Nawab Ali Verdi Khan, the last of the great Nawabs of Bengal, had bent before the storm and granted the invader's demands. Though victorious in the field, he had recognised that his tottering power was in no position to sustain a long-continued contest. The burning question of the succession needed all the attention of his declining years—a question doubly important now that the Mahrattas had at last wormed their way into the very heart of his dominions, presenting a complex problem that it must be left to his successor to solve. It appeared as if a great Mahratta empire were about to rise on the ruins of the Moghul dynasty, just as five centuries before that power had planted its foundations on the fallen greatness of the Hindu kingdom that had gone before. It was a dramatic moment in the history of Bengal, and the fate of the province trembled in the balance as the men who were destined, as time showed, to reduce it at last to law and order still looked out doubtfully from behind the ramparts of Fort William, appalled at the gigantic task that lay before them.

Nothing can well give a better idea of the state of confusion that reigned among the princes and people of Bengal at this time than the exhaustive minute sent home by Warren Hastings on November the third, 1772. It was small cause for wonder that many a heart failed at the almost insuperable difficulties before those who should be called upon to undertake the imposition of law and order upon chaos. The growing weakness of the central power had been the opportunity of princes, zemindars, farmers of the revenue, and a whole hierarchy of lesser instruments of oppression. Each man for himself exacted as much as he was able from those beneath him, caring nothing for the principles of humanity and justice. England in the reign of Stephen, when, as the chroniclers record, God and His saints slept, but faintly portrays something of the state of Bengal one hundred and fifty years ago. 'The Nizams,' to borrow Warren Hastings's own words, 'exacted what they could from the zemindars, the great farmers of the revenue, whom they left at liberty to plunder all below them, reserving to themselves the prerogative of plundering them in their turn when they were supposed to have enriched themselves with the spoils of the country. The Muttisidees, who stood between the Nizam and the zemindars or between them and the people, had each their respective shares of the public wealth. These profits, being fixed by no rate, depended on the temper, abilities, and power of each individual for the amount.' The safety of the person was as little regarded as the safety of property. Each man was a law unto himself, and encompassed his neighbour's death as easily as he devised new schemes to fleece him of his goods. The court of Murshedabad had become a hotbed of intrigue, where even political ambition was discarded in the race for wealth and its attendant luxury. Political advancement had come to be desired only because of the vast opportunities it provided for the acquisition of wealth, and such an atmosphere sapped the courage and the manliness of a race which had once swept over the land in an irresistible tide of conquest. The men of these latter days of Musulman rule had fallen from their high estate. Effete, effeminate, given over to luxury and greed, to them the desire for military glory upon which their empire rested was unknown. They who held by the sword were rapidly forgetting the use of the sword, and the end was not far off. So drew to its close the final scene in the history of a great empire—a scene made familiar by other and still greater empires in the West.

Such was the state of Bengal in the middle of the eighteenth century—ample justification, if such were needed, for the step the East India Company was about to take. The terrible events of June 1756 showed it to be a matter of life and death. It was a question either of the abandonment of their settlement and of their trade—which another Western nation would most assuredly and promptly appropriate—or a full recognition of the fact that the administration of justice and the direct collection of the revenue by the Company were essential to the continuance of its trade. To a nation with such traditions as those that stood behind the defenders of Fort William there could be no choice, and seven years after Clive's victory at Plassy the Company stood forth as the Dewan of Bengal, Behar, and Orissa. It was the first momentous step in the direction of immediate control, but still for four years more the Company hesitated to take up its new responsibilities, leaving the actual work of government in the hands of native officials. By the treaty of 1765 the Company had only taken over the fiscal administration, leaving all matters of criminal justice and police in the hands of the Nawab, for which he was allowed a sum of no less than 360,000*l.* But gaining confidence as the need grew imperative, the Company in 1769 appointed English Supervisors to each of the great divisions of the province. In that year Mr. William Harwood, endowed with vague powers, was appointed to Rajmahal to supervise the surrounding district, corresponding roughly with what is now South Bhagalpur and the Santal Parganas. But even the appointment of Supervisors was only a temporary measure, a feeler, as it were, put out in the effort to determine what the needs of the province actually were, and how best those needs might be met with the limited means at the company's disposal. The functions of the Supervisors were truly varied and numerous. They were to collect all the information possible, fiscal, social, and historical, concerning the districts through which they passed, and, above all, to attempt to put a stop to the enormous peculations that diminished the revenue. But it was soon evident that the Supervisors had been set an impossible task. Their inexperience and ignorance of the numerous races within the enormous districts under their control, the lack of speedy means of communication, and political disorders hampered them from the first. Instead of being able to enter upon the wide range of duties expected of them by the Company, they found their time more than fully occupied with the collection of the revenue alone. This was the most important of their duties, and all others had of necessity to be sacrificed to its demands. Consequently they were unable through want of time to take the administrative and executive measures that in fact would have facilitated the collection of the revenue. Finally, recognising the futility of half-measures, the Company under the energetic presidency of Warren Hastings stood forth as the direct governors of Bengal in 1772.

Nowhere was the confusion greater or the difficulties that met the Company's servants more formidable than in the district bordering on the headquarters of the rapidly declining Moghul power. Here the worst abuses that spring up round a corrupt and decaying court were in full evidence. Moreover here the wild hillmen of the Rajmahal Hills and the aboriginal races that peopled the surrounding country added their quota to the general confusion. These had not been slow to gauge the growing weakness of Musulman authority, and they seized the opportunity to insult it with even greater boldness than of old. Robbery, dacoity, and murder went on unchecked even up to the very gates of the citadel where the last of the Moghuls under British protection still held his puppet court.

What the relations between the Paharias and the Musulmans actually were can only be gathered from the position in which things were found at the intervention of the British. That the presence of the headquarters of Moghul rule in Bengal within a few miles of their borders had exercised no influence on their manner of life and political organisation has been already dwelt upon, forming as it does one of the strangest pictures in the extraordinary panorama of Indian history. All the evidence that remains goes to show that they never at any time acknowledged imperial supremacy. Directly with the Government they appear to have had no relations at all. As so continually illustrated in Indian history, empire had succeeded empire without at all affecting the mass of the people, who but passed from beneath the oppression of one ruler under that of another with true Oriental indifference. It mattered little to the Paharia, who desired only the seclusion of his rocky home, whether Hindu, Afghan, or Moghul reigned at Gaur, Rajmahal, and Murshedabad. Only with the neighbouring zemindars at the foot of the hills was he forced to come into close contact. Between these two races, differing in language, thought, and tradition, there existed always a spirit of fierce antagonism. The zemindars coveted the fertile lands that skirted the foot of the hills: the Paharias desired only to keep back the hated foreigner as far as might be from the country they had so long held. But the wild lawless character of the hillmen had

A TYPICAL SCENE IN THE RAJMAHAL HILLS

put a check even on the greed of the Hindu and Musulman zemindar, and between the hills and the plains a more or less wide strip of neutral ground bore evidence of the constant antipathy and suspicion that reigned on either side.

When the British first arrived to undertake the administration of the Rajmahal district they found that Paharias and zemindars had made a temporary compromise. Among the former a rude indigenous system founded on patriarchal lines was in existence. While owning the nominal supremacy of Manihari, a chieftaincy founded by the Katauri—an advanced section of their own race—with its dependent *tappas* of Patsanda, Barkop, Usila, and Hendue, the Paharias brooked little interference from without, each locality forming a small independent state within itself. Over certain stretches of country or groups of villages presided the Sardar, the divisional headman, with powers vague and indefinite, but respected and far-reaching. It was a monarchical system pure and simple—a despotism more or less benevolent, as the case might be, in which the Sardar was supreme within the limits of his influence. In each village, subordinate to him and acting as his deputy, was the Manjhi. Beneath these all were equal. There was no aristocracy, no clearly defined ranks and grades, each with its own household duties and political responsibilities such as made each Santal village a commonwealth complete within itself, giving it a clannishness and cohesion unknown among the Paharias. Such cohesiveness as the Mals possessed was due rather to the physical conditions of their mountain homes than to their internal forms of government.

The Sardar, the highest authority, and supreme within his own sphere of influence, played an important part in Paharia history. He it was who organised and incited the raids upon the zemindars of the plains, who administered a rude justice, and who was the authority on every question of custom and tradition that arose within the tribe. It was thus to the Sardars, the supreme power in the Paharia political system, that the zemindars finally appealed when time after time the wild tribesmen had descended on their fields, and attempt after attempt to pursue them into the hills had failed. Recognising the impossibility of resistance, they determined to open negotiations and effect a compromise. Such depredations must be stopped, cost what it might. They had brought bribery to a fine art in their own political organisation, and none knew better than they the effectiveness of a bribe where force and diplomacy had failed. Consequently they made an offer to the Sardars.

Portioning out certain of the fertile lands that they had already cultivated at the foot of the hills, they offered them to the Sardars on jagir, or service tenures. The condition of their holding them was to be the service rendered to the zemindars by preventing any further invasions of the Paharias beyond their limits. It was an attempt to secure a buffer state—a ring-fence of Paharia landholders between themselves and the hills. The zemindars hoped that the Paharias would not attack the lands of their own Sardars, and that they themselves might lie securely ensconced behind this effective barrier. As a further condition, the Sardars were to maintain guards at the passes that led down into the plains in order to keep a check upon any of the wilder hillmen with whom persuasion might fail, while the zemindars on their side of the line placed their own police outposts in the hope of making assurance doubly sure.

But a purely personal and local agreement such as this, based on mere verbal assurances and on assumed mutual confidence which did not exist, formed but a frail barrier between the two races. It was a case of each man for himself, and each zemindar was forced to make his own terms with the Sardar of the hilly tract that threatened his estate. Once every year the agreement was renewed. Down from the hills to meet the zemindars came the

Sardars of each *tappa* attended by all the village Manjhis who owed them allegiance. The time chosen for this meeting was the Dasahara Festival, and with much feasting and drinking—the invariable accompaniments of every important act of the Paharia's life—the agreements were annually renewed. It was the one visit of the Paharias to the plains throughout the year, when they came on a peaceful errand intent, and they descended in huge numbers, whole villages and *tappas* together, to celebrate fitly the renewal of the agreement they had often kept with so little fidelity. The zemindars provided the hospitality, and the Paharias, troubled by no pangs of conscience, enjoyed it to the full. The Sardar received a turban from the zemindar as a sign of his adherence to the renewed agreement, and the feasting done he returned with his following to keep the promise with more or less fidelity as circumstances or inclination might dictate. The zemindars, on their part, knew but too well that they were absolutely at the hillmen's mercy. The rocky tree-clad range that stretched for miles on either hand protected them now as ever from all danger of retaliation, and the plainsmen, no match for them in strength and endurance, had no resort but this futile annual bribe. How futile it was none knew better than the zemindars, yet once begun they dared not discontinue it, lest worse might befall them. Willing enough to take the money and the lands, and feast once a year at their enemy's expense, the Paharias had but the most rudimentary notions of the sanctity of an oath. Scarcely a year passed but roaming bands swept suddenly down on the lowland homesteads and as suddenly disappeared laden with spoil and leaving desolation in their wake. Yet year after year these same Sardars and Manjhis with shameless effrontery appeared at the time of the Dasahara Festival, and the unfortunate zemindars, in the full knowledge of repeated breaches of good faith, had no other alternative than to renew the engagement in order to avoid an open rupture.

But at last a crisis came. The year 1756 was a memorable one for Bengal. Surajah Dowlah, scarcely secure upon the gadi, had marched with an immense force against the English settlement on the Hooghly, and wild rumours were afloat. Everywhere there was a spirit of unrest which reached even the hillmen on the far-off Rajmahal Hills. The wild depredatory instinct that their yearly agreement with the zemindars had held within some slight check broke loose, and the Sardars and Manjhis, disregarding all their obligations, not only exercised no restraint upon the more turbulent spirits of their race, but in many cases themselves joined openly in raid and foray. Yet, with a supreme contempt for the lowlanders and finely ignoring past offences, they appeared as usual at the next Dasahara Festival. But their insolent complacence was destined to receive a rude shock. Even the despised lowlander had lost patience at last, as the highlander was to find to his cost. Cunningly meeting treachery with treachery, the zemindars made no sign, but set the usual feast before their unsuspecting guests. Then, when the strong liquor had taken effect and they were willing to swear eternal friendship and recognise a fine sense of distinction between 'mine' and 'thine,' the lowlanders, sober and relentless, fell upon them, and few escaped to tell the tale. It was a ghastly scene of massacre and bloodshed, prompted by the desire of retaliation for injury and perfidy long endured. But for the lowlanders themselves it was a fatal mistake. So treacherous an act, outraging their primitive instincts of hospitality, fired the ever-ready martial spirit of the hillmen. Swiftly the news spread into the far recesses of the jungle, and the flower of the Paharia youth burned with the mad passion of revenge. Banding together in huge companies—practically the whole fighting force of the clan—they swept down upon the plains, and raid after raid taught the much-suffering zemindars the worse than futility of their treacherous act.

It was an evil day for the dwellers in the plains. Exhausted with the struggle to drive off the hillmen from their lands, they fell a prey to another and still more deadly evil. Hitherto their lands had been rich and fertile, and even the depredations of the hillmen, though a heavy tax, had not been sufficient to drive them from their homes. But yet another of the most deadly evils that can befall a nation was at hand. Plague and pestilence, battle and murder, had swept over the great cities and plains at the foot of the Rajmahal Hills, leaving their mark on all that they had touched. Now a scourge no less dreaded, and coming, as those that had gone before had done, with dramatic suddenness, was about to lay its heavy hand upon the people of Bengal. The famine of 1770, coming just at the moment when the British were entering upon full possession of their new inheritance, was one of the most severe that have ever laid waste even this sorely tried land.

The partial failure of the crops of 1768 was the beginning of evil days, and high prices for grain ruled in the early part of 1769. A plentiful harvest in that year would have quickly made good the previous year's deficiency, and the first half of the rainy season seemed to promise an abundant crop. The Supervisors had but lately arrived in their various districts, and new to their tasks, and not as yet in touch with the people, the terrible catastrophe that was about to fall was unforeseen. Even the zemindars and the people themselves were deceived by the abundant rainfall of the months of July and August. Everywhere was fancied security, and none foresaw the coming of distress. Suddenly in the month of September the rain ceased. Calamity with that appalling swiftness that one learns to associate with the East fell upon the people. Day after day the cultivator watched his fields, waiting for the rain that never came. Days passed into weeks, and the corn, half grown, began to wither in the fields. Weeks passed, and eagerly as men looked and prayed the brilliant scorching light of the sun was never for a moment veiled by the clouds that would have brought salvation. Idle perforce, depending upon the elements, the unfortunate people watched with despair the passing of a rainless September and their slowly dying crops. It was a heart-breaking sight to this people of the soil. They had cast their bread upon the waters in unquestioning faith, and Nature, forgetful of her duties, threatened to withhold her hand. To them it was an affair of life and death. Living from hand to mouth, dependent on each year's crops, they saw pass away before their eyes the only hope of subsistence that was theirs, and as they watched the tender green of the young rice just breaking into the ear arrested in its growth and slowly withering until the fields became but yellow masses of stalks and straw, they looked forward with blank and numb despair towards the coming year.

But such was the nature of this long-suffering people, and so accustomed had they become to misfortunes and national calamities, that they sat down helplessly and uncomplainingly to await the inevitable. Long years of subjection and a fatalistic creed had broken their spirit, and they uttered no complaint. The few English officials absorbed in the herculean tasks that the Company had set them failed to realise the tragedy that was at hand. Alarmist reports, it was true, came in, but the absence of all sign of distress among the people themselves upon whom the first blow must inevitably fall discredited them at headquarters. It was the first time since the British Government had assumed responsibility that it was brought face to face with a great national calamity among the people of India. The difficulty had arisen, too, at the most inopportune moment. The first tentative step to acquire a greater knowledge of the people and a closer insight into their daily life had but just been taken by the appointment of the Supervisors, and the Government, fearful of responsibility, was inexperienced as yet in dealing with matters of great import in the administration of an enormous tract of country. Always pursued by the knowledge that the question of revenue loomed larger than all others in the eyes of the Court of Directors at home, this sudden catastrophe at the outset of their direct rule found them totally unprepared to meet it. Occupied with other matters, it was not until too late that they realised the appalling nature of the danger that was upon them. Then the difficulty of communication, the lack of knowledge of the province, and the still denser ignorance of the character of the innumerable tribes and castes that peopled these newly acquired possessions, made any adequate measures of relief wellnigh impossible. A conquered, dispirited people, who regarded famine with unquestioning despair as the result of one of Nature's inexorable laws, quietly accepted its fate. The rain had failed, there was no harvest, their food supply was rapidly diminishing and they must die—it was a natural sequence of events, and nothing could avail them. Their creed taught them that what the gods send, they send, and no man can uplift his hand against their stern decree. When to this deadly apathy and fatalism caste prejudices were added, something of the difficulty of a far-off government, ignorant of these things, in attempting to stem the tide of calamity may be imagined. Even a hundred years later the Santals preferred to die in hundreds with food spread out before them simply because that food had been cooked by the Brahmins, whom they hated and despised. Inexperienced in the methods of famine relief, the English officials were absolutely at a loss among the tribal prejudices of these strange peoples, of the very names of whose castes they were often entirely ignorant. Passive, dumb with despair, the wretched cultivators died by thousands, welcoming, open-armed, the death that released them from the pain and horror of starvation; while upon the Government, pathetic in its eagerness to help, was being forced the bitter knowledge of its inexperience and inability to stem the tide.

But while the plains lay stricken at their feet, the hills afforded sustenance to the wild race which had clung to them so long and with such passionate enthusiasm. Yet once again the hillmen saw calamity overtake the cities of the plains. Empire had succeeded empire, pestilence had laid low the proud capital at their very gates, and now famine, like the angel of death, was hovering over the land. Yet all these things passed by and left this wonderful people untouched. All through that fatal summer of 1770 the hillmen held out. Such crops as they cultivated on the lower slopes of the hills might die, but the dense jungles that lay beyond furnished them with an inexhaustible supply wherewith to weather the storm. They had always demanded little of life. What Nature gave sufficed. Even rice was to them a luxury, and so it came to pass in the day of adversity, when famine fell upon their neighbours in the plains, that these people of few wants escaped unscathed. When roots and herbs and fruits failed, there remained the countless forms of life that infested the remoter jungles to fall back upon, and the Paharia was a born huntsman to whom the toils of the chase came never amiss. Thus while among the dwellers on the plains there was everywhere ghastly evidence of the work of famine, the hillmen pursued their daily round of immemorial custom and routine that no event in the outside world seemed to have the power to turn from its accustomed way.

Secure themselves, the desolation in the plains was a chance such as the Paharias were not slow to take advantage of. Descending from the hills they found the zemindary police outposts deserted. The famine had fallen with particular severity on the strip of land that lay between the Rajmahal Hills and the Ganges, and death had laid a heavy hand upon the ryots. Even when years of plenty followed there were few left to cultivate. Whole tracts of land lay fallow, and the police posts unoccupied again by the zemindars fell into decay. Even for miles beyond along the plains cultivation had receded, not fully to recover its lost ground for many a year to come. When, added to the ravages of famine, the whole country side was harassed by the long-dreaded hillmen, its cup of misery was full. Not even the old weak defences remained between the Paharias and their prey, and the years that followed were years of dire distress for zemindars and ryots. Even the abundant harvests, by which Nature seemed to be endeavouring to repair the damage she had done, failed to yield their full return. Time after time the Paharias swept down upon them and levied heavy toll. The treacherous murder of their Sardars and Manjhis had not been forgotten or forgiven, and hate for the lowlander which had long been a tradition was now intensified by a spirit of revenge. In the old days they had plundered and robbed: now they wantonly burned whole villages and slaughtered women and children like cattle in cold blood. Riot and murder ran wild and there was none to check them. It was the interval of chaos between the fall of the Musulman power and the final establishment of British rule.

Already in 1763 a British force had penetrated far towards the Rajmahal Hills, and the first battle in the oncoming tide of victory had been fought and won within their view. The following year brought the hillmen at last into direct contact with the great White Raj. Up the broad highway which had witnessed so many changing scenes came the Government dâk runners communicating with their most westerly possessions in Behar. Along the banks of the Ganges, through the Teliagaria Pass, their way lay, but there were many to whom their destination was a goal unreached. The hillmen hurrying down to the plains were no respecters of persons, and the dâk runners of the far-off power which to them as yet was but a name were legitimate and often desirable prey. Time after time the Government despatches were destroyed and their carriers robbed and murdered. It was a matter that could not be lightly overlooked. Whatever else failed, the means of communication with their furthest possessions must be kept secure, and the authorities at Fort William took prompt action. In 1772 Captain Brooke of the Company's service was entrusted with the raising of a corps of light infantry especially adapted for hill fighting. It was expressly designed to protect the means of communication and the unfortunate lowland cultivator whom an accumulation of misfortunes had wellnigh overwhelmed. But the new corps, hastily raised, soon found that it had no light task before it. A rough untrained body of men upon whom British leadership and discipline had not yet had time to take effect, it fared ill at the hands of the Paharias, skilled as they were in skirmishing and harrying armies on the march. Simulating retreat before the advance of the enemy, they drew them into the patches of jungle that lay at the foot of the hills. Then, with all their intimate knowledge of the ground and their inimitable skill as mountaineers, they held the invaders in the hollow of their hand. The most modern firearms and weapons of warfare were of little use in this country that afforded such difficulty of passage and such unlimited opportunities for ambush. The bows and arrows of the Paharias for their part never failed of deadly effect. Concealed behind the huge boulders on the outskirts of the jungle they marked down their adversaries with unerring aim. The arrows of the Paharias too were often poisoned, and the men of the light infantry regarded them with a deadly fear. It was a hopeless contest. Roads there were none, and progress was only to be made by cutting a way for the troops through the forest as they marched. The difficulty of securing supplies increased with each advance, the jungle, though furnishing all the limited needs of the hillmen, offering no adequate subsistence to the men of the plains. Added to all these disadvantages was the unhealthy climate of the Rajmahal Terai. On the hardy Paharia, inured by long residence, the fatal miasma had no effect; but upon the foreigner of another race and land it worked disastrous results. Sickness was rife among the troops, and many died before they could reach the more salubrious air of the plains beyond. Harassed on every side, the troops were at last forced to retreat, their object unaccomplished. So from the first encounter with the British Raj the Paharias emerged victorious even as they had done from many similar encounters through all the centuries that had passed since they had settled on the Rajmahal Hills.

But the time of their subjection, long delayed, was at last at hand. For six years the Corps of Light Infantry continued to do what it could to protect the surrounding country, assuming after its first disastrous attempt a strictly defensive attitude. But in spite of its efforts, so daring became the depredations of the hillmen, threatening so greatly the lines of communication, that in 1778 Captain Browne, who had succeeded to the charge of the Light Infantry Corps, was directed to devise some fresh means of bringing them to submission. Warned by the experiences of six years before, all idea of military operations was abandoned. Conciliation and not conquest must be looked to if peace was to be brought to this sorely tried district. Captain Browne devised a scheme something on the lines of that which had formerly held between the zemindars and the hillmen, but with important additions to render it of more effect. The Sardars were to be propitiated by being acknowledged as chiefs of the tribe, and *sanads* were to be granted to them by Government, they in their turn engaging to keep the peace, report at once all outbreaks on the part of the hillmen, and generally use the great influence they possessed over the latter in the interests of law and order. The Manjhis were to make similar engagements with the Sardars, and by this means it was hoped to spread a spirit of obedience and discipline throughout the tribe. Those Sardars who lived nearest the river and the lines of communication were to be paid a fixed sum to protect the mail runners. It was a bribe pure and simple as in Musulman days—the offer of a permanent allowance to forego the chance of an occasional haul. As a further precaution the old zemindary police outposts were to be re-established at regular intervals all along the foot of the hills, but they were no longer to be left in native hands. Government was to undertake direct control of police duties by means of Thanadars—local police officers under the supervision of Divisional Superintendents. Captain Browne's scheme thus interposed a third party between hillmen and zemindars, independent of either and backed up by an authority whose power was daily increasing in the land.

But there was one new and important element in Captain Browne's scheme which was destined to prove the wisest measure of all. Suitable lands at the foot of the hills were to be portioned out to retired or disabled sepoys who had completed their years of service or had been compulsorily retired through ill health, wounds, or other physical disability. These lands, known as Invalid Jagirs or Ghatwali tenures, were acquired by Government and allotted rent free on condition that the holders settled upon them and gave assistance to the local authorities in case of need for the maintenance of law and order. It was a bribe of the most permanent and effective kind. A ring of lands such as these round the foot of the hills formed the best possible protection to the lowlanders. The sepoys of necessity were men who had seen military service and to whom fighting had been the main business of their lives. Here they were settled on their own land which was theirs for all time, and they naturally defended it from attack with all their might, as a man only will defend his own home. Their interests and those of the authorities were at once synonymous, their stout resistance to attack springing partly from

A PRIMITIVE MODE OF IRRIGATION

PLOUGHING

selfish motives, yet having all the effect of loyalty to the British Raj. It was the soundest measure of policy and the cheapest form of police.

But Captain Browne, though securing Government's sanction to his plans, was not destined to see his reforms fully carried out under his own eyes. The completion of the work that he had so well begun was reserved for another—an Englishman young in age and in experience who yet in five short years so won the confidence and fired the imagination of this wild hill people that to-day, after the lapse of more than a century, his name is still revered among them as a household word.

CHAPTER IV

AUGUSTUS CLEVELAND

The Paharias have but one national hero, and he was an Englishman. Producing among themselves no name worthy of remembrance above its fellows, it was left for one of another race so to impress them with his genius for administration, his justice, and his sympathy for their needs, that they have ever since regarded him as the greatest benefactor of their race. The name of Augustus Cleveland, well-nigh forgotten among his own countrymen, has been handed down from generation to generation among this wild hill people with touching fidelity and reverence. The memory of the great 'Chilmili'—the nearest they can get to the unaccustomed English name—is now enshrined for all time among the legends and traditions of their race.

As one reads the records of these few short years of Cleveland's wise administration, it is difficult to realise that the central figure is that of a young man of an age at which the civilian of the present day is only just beginning his career in India. When appointed to the important post of Collector of Bhagalpur—and the Collector in those days was administrator, lawgiver, and commander-in-chief in one—he was barely twenty-five. But those were the days—the early days of our Indian Empire—when to the strong man all things were possible. Before the young Collector of Bhagalpur vast opportunities rose up in line. To him was given the magic charm of moulding and shaping the province yet to be, of building order out of chaos, of stamping the first imprints of a high civilisation upon a wild and hitherto untamable people, and, greatest feat of all, of leaving his memory enshrined in the hearts of the conquered race—an ignorant, suspicious, turbulent people into the mouth of whom the name of foreigner hitherto had never come but with a curse. Arriving in India before completing his seventeenth year—there were no examinations in those days, and the days of cramming were not yet—he had the best possible training for his great work—five years as Assistant Magistrate in the district which he was afterwards to govern as Collector. Rapid transfers were unknown, and the whole of Cleveland's Indian career, with the exception of the first two years, was passed either at Rajmahal or Bhagalpur. It was this that accounted in large measure for his marvellous success in the administration of the province. He knew thoroughly the country he was called upon to rule: he had travelled through it with the Collector and alone: none knew better than he its grievances and needs. Then when the time came, his tact and wisdom and genius for administration enabled him not only to mitigate temporary evils, but to impress his own individuality upon one part of the province at least for all time. To-day the aims for which such men as Cleveland worked have been in great measure accomplished. The law, more and more adapted to the people's needs, is fixed, and backed by all the forces of the British Empire runs undisputed to the furthest recesses of the jungle, and the Civilian of the twentieth century has but to punish disobedience to that law and tread the routine paths of administration that others have made straight. To the Civilian of to-day, after the passing of more than a hundred years, the career of Augustus Cleveland offers a special interest, showing what manner of men his predecessors were and what work it fell to them to do, while to his fellow-countrymen at large it serves well to recall to mind the greatness of the task accomplished and to afford a hopeful outlook towards the many problems that still await solution at the hands of the ruling race.

It was in 1773 that Augustus Cleveland, two years after his arrival in India, was appointed assistant to the Supervisor at Rajmahal. The Bhagalpur district had been formally severed from Behar that same year, but as yet its eastern boundary stopped short at the foot of the Rajmahal Hills. Between it and the Ganges there lay the narrow strip of wild unsettled country, peopled by the Paharias, and destined later to form the nucleus of the Santal Parganas, which at the first rough division of Bengal under the Supervisors had been placed with Rajmahal under the jurisdiction of Birbhum. Hitherto the chief interest of this district had lain towards the east. Here almost within its ken there had risen the great cities of Hindu and Musulman, and it was on this side that the Paharias had seen the imperial power advancing step by step until at length it crossed the Ganges and raised its headquarters at their very gates in Rajmahal. Towards the west, authority, further removed, had caused them less anxiety. Patna and Bhagalpur had never been the standing menace that Gaur and Pandua, Murshedabad and Rajmahal, had been in days gone by. Consequently it had been upon the eastern slopes of the hills that they kept their closest guard, knowing that on this side lay the greatest danger to the independence they had so long preserved. But with the gradual settling down of the province under British rule the centre of interest veered round towards the west. Slowly but surely this new empire was closing in around the Rajmahal Hills, equally strong, tenacious, and organised on every side, and the physical characteristics of this narrow strip of land which had played so important a part throughout its history were determining the formation of the new province and uniting it, not with its neighbours to the east, but with those to the west. Rajmahal, at the outset the seat of one of the Supervisors, was soon found to have none of the conveniences of Suri in Birbhum, and the Supervisor withdrawn, the former Musulman capital rapidly sank into a place of but little importance. Left thus without a headquarter station near at hand, the traditional interests of the district caused it for the moment to be attached to Birbhum, but it was not long before geographical and political considerations made its transference to Bhagalpur and the western province imperative.

The first five years of Cleveland's assistant magistracy in the district introduced him to the state of affairs he was afterwards to do so much to settle on a peaceful and permanent basis. The Corps of Light Infantry, especially raised to reduce the wild hillmen to submission, had made its first attempt and failed. Though affording some measure of assistance to the unfortunate lowlander, it was an impossible task for it to protect adequately the immense stretch of country that encircled the hills. Safe in the knowledge that the light infantry could not force its way through their jungles and across their hills, the Paharias had but to take advantage of its absence on either side to rob and plunder at their will, retiring long before the troops could cover the circuitous route that they must take to reach the scene of action. The confusion and disorder on the western slopes was no less great than on the Bengal side, and here the authorities were further handicapped by the fact that their jurisdiction extended only to the foot of the hills, which thus furnished a doubly safe retreat. Warrants in those early days met with sufficient difficulty in execution within close range of the source from which they emanated. To pursue the fugitive from justice into a neighbouring jurisdiction was a source of much trouble and infinite delay. To expect redress from distant Suri in Birbhum against a band of robbers on the western slopes of the Rajmahal Hills was hopeless. Yet the extraordinary official jealousy that existed between neighbouring government officers in those days precluded all attempts on the part of the Bhagalpur Collector to redress the wrongs on his own boundary almost at his very doors. Once the banditti reached the slopes of their hills they were safe, and could well afford to laugh at the authority that dared not follow but must pursue the cumbrous method of sending miles away to Suri to put the law in force against them. Long before the Collector there could make his power felt in this remote corner of his district, the hillmen had contemptuously added further dacoities to their record.

There was yet another element of disorder on the western side of the hills. Here at the foot lived several powerful zemindars who proved a scarcely less vexatious source of trouble to constituted authority than the Paharias themselves. Among them all, none was more notorious than Rup Narayan Deo, zemindar of Chandwa. Involved in constant quarrels with his neighbours, he had been nothing loth to enlist the help of such redoubtable fighters as the Paharias had proved themselves to be in many a raid and foray. These new allies, always spoiling for a fight, eagerly followed where the hope of booty led, and with Rup Narayan at their head ravaged the whole south of the district far and wide. Further to the west lay the rich zemindary of Kharakpur, founded a hundred and seventy years before by a Pathan adventurer on the ruins left by the Bhuiya invasion. Its Raja, catching the spirit of the times and viewing with distrust the growing English power at Bhagalpur, threw in his lot with those who strove against the forces of law and order. Away to the south in Sultanabad ruled the high-spirited Rani Sarbeswari. head of an important house of acknowledged Rajput purity. Petty feuds with neighbouring chiefs had long been smouldering, and, joining with the Paharias and Rup Narayan Deo, she held the whole southern portion of the district in a state of terror and alarm. During two months of the winter of 1777 no less than forty-four villages were plundered and burnt to the ground, few of their inhabitants so much as escaping with their lives. Three zemindars of Godda had shown themselves well disposed towards the authorities at Bhagalpur, having lent assistance in bringing some of the worst local offenders to justice, and they had thus incurred the bitter hostility of Rup Narayan and his insurgent faction. Time after time raids were made upon their lands, and they were themselves finally murdered in cold blood within their own homes. Growing bolder with success a lawless band swept the country almost up to Bhagalpur itself, showing their contempt for the Collector and his authority by carrying off his tents which had been pitched in a mango grove a few miles south of the town. River dacoity was as common above Rajmahal as below, and terror reigned along the Ganges from Bhagalpur to Rajmahal. Nowhere by land or water within sight of the Rajmahal Hills was there any safety for person or property.

Such was the state of affairs when Augustus

Cleveland took over charge as Collector of Bhagalpur in 1779. Few districts in Bengal at that time presented greater difficulties, and few had greater need of the strong hand of an able administrator. Everywhere since 1772, when the Company under the guidance of Warren Hastings had stood forth as the direct ruler of Bengal, the first signs of the new reign of law and order had become apparent. The time had come when they should reach even the remote recesses of the jungle on the Rajmahal Hills. The inadvisability of leaving this narrow strip of turbulent hill country between the Bhagalpur border and the Ganges subject to another jurisdiction had been fully brought home to the local authorities. The river undoubtedly formed the natural boundary, and the first great step towards the reduction of the independence of the Paharias was taken in its transference to Bhagalpur in 1779, the year of Cleveland's appointment to the Collectorate.

With the wisdom born of experience, Cleveland's first efforts were at conciliation rather than conquest. He found his office at Bhagalpur already too greatly involved in difficulties and disputes to allow of any punitive expedition against the newly acquired strip of territory, even had that been deemed advisable. Busy with his multifarious duties, his first year at the head of the district must have been fully occupied. Yet in 1780, scarce twelve months after he had taken over charge, he was able to report favourably of his first attempts to pacify this new portion of his district which had so long escaped subjection. Following the lines laid down by Captain Browne, he had endeavoured to secure the goodwill of the Sardars and Manjhis. This was only to be done at that stage by the old time-honoured means of a bribe. Short of actual conquest at the sword's point, nothing else would induce them to give up their predatory habits and throw in their lot with the British Government. But to gain them, as Cleveland divined, was to gain the whole tribe. Their influence with the rank and file was paramount. There was no option but to secure their fidelity by the only means that appealed to them, and to insist that the payment of the subsidy was dependent on their maintenance of the peace within their jurisdictions. To every Sardar and Naib and Manjhi who accepted these conditions, a permanent annual money payment was allotted. Each holder of a pension was bound to assist the authorities when called upon, report all crimes within the villages under his control, and generally use all the influence he possessed in preventing a breach of the peace. In 1780 Cleveland was able to report that forty-seven hill chiefs had given in their submission on these terms. The pensions allotted by him in this and succeeding years amounted to fifteen thousand rupees per annum; and though fixed by Cleveland, doubtless with little idea of any prolonged duration, they were destined to survive absolutely unchanged in amount for wellnigh a hundred years, until within a comparatively recent date. It was not until 1879 that they began to be resumed.

But, knowing full well the wild nature of the hillmen and the very partial measure of success that this subsidising system had already met with, Cleveland foresaw that their voluntary submission would need to be carefully cemented before reliance could be placed upon it. A primitive people, with the most rudimentary conception of the nature of an oath, it was difficult to know what appeal could be made to them with any hope of success. Fighting was the only trade they knew, but in that they excelled. Hardened by exposure and accustomed from their youth up to the use of weapons for the chase if not for raid or foray, they were adepts in the irregular warfare that was all their native hills allowed. Hitherto this fighting capacity had been ranged against the forces of law and order: it had been the terror of the lowlander and the scourge of the country for miles around. To Cleveland occurred the idea of using this military instinct, as it were, against itself. If it were possible to turn it into legitimate channels, a powerful force might be placed at the disposal of Government, bringing the peace and quietness they had never yet had down to the Rajmahal Hills. To secure this great result became the guiding principle of Cleveland's policy. A body of these highlanders armed for hill fighting would prove invaluable if once they could be induced to accept discipline, and dependence could be placed upon their loyalty and good faith. But there the difficulty lay. Regardless of the most solemn undertakings and ignorant of the first principles of obedience, their splendid military qualities had as yet found outlet only in impulsive individual action, typical of savage warfare and guided by none but purely selfish considerations. Moreover, shy and suspicious of strangers, to gain their confidence so as to impress upon them loyalty and good faith on the one side and discipline and obedience on the other was no light task.

But now that forty-seven chiefs had given in their submission of their own free will an opportunity that Cleveland was not slow to take offered itself of putting his scheme to the test. Warren Hastings was at the helm of affairs, and there was every hope of support from the broad statesmanship of that great administrator whose views, unlike those of the Company, were based on a wide and far-reaching imperialism that foreshadowed the events of later years. Drawing up a scheme which it was hoped would inaugurate at length a reign of law and order for the long-suffering province, he submitted it to the Governor in Council for approval.

It was a notable scheme. A corps of hill archers, some four hundred strong, was to be enrolled from among the followers of those forty-seven chiefs who had given in their adherence. The Paharias were to be their own police. Not the hated foreigner, but they themselves were to be the guardians of their land. The only outside element was to be the Collector of Bhagalpur himself, who was to add to his numerous other duties the command of the corps when raised. Eight of the most trusted Sardars were to be placed in command of detachments: each was to be practically supreme within his own sphere, the guardian of the peace and the dispenser of a rough justice among the members of his troop and his own people. In order to induce *esprit de corps* there was to be provided a special uniform of purple jackets and turbans, soon destined to become a dearly prized distinction among a people with a primitive instinct for the outward and visible symbols of authority. Every village headman was to be encouraged to furnish recruits, and he was to be paid two rupees per month if he supplied the required number. The eight Sardars in charge of detachments were to be paid five rupees, and the rank and file three rupees per month, while the whole annual cost was estimated at 3,200*l*.

It was not a large sum compared with the results that might have been expected from the outlay if success favoured the scheme. But at headquarters, amid greater and more pressing interests, it was easy to overlook the needs and dangers of a far-off corner such as the Rajmahal Hills. Neither the lawlessness of the district nor the necessity of devising some special scheme to cope with it was fully understood. The Bengal Government, whose credit with its masters at home depended almost entirely upon excess of receipts over expenditure in its annual returns, looked bitterly askance at every fresh outlay demanded of it locally. It was an unfortunate time, too, to press for even so small a disbursement as Cleveland's scheme required. Warren Hastings was beset on every side with difficulties. Bengal had not yet recovered from the disastrous effects of the famine of ten years before, and innumerable problems demanded the attention of the Company. The province, it was calculated, had lost no less than one third of its native population during the fatal summer of 1770, and one third of its arable land had fallen out of cultivation. Depopulation had naturally taken place on the largest scale among the lowest peasant class, depriving the landlord of his labourer, and forcing him to let his fields lie fallow. Much the same state of things existed in Bengal in the years that followed as prevailed in England after the Black Death in 1389. A vast agrarian problem presented itself which needed all the Company's resources to meet. Fortunately for the British Government, the Bengali ryot had none of the spirit and power of combination that inspired the Peasant Revolt of his English counterpart four centuries before. Now, as always during the early years of British rule, it was the fiscal rather than the political question that presented the greatest difficulty. Still reluctant to leave their first position as a trading company and constantly reminded by the Board of Directors at home of the urgent necessity of large financial profits, it is not to be wondered at if the group of officials at Fort William looked with suspicion on any expenditure that did not promise an adequate return. Cleveland's first scheme, coming before them at such a time, gave only the uncertain hope of pacifying a wild hill district, a mass of dense jungle and untilled lands which then afforded but little expectation of the rich harvest they were destined to yield in years to come.

Consequently, in the press of more important

matters, the scheme met with scant consideration, and was vetoed by the Governor in Council. But Hastings, vigilant and foreseeing, showed his appreciation of the need that prompted it by approving a smaller scheme subsequently submitted by Cleveland, who though once rebuffed did not cease to press forward a measure of whose wisdom and necessity he was convinced. Sanction was obtained to a grant of ten rupees per month to each Sardar and five rupees to their Naibs, but no grant at all was to be allowed to the Manjhis. It was only the most temporary of expedients. But, fortunately, before the end of the year the Commander-in-chief of the British forces in Bengal passed through Bhagalpur on his way up country. To him Cleveland unfolded his scheme. In the light of local investigation there could be little doubt of its advisability. The Commander-in-chief had just marched along the foot of the hills, and although, at the head of an army, he had experienced little of the dangers of the road, the rugged and difficult nature of the country, and the terror which the hillmen inspired could not fail to be brought home to the most casual passer-by. He warmly supported the measures proposed by Cleveland, and his recommendations to Government secured the adoption of the original scheme almost in its entirety.

At the end of the year 1780 the Corps of Hill Archers was enrolled. When first approached the forty-seven Sardars who had given in their submission were doubtful and suspicious of this new thing. But when the scheme was explained to them in detail by its originator himself, they grew more interested. It was the first sign of the wonderful magnetic influence Cleveland was destined to acquire over this wild hill people. From the outset he gained their confidence—that first essential in dealing with a native race. He inspired them with a sense of his own truthfulness and his own honourableness of purpose, and above all of his entire sympathy with their needs. These things the Paharias had never met with hitherto in all their history. So for a time they wondered and held back, scarce believing that these things could be. Hatred of the foreigner had long since become a tradition: was it possible that any good thing could come from association with such a one? Yet, after all, were these determined white sahebs who ate flesh of all kinds, clean and unclean, and admitted no caste prejudices, altogether the strangers that they seemed? They were not Hindus, for they killed the sacred cow. They were no true Musulmans, for they ate swine's flesh and had no fear of forbidden things. Was it not possible—nay more, probable—that they might claim descent from that one of the seven brothers in the legend of their genesis who at the first great feast took flesh of all kinds and wandering off into a far country had been no more seen? All these things were pondered and discussed in many a village gathering, convened by Sardar and Manjhi beneath the wide-spreading trees of their primæval forest to weigh the merits of this new scheme. Doubtfully at length they signified their assent, and recruiting for the new corps was at once begun. The first hesitation overcome, there was little further difficulty. Where one led the way, others followed, and when they fully understood what was required of them they entered into the spirit of it with eager zest. The carrying of arms and hill fighting were what they had been accustomed to from their youth up. Cleveland's scheme, as they joyfully put it, gave their warlike instincts a legitimate outlet that they had never before possessed. To them it was a new game, and the Corps of Light Infantry at the outset was not lacking in recruits.

But Cleveland was quick to recognise that it was absolutely essential to move slowly and only introduce outside influences by degrees. Left, therefore, of necessity almost entirely to the Sardars, very little order and discipline could be expected from the new body of troops. If they proved loyal in time of need, and carried out the orders given them, it was the most that could be expected. The rest must be left to their rough methods of warfare which had so often proved successful in the past.

It was not likely to be long in the disturbed state of the country before their effectiveness was put to the test, and an opportunity soon occurred. To the south the more turbulent of the hillmen broke out on one of their old raiding exploits, plundering villages and laying waste the land far and near. Cleveland, eager to try the mettle of his new troops and to prove the value of his scheme, marched at the head of the Hill Archers to be present himself as sponsor at their baptism of fire. It was a difficult task to hold them in restraint; but even such slight discipline as they had already learned proved effective, and showed how efficient a force they might become with adequate training under European supervision. Sweeping down upon the marauding hordes that infested the foot of the hills, with all their old spirit and something of a new and better-organised plan of attack, they carried all before them. The raiders, astonished at the strength of this new fighting force, which seemed to have sprung up in the twinkling of an eye, were driven back with loss and pursued far into their own country, where the sight of this well armed and equipped body of men, led by authority and obedient to the commands of a single leader, inspired them with awe and respect and a grudging admiration. This fighting in a disciplined body of their late companions in arms, with whom in old days they had made many a raid and foray, appealed to their imagination, and recruits came in rapidly from among those who until now had been among the most formidable foes of law and order.

So completely successful was this first crucial test that Cleveland urged Government to recognise the corps as a permanent and properly constituted fighting force. Great as their effectiveness had been proved to be, even in their present untrained, half-organised condition, it would be enormously enhanced were the men disciplined and armed like a company of regular sepoys under an efficient military officer. The promise of a loyal and useful force, capable of dealing with local disturbances, induced Government to sanction Cleveland's proposal, and Lieutenant Shaw was appointed as Adjutant to construct the new corps. Almost all its first conditions were to be retained. Recruited entirely from among the Paharias, its chief object was to form an effective police force to keep the peace on the Rajmahal Hills. Stationed at Bhagalpur the corps was known henceforth as the

Bhagalpur Hill Rangers, and for over seventy years it continued to exist, well justifying its existence until, the special need for which it had been constituted having passed away, it was finally disbanded on the reorganisation of the native army after the Mutiny of 1857.

But the new corps was destined by Cleveland from the first to be far more than a mere military organisation of police. Through it he hoped to secure the better administration of justice, making it fulfil the functions of the ordinary courts and enforce the punishment of crime and evil-doing which as yet they had so signally failed to do. Nominally the Paharias were subject to the regular course of law that held good for all the province. But so far as they were concerned it might never have existed. Crime had hitherto gone on unchecked. No government peon or process server dared venture within sight of a Paharia village, and no warrant had yet been executed on the Rajmahal Hills. It would be long before the cumbrous machinery of the law could reach this wild hill people, and to accustom them first to a rude form of justice through their own primitive institutions was the easiest and most effective course that could be pursued.

The new corps was to be a body complete in itself, and the old tribal conditions of life to

A GROUP OF PAHARIA WOMEN

which its members had always been accustomed were to be interfered with as little as possible. The old patriarchal system, wherein the power to punish lay in the hands of the Sardar and Manjhi, was adopted in the form of a court-martial of the officers—themselves headmen—to try all petty offences committed by members of the corps. Intensely jealous of outside interference, they would have strongly resented any attempt to bring them into direct relation with the ordinary courts, and Cleveland, wisely recognising this, refrained from jeopardising the whole scheme by trying to force upon them a system not adapted to their needs. From the first the district had been marked out as apart from the province to which it officially belonged. Already the non-regulation system was in its infancy.

But, trusted as this roughly organised court-martial of the officers might be to punish petty offences, some further check on serious crime was soon found to be necessary. In 1782, two years after the formation of the corps, the first heinous offence among its members occurred. One of the Hill Rangers murdered a woman of his tribe, and the headmen, not feeling competent to act in so grave a matter, actually reported the crime at head-quarters. The very fact that they had come to regard murder as a grave offence against the law, and were willing to hand up one of their number to justice at headquarters, was a striking instance of the confidence and respect that Cleveland and his system had inspired among them. No sooner, it appeared, were they convinced of his sympathy and justice than this exclusive and jealous people quietly submitted themselves and their affairs into his hands. It was a splendid tribute to the man and to those broad principles of right and justice, and, above all, of sympathy, upon which his rule was based.

To meet such cases of serious crime in future, Cleveland determined to form a special court among the Hill Rangers themselves, reserving only the ultimate power in his own hands. It was to consist of a small number of officers of the corps—not less than three—who were to be appointed by the Collector. They were only to meet when called together by him, and to him was reserved the right to veto or amend all sentences passed, except in the case of capital punishment, when a meeting of all the hill chiefs was to be convened and their decision alone held final. Thus was originated the first germ of the famous court of justice known far and wide as the Hill Assembly.

So well was this scheme received by the members of the corps, whose natural suspicions of change in any form were lulled by the freedom from outside interference which it maintained, that Cleveland determined to adapt it to the whole of the hill district which had so far given in its allegiance. The maintenance of peace and justice was far more important than the maintenance of a system of law. The ordinary courts were powerless to contend against special needs and special evils, while a less regular method promised every hope of effectively dealing with them. Absolutely ignorant of all form of law and procedure, and altogether unfitted in mental capacity to fight on equal terms with the plainsman in craft and cunning, not even the severest injury or the deepest grievance would induce the hillman to seek redress in the Bhagalpur courts. He preferred to resort in case of need to the most primitive of all arguments, where he was on surer ground and seldom failed to win the day. It was hopeless for many a year to come to expect a change. Yet if approached with tact and sympathy, and shown the paths of peace and justice along lines he understood and had long imperfectly followed, he had proved himself eminently amenable. Representing all these things to Government, Cleveland finally, in April 1782, obtained sanction to withdraw the whole of the Rajmahal Hill tract from the jurisdiction of the ordinary courts, and the same rough system of local control which had proved so successful with the corps was further elaborated and extended throughout the district. A council of Sardars was to meet twice a year forming a sessions court to try all offences that had occurred during the previous six months within its jurisdiction. The Collector might modify or reverse its decision on appeal, except in the case of capital punishment. None had the right to inflict or rescind the sentence of death save the Hill Assembly itself. The Paharias, who had kept their native hills untouched through each succeeding wave of conquest, had won at length this great acknowledgment of their independence from the last and greatest conqueror of all.

The report submitted to Government of the first meeting of the Hill Assembly in 1782 forms an interesting record. There was no lack of work for this earliest Paharia Court of Sessions. The hill-men of the further highlands had not ceased to give trouble, and the early years of the Bhagalpur Hill Rangers were full of activity. As yet but half of the Sardars and Manjhis had given in their allegiance, forming the nucleus of the corps. Those on the outskirts of the district towards the south had not yet come in, and a large portion of the hill tract still remained untouched. Scarcely had Lieutenant Shaw had time to work the raw material at his disposal into the semblance of a regular corps when it was called upon to face one of the most determined incursions that had yet taken place. The wild tribes from far back in the jungle, alarmed at these strange signs of coming law and order, and resenting the part that their fellow tribesmen were playing as treachery to the common brotherhood, organised a raid, not only on the peaceful farmsteads of the plains, but also on those Paharia villages whose Manjhis had taken service under the hated foreigner. Rup Narayan Deo, zemindar of Chandwa, and Sarbeswari, the restless Rani of Sultanabad, eagerly welcomed their overtures, and joined in the foray on their neighbours' lands. Burning the villages of the loyal Manjhis on the way, they passed on to more promising fields of booty. The Pargana of Kharakpur was a stretch of fertile well-cultivated land, and promised a rich harvest of plunder. Its chief had given in his submission and deserved the worst that might befall. With all their old dash and courage, they swept down upon his lands, and with nine hundred head of cattle as their share of the spoil they returned in seeming triumph. But their confidence and self-satisfaction were destined to receive a rude shock. They were soon to learn once for all that the old days of unbridled licence were past for ever. Justice pursued them with unexpected speed. It was for such raids as this that the Hill Rangers had been organised, and following the raiders into their own homes among the hills they arrested no less than one hundred and ninety-five. Of these one was a Sardar, Bidji of Titoria by name, and as many as seventy-four were Manjhis. The remaining one hundred and twenty had formed part of the rank and file of the foraging party who had followed where their Sardar and Manjhis had led.

The trial of these offenders formed the first duty of the newly constituted Hill Assembly. It was a striking picture of a patriarchal gathering. There was no hall of justice but the wide expanse of sky or the shade of some mighty monarch of the forest. Though only a selected number of the chiefs were to act as judges, a dense crowd of hillmen had come from the recesses of the forest in awe and wonder at this new departure whereby quick justice was to be meted out to those who had done evil. In the centre, cross-legged on the ground, sat the judges, stolid, immovable, deeply impressed by these new formalities and the solemnity of the decision they were to be called upon to give. Cleveland himself presided, and facing him and their judges, guarded by the Hill Rangers in their smart uniform of purple coats and puggarees, were the prisoners, a ragged group of wild hillmen, unclothed save for a strip of cloth about the loins and with tumbled masses of coal-black hair half hiding their rough uncouth features. Scarcely distinguished from the rank and file stood the Sardar, the chief accused—no better clothed and with only an indefinable distinction in his mien and bearing, born of the right to lead and command. Behind and around all these, squatting on the ground, close packed, shoulder to shoulder, line on line, sat the rank and file who had travelled far to see this great thing: while hovering on the outskirts of the crowd stood the wildest and most untamed of all the hillmen, some, doubtless, friends and relatives of the accused themselves, fearful and suspicious, with many a raid and foray on their dawning consciences which the near approach of punishment had now first wakened into being.

For three days the judges sat, hearing all the evidence that was to be obtained on either side. 'It was conducted,' writes Cleveland, referring to the trial in his official report, 'with as much ceremony and formality as the nature and disposition of the people would admit of.' Upon the minds of the spectators the passing of those three days made a lasting and ineffaceable impression. Since the beginning of time in all their history no days had been so memorable. The progress of the trial before their eyes, even as an object-lesson teaches children, taught them a truth that it had been hard for their lawless and untrammelled instincts to accept, that a power had arisen in the land above and beyond their tribal organisation—a power whose mainstays were justice, fairness, and equity which it was necessary that they should obey. It was the beginning of the final triumph of right over might in the Rajmahal Hills.

The judges whom Cleveland had chosen to be the centre figures in this first court of justice that the hillmen had ever known were no less impressed than the rank and file. 'I have the pleasure to observe,' continues the official report of the Collector, 'that the chiefs appeared to conduct themselves throughout the trial with the greatest attention and impartiality.' They fully realised the importance of their position as the source of justice, and to their patriarchal instincts and independent spirit the freedom of judgment that had been left to them made an especial appeal. The Great White Saheb sat by, it was true: but he had generously placed the decision in their hands. Already his influence over them had taken firm root, and the trust he thus reposed in them they determined he should have no cause to regret.

At the end of the third day the great trial closed. For a space the judges consulted apart among themselves, but on this first Paharia Bench there was no indecision or disagreement. Amidst the awed silence of the clan they gave their award—an award that struck terror into the hearts of evildoers. Sardar Bidji of Titoria was to be hanged immediately, so ran their judgment, and one of the rank and file, Chandra of Pupat, was to share his fate. Twenty days hence Manjhi Jaura of Tatakpara should be hanged and seven other Manjhis imprisoned for life unless the whole of the nine hundred cattle that had been carried off were delivered up within that time. If the cattle were restored Jaura Manjhi and the other seven were to receive a free pardon for all past offences.

At once, in the presence of the full strength of the Corps of Hill Archers, of the Sardars and Manjhis, and of the vast gathering of men of the tribe, the first part of the sentence was put into execution. Preparations having been hastily made, the assembly awaited in breathless awe the consummation of this summary justice. On a branch of one of the trees that had looked down on the first Paharia court of justice Bidji, Sardar of Titoria, and Chandra of Pupat paid the extreme penalty of the law, furnishing before the eyes of the whole tribe a solemn warning to all evildoers. The judges had not erred on the side of leniency, and it was well that all should see and know the swiftness of the fate that lay in store for such as should in the future be guilty of a like crime. The first act of justice of the Hill Assembly completed, the hillmen dispersed to their own homes, pondering on these strange things that had come to pass, and spreading even to the most remote recesses of the jungle the fame of this Great White Saheb who had arisen to rule the tribe.

But Cleveland's efforts for the Paharias went far beyond the Hill Rangers and the Hill Assembly. To protect them once for all from the outside interference that they brooked so ill, he formed the lands they held into a government estate. No longer need they fear the encroachment of the hated foreigner. Henceforward there was a line protected by the full force of British law which he could never cross as zemindar. The Paharias held direct from Government, and they were to hold absolutely rent free. Such favourable conditions made even the most exclusive among the Paharias anxious to be included within the hill tract, and the chiefs of Ambar and Sultanabad, still under the old district of Rajshahi, refused to give in their allegiance unless similar terms were offered to them. Further to the south, across the Brahmini, lay the Pargana of Belpâtta, including the Mal state of Sankara, ruled by its turbulent chief, Tribhuban Singh. The latter, seing the advantages that might be gained from inclusion within the hill tract, strongly urged the claims of Belpâtta to receive the same privileges as the northern states. Consequently these lands were withdrawn from the districts to which they had hitherto belonged and included within the limits of the privileged Paharia tract, their chiefs receiving stipends like their neighbours. The vast government estate was thus consolidated, and became known for all time by the picturesque name of the Daman-i-koh—the Skirt of the Hills.

Within the limits of this new district were wide stretches of fertile land, low lying, at the foot of the hills, and admirably fitted for cultivation, only awaiting the touch of the plough to return a hundredfold of all that might be committed to their care. If the Paharias could be induced to leave their homes on the rocky slopes of the hills and descend to cultivate these lands of so much promise, it would be a great step towards their adopting something of the higher civilisation that lay around them on the plains. The most backward people with whom the British in Bengal had yet come into close contact, it was obvious that but little hope of their advance could be entertained so long as they refused all intercourse with the more advanced races in their neighbourhood, and neglected cultivation for the wilder pursuits of the chase. Still less, now that Government had especially protected their lands, could any higher influence from the outside world penetrate to their mountain homes. Nothing but their descent into the low-lying skirts of the hills, and their adoption of the life and interest of the plains, could raise them from their backward state.

It was to accomplish this end that Cleveland devoted the efforts of the last years that were left to him. Twice a year under his control the Hill Assembly met, faithfully fulfilling its functions and growing more and more accustomed to intercourse with the foreigner. How far the confidence that he had inspired might have induced them to adopt further reforms was never to be known, for at the very moment when his plans, well devised and well executed, were promising success in full measure death came. Aged only twenty-nine, he died suddenly on January 13, 1784, in the midst of his schemes for the welfare of his people, deeply regretted by all with whom he had come in contact. The stone monument that the Board of Directors sent out from home still stands in front of the house he occupied at Bhagalpur, fitly describing the great service he had done, alike to his own government and to the Paharias for whose good he had so constantly and so ably striven. The inscription runs:—

TO THE MEMORY OF
AUGUSTUS CLEVELAND, ESQ.,
LATE COLLECTOR OF THE DISTRICTS OF
BHAUGULPORE AND RAJAMAHALL,
WHO, WITHOUT BLOODSHED OR THE TERROR OF AUTHORITY,
EMPLOYING ONLY THE MEANS OF CONCILIATION, CONFIDENCE,
AND BENEVOLENCE, ATTEMPTED AND ACCOMPLISHED
THE ENTIRE SUBJECTION OF THE LAWLESS AND SAVAGE
INHABITANTS OF THE JUNGLETERRY OF RAJAMAHALL,
WHO HAD LONG INFESTED THE NEIGHBOURING LANDS BY
THEIR PREDATORY INVASIONS,
INSPIRED THEM WITH A TASTE FOR THE ARTS OF CIVILISED LIFE
AND ATTACHED THEM TO THE BRITISH GOVERNMENT BY A
CONQUEST OVER THEIR MINDS—
THE MOST PERMANENT AS THE MOST RATIONAL
MODE OF DOMINION—
THE GOVERNOR-GENERAL AND COUNCIL OF BENGAL,
IN HONOUR OF HIS CHARACTER AND FOR AN
EXAMPLE TO OTHERS,
HAVE ORDERED THIS MONUMENT TO BE ERECTED.
HE DEPARTED THIS LIFE ON THE 13TH OF JANUARY, 1784,
AGED 29.

At the other end of the station, not far from the government offices, the zemindars of the district raised an imposing monument to his memory in the form of a Hindu pyramid surrounded by a wide arched gallery wherein the sacred lamp attended by a priest still burns. But among none was grief more genuine and sincere than among his own especial people of the Rajmahal Hills. They raise no monument in stone to their respected dead, but for him they have raised a still more lasting memorial in their hearts and in the traditions of their tribe. At the time of his death they solemnly performed for him all the funeral rites with which they honour their departed kinsmen. 'Lo!' they said, 'we have lost a father.' 'Yea,' was the reply, 'the father and mother of the tribe,' and the weird wailing notes of the Paharia death-song echoed along the hills across the valleys from range to range as village after village caught the news and sadly hastened to join in the performance of the one universal funeral rite of national mourning that the tribe has ever known.

CHAPTER V

THE DAMAN-I-KOH

THE strength of the master hand was quickly seen when once its hold had been relaxed. Cleveland's forceful personality alone had made such rapid progress possible, and it was but a natural consequence that, the guiding influence removed, there should be some falling back among the hillmen into their old ways and habits of life. Other Sahebs succeeded, just and wise administrators and honoured servants of the Company in their day and generation, but they were not as 'Chilmili.' They lacked the magic of his personal influence and name, and none inspired them with the entire confidence that they had given to him. It was not to be expected that a few short years could change the nature of a race, itself the growth of centuries, and it was small wonder if the old lawless spirit of the highlanders here and there asserted itself again in the days that followed.

Cleveland had never intended his measures to be anything but of a temporary nature. They had been especially designed to meet special needs and to guide the first uncertain steps of a primitive people along the paths of peace and justice. Had he lived he would doubtless have modified many of his earlier schemes as the hillmen showed themselves capable of better things, or as the pressing need to which they owed their origin grew less or ceased altogether to exist. Some, as the years passed, there can be no question, would have been better abolished or curtailed. Yet by a strange turn of Fate, owing partly to the entire ignorance of this remote hilly tract that prevailed at headquarters, amid the weightier affairs that were agitating Bengal, and partly to the difficulty of interfering with the hillmen themselves, it happened that Cleveland's avowedly temporary measures were destined to remain for long untouched, exactly in the same state in which he had left them.

For over thirty years following Cleveland's death the Daman-i-koh was controlled by his Sazawal and successor, Abdul Rasul Khan. During all this time scarcely a single change occurred. The Hill Assembly still met regularly, executing its rough form of justice ; and twelve years after his death the rules that Cleveland had drawn up to regulate its meetings were made law in Regulation I. of 1796. All offences committed by the hillmen were to be tried by the assembly presided over by the

Collector, who had power to confirm or modify any sentence under fourteen years' imprisonment. For any higher sentence that might be passed the approval of the Nizamat Adaulat—the Supreme Criminal Court—was made essential. With this one small proviso the Daman-i-koh was absolutely exempt from all connection with the ordinary courts. So little power had the Collector that he was unable on his own motion to try and punish even the most petty offences of the Paharias. It was a strange anomaly even in British India at the beginning of the nineteenth century. A small tract of some fourteen hundred square miles surrounded by a province to which it bore the relation of a single blade to a field of corn, it yet preserved a form of government all its own, wresting even from the most powerful conquerors that Bengal had yet known practical acknowledgment of its independence.

But left without Cleveland's commanding influence to restrain it signs of disorder were not long in appearing. The Hill Assembly, increasing in size as the fame of its meetings grew, gradually fell from its first high estate and became a prey to quarrels and dissensions. Its members, gaining confidence as they grew accustomed to their powers, became inflated with an undue sense of their own importance. Intrigues and bribery crept in to destroy the strict impartiality of their decisions, while disagreements among themselves interfered with and delayed the course of justice. Finally things came to such a pass that the assemblies fell into disrepute among the hillmen, and many of the Sardars refused to attend. It was only by bringing strong pressure to bear upon the chiefs that the assembly could be held at all during its last years, and had Government had more time at its disposal to deal with the affairs of this remote province it would hardly have existed so long as it did. Almost uncontrolled power in the hands of a semi-civilised people needed the strong hand that had given it birth to guide it into the right paths, and that hand relaxed a certain reaction was bound to come in the ordinary course of events. That the Hill Assembly should have so long performed its functions after Cleveland's death is a tribute to the personal influence that had made it in its early days so effective a weapon in the cause of peace.

Suspicion on account of the falling away of the Hill Assembly fell upon the Sazawal Abdul Rasul Khan. Several charges of encouraging lawlessness among the Paharias and not faithfully enforcing their obligations were made against him. To inquire into the truth of these charges Mr. James Sutherland, a Civil Servant, was deputed, and he was further asked to report on the general condition of affairs in the Daman-i-koh. But in 1818, before he could begin the inquiry, Abdul Rasul Khan died after thirty-four years of undisturbed and unquestioned authority. The exact nature of his powers seems never to have been defined, and during the whole course of his tenure of office not a single periodical report was ever made by him. Both he and the hillmen appear to have been entirely overlooked by Cleveland's successors in the Collectorate of Bhagalpur, and this small hill tract pursued the even tenor of its way during thirty-four years with practically no reference to the doings of the world beyond. The Paharias during all this time were almost as completely their own masters as when they watched the rise and fall of Hindu and Musulman empires without their gates.

It is thus difficult to speak of the merits or demerits of Sazawal Abdul Rasul Khan's conduct of affairs. The only criterion is the condition in which he left the Daman-i-koh, as gathered from Sutherland's graphic and interesting report submitted on June 8, 1819. Therein the defects of the system then in force were clearly pointed out, and the abolition of the office of Sazawal recommended. The total exemption from the criminal code and the uncontrolled constitution of the Hill

Assembly were strongly commented upon. 'Collected with difficulty,' writes Sutherland, referring to the members of the Assembly, 'they manifest an impatience in being employed in duties for which their disposition and habits so ill adapt them. The sentence unregulated by any fixed principle is often the hasty and capricious suggestion of the first individual whom lassitude induces to speak in the hope of closing the business of the court.' A striking example is given of the unreliability of the Sardars with whom such great judicial powers resided. One Somija Paharia had been charged with the murder of his wife. 'He was convicted,' so runs the report, 'of illegally and forcibly striking her four times with the open hand, whereby she died. This man would have been only sentenced to receive ten rattans had not a hill Naib, whilst one of the Sardars was repeating the judgment of the court, suddenly added a year's imprisonment, which amendment was immediately adopted by the whole assembly.'

Another important question raised by Mr. Sutherland in his report was that of the stipends payable annually to the Sardars and Manjhis. As he pointed out, Cleveland had only intended these as a temporary measure, and this fact had been impressed upon the chiefs themselves at the time of their first distribution. It had been recognised as in the nature of a bribe to keep the peace, and it had since become evident that while in many cases such a bribe was no longer required, in other cases it was being grossly abused, the Sardars accepting the stipends and openly breaking the conditions on which they had been granted. This was particularly the case with the Sardars to the south, where, the boundaries never having been clearly defined, constant friction with the neighbouring zemindars took place. The latter were in many instances extremely jealous of the numerous lands which Cleveland had withdrawn from their estates to form the Daman-i-koh, and they were ever on the watch to recover what portions they could by fraud or stealth. Disorder and confusion reigned along all the southern border.

But in spite of the state of affairs disclosed, no notice seems to have been taken of Sutherland's report for the next six years. The Bengal Government had many other things to occupy its attention, notably the First Burmese War, and it was not until 1826 that orders were passed upon it. The stipends were condemned, but it being considered inadvisable to abolish them straight away they were to be resumed as opportunity offered. To put a stop to the confusion that reigned owing to the ill-defined boundaries, the Hon. John Petty Ward, with the help of Captain Tanner as surveyor, was appointed to demarcate clearly by means of stone masonry pillars the land properly included within the Daman-i-koh. But beyond this special duty no further control over the hill tract was entrusted to Mr. Ward. He had consequently nothing whatever to do with the stipends, and, partly as a consequence of this, the order for their gradual resumption remained a dead letter, and they survived quite untouched for more than fifty years longer. Had he been entrusted with more extended powers, they and many another tradition of the Paharias would have met with scant respect.

Mr. Ward, who was the younger brother of the third Viscount Bangor, had entered the Civil Service in 1810, and was consequently an officer of sixteen years' service when appointed to demarcate the Daman-i-koh. An extremely able officer, he soon made it evident that the strong hand was once more shaping the destinies of the Paharias. But his was not the sympathetic hand of Augustus Cleveland. His writings, terse, graphic, and incisive, standing out like veritable oases in the desert of dry and voluminous record-room literature, disclose him a man of decided opinions, and sound common sense. Sympathy and respect for tribal prejudices, which had played so large a part in guiding his predecessor's policy, troubled him

THE HONOURABLE JOHN PETTY WARD

not at all. He considered the whole system of setting aside land especially for the benefit of the Paharias to be unsound and contrary to general policy. For Cleveland's generous system of protection he had no word of approval, and in his reports he writes in his straight outspoken way of 'the preposterous claims of the Paharias.' He looked upon the situation from an entirely opposite point of view. That a race of robbers and free-booters should have special laws enacted for their benefit, receive stipends, and live rent free, appeared to him an utterly mistaken line of policy. He would have brought them at once, if he had had his way, under the ordinary law that ran in the rest of the province, sweeping away at one blow stipends and privileges alike. But, sound as his arguments undoubtedly were theoretically, he entirely over-looked the fact—fortunately not forgotten by the British Government in India—that special cases do arise which call for special laws, and that it is the duty of the ruling power to adapt the law to the needs of the people, and not the people to the law.

It was owing to his efforts that, in the year following his appointment, Regulation I. of 1796 which had legalised Cleveland's rules for the hill assemblies was repealed by Regulation I. of 1827. For the first time the hillmen were brought under the ordinary courts, but still with exceptions in their favour which differentiated them from their neighbours without their limits in Bengal Proper. A committee of Hill Manjhis was allowed to sit at the trial of all cases in which a hillman was concerned, and to them it was given to declare the *fatwa*—the decision as to the guilt or innocence of the prisoner or as to the law applicable under the circumstances. This still left the administration of justice largely in their own hands. Only men of their own race were to give the verdict, and the discretionary power left in the hands of the court was small. Further, the Manjhis were authorised to adjudicate summarily in disputes with regard to land succession and claims to money when the value of the claim did not exceed one hundred rupees. The Paharias, though they were no longer to enjoy the unbridled independence of the old days of the Hill Assembly, were thus left with only a minimum of control on the part of the ordinary courts, which they enjoyed for nearly fifty years longer. Regulation I. of 1827 was not repealed until Sir George Campbell's Act for the better government of the province was passed fifteen years after the close of the Santal Rebellion—Act XXIX. of 1871.

It was in the same spirit of determination to curtail in every possible way the privileges of the Paharias that Mr. Ward had set out to demarcate the boundaries of the Daman-i-koh in 1826. The history of that demarcation, lasting over seven years and fruitful of many folios of correspondence, is of the most chequered description and one difficult to follow. There are occasional blanks in the records which cannot now be satisfactorily filled in, and the whole work seems to have been carried out in the most unsystematic way, though this cannot be altogether laid to the charge of Mr. Ward, who was transferred to other duties on two or three occasions during the progress of the demarcation. Beginning in 1826, a start was made at the northern limit of the Daman-i-koh in Manihari, the first stone pillar of the ring that was to surround this promised land being placed a few miles south of Pirpainti. Thence the demarcation was continued towards the east, and for the next two years the ring-fence of pillars continued to extend. The reports of these two seasons' work are full and interesting, throwing as they do many sidelights on the history and associations of the locality. But Mr. Ward's view of the undesirability of the demarcation was soon apparent in his endeavour to restrict it to the smallest possible limits. With no apparent reason, all mention of the Colgong Hills had been omitted from Mr. Sutherland's report. Taking advantage of this, Mr. Ward arbitrarily cut them off from the

Daman-i-koh. It is particularly inexplicable why no reference was made to them in the report of 1819, since at that time they were receiving stipends, and continued to do so until 1881, though, owing to Mr. Ward's action, they were never included in the Daman-i-koh, as finally demarcated. It is a striking instance of the anomalies and illogical conditions that are to be constantly found in the eventful history of the Paharias and the Rajmahal Hills.

But one useful and salutary measure was the result of these early years, when Mr. Ward brought common sense and firmness if not sympathy to deal with Paharia affairs. One of the chief abuses that had crept into Cleveland's system was instanced in the person of Sumar Singh, the self-styled Raja of Sankara. More than forty years before Tribhuban Singh, the father of Sumar Singh, had become Cleveland's stipendiary Sardar for the Sankara Hills. Lying adjacent to the plains and easily accessible, Sankara had been hitherto contained in the Birbhum zemindary, and Tribhuban Singh had little in common with the wild hillmen of the northern hills, and was in fact a petty Talukdar of the plains. But, foreseeing great advantages to himself, he had induced Cleveland to include not only Sankara but the huge *tappa* of Belpâtta, of which it formed a part, within the Daman-i-koh.

Belpâtta lying to the extreme south, Cleveland knew little of it, and deceived by Tribhuban Singh's representations and led on by his desire to protect the hillmen on their southern boundary, he had secured from Government its transfer from Birbhum to Bhagalpur, and appointing stipends to its chiefs had included the whole *tappa* within the hill district. In the years succeeding Cleveland's death Tribhuban Singh and his son Sumar Singh had turned the special privileges thus gained to good account. To the lawless predatory habits of the Paharias, to whom they were really allied by birth, they added all the craft and cunning of the plainsmen, to whom through long training and association they had become akin. Both were men of singular determination and force of character standing out pre-eminently—unfortunately chiefly by their evil deeds—from among the men of their race which has left but few individual names on record. With the absolute immunity from the ordinary courts gained by their inclusion within the Daman-i-koh and situated on the edge of some of the most fertile lands in Bengal, their opportunities for evil were unrivalled. A raid across the border carried no fear of future reprisals in its wake. Once back again within the limits of the Daman-i-koh the ordinary law of the plains could not touch them. They were within safe sanctuary. Long before

Mr. Ward's coming the name of Sumar Singh had become a terror to all the surrounding district. So audacious had his forays become that they threatened at last even the headquarters station of Birbhum at Suri. Yet the authorities were impotent, for no writ could follow him to his own home. There he was triable only by his peers in the Hill Assembly, and that body in its latter days was no longer the impartial court administering stern justice that it had shown itself to be at its inauguration. Sumar Singh was strong and rich, and justice never came his way. His lands slowly but surely increased, anything he was able to appropriate from his neighbours becoming at once privileged property as part of the Daman-i-koh. The stipend his father had received was now of small account, and he contemptuously bestowed it on a relative, deeming the receipt of it unbecoming to the dignity of the title of Raja which he had arrogated to himself.

For years Sumar Singh had flourished, his evil doings far from headquarters apparently escaping the notice of the English authorities. But to Mr. Ward, unsympathetic to the protective system at its best, such an abuse of it was not to be tolerated. With a stroke of the pen he cut off Sankara completely from the Daman-i-koh. It was doubtless a wise reform, but, like so many reforms before and since, it involved a certain amount of hardship where it was least deserved. With Sankara, by Mr. Ward's sweeping order, went the hills to the south-west, genuine Paharia ground which Cleveland had expressly recognised, and to which he had granted stipends. The whole of this country, comprising all Belpâtta except the hill *tappas* Marpal and Dampal, was restored to Birbhum, losing all its special privileges, though, strangely enough, in spite of his indignation at Sumar Singh's conduct, Mr. Ward made no attempt to withdraw the stipends, which still continued to be paid to him until his death, nearly thirty years later, and to his successors after him. Sumar Singh in fact lost nothing but the privileges of the Daman-i-koh. He still retained his ill-gotten gains and the Sankara estate, and flourished till the end of a long life of evil doing, his death occurring just in time to save him from the wrath of the outraged Santals when they rose in revolt against such oppressors as he.

After two years of constant systematic labour Mr. Ward's work of demarcation met with a sudden check. Why it should have been stopped remains an unsolved mystery, and though the whole establishment for the work appears to have been retained, the records are silent as to further progress made in the years that immediately succeeded. Mr. Ward is known to have been sent on special duty to Purneah, and in 1830 he was appointed Commissioner of Aligarh, which appointment, however, he could not have long held, as he was acting Collector of Bhagalpur during that year. But although Mr. Ward was back again as head of the district, the work of demarcation did not proceed. Suddenly, in 1832, Government at headquarters seems to have become alive to the fact that not a fourth of the demarcation had been completed. Then followed a long acrimonious correspondence, prolific of explanations, censure, and recriminations. Government called upon the Board of Revenue to explain the delay, the Board of Revenue turned to the Commissioner, and the Commissioner endeavoured to fix the blame upon Mr. Ward. The latter's reply to the Commissioner is by far the most striking letter of the whole correspondence, and for contemptuous insubordination from a civilian to his superior officer it would be hard to find an equal.

As a result of this passage of arms, Mr. Ward was ordered to commence the work again at once. But utterly unsympathetic to the principles of the task before him and with his own grievances against Government, he appears to have taken little further interest in the work of demarcation. There is no record of progress made after this date except the map, from which it would appear as if the line were arbitrarily drawn by a mere stroke of the pen. Little or no inquiry could have been made on the spot, or the extraordinary inclusion of certain lands and the exclusion of others would hardly have taken place. On the east the line of demarcation has been drawn straight as a die on the map, absolutely careless of the claims of the lands on either side. Through Ambar and Sultanabad straight down to the Brahmini River it runs, turning neither to the right nor to the left, regardless of obstacles in the way, actually cutting through many a Paharia village, and excluding many a Paharia hill and homestead. On the south the Brahmini River formed a convenient natural boundary and avoided the difficulties of demarcation. It weighed little with Mr. Ward that it excluded the Ramgarh and Sankara Hills, and these were entirely ignored though their stipends were left to them untouched. From the Brahmini again the line was taken due north till it rejoined the first pillar near Pirpainti.

Great was the confusion that arose from this arbitrary demarcation. Mr. Ward retired from the service in 1834, disgusted with the treatment he had received, though it is only after his retirement that official blame seems to have been showered upon him, when the results of his hasty methods became apparent. The Resumption Commissioner, however, to whom was entrusted the duty of settling the disputes that naturally arose after Mr. Ward's departure, seems to have studied the rights of the parties with little more attention. He practically ignored the imaginary boundary line just drawn by awarding to Pargana Ambar, outside the pillars, the whole hill *tappa* of Sumarpul, which Cleveland in 1781 had taken from it to form a portion of the Daman-i-koh. This was almost as great an injustice as Mr. Ward's withdrawal of the hills to the south of the Brahmini, and though it was strongly protested against at the time Sumarpul was lost for all time to the Daman-i-koh.

But it was soon apparent that the demarcation—the cause of so much official heartburning—was in vain, so far as the Paharias were concerned. Though this fertile land lay at the Skirts of the Hills, theirs for the taking, they still held back. So long as the hated foreigners, Musulman and Hindu zemindar and mahajan were kept in check, and their own independence secured, that was all they asked. They were content with their homes on the rugged slopes of the hills which had faithfully sheltered them from so many of the vicissitudes that had overwhelmed their neighbours of the plains, and which promised them the few necessaries that they demanded of life for all time to come. The low-lying portions of the Daman-i-koh, securely guarded within the circle of stone pillars, remained untouched, all its allurements of fertility and plenty and exclusiveness failing to draw down the hillmen from their hills. So for a space it seemed as if the demarcation had been in vain, and the great white boundary pillars that the British Government had built looked upon a land of untouched hill and jungle whereon the hand of man had never yet laid its impress.

But it was only for a brief space. Already another tribe, aboriginal like the Paharias, but with a history strangely unlike theirs, of constant movement and restless wanderings, was slowly but surely making its way towards the Daman-i-koh. The Santals, the most numerous aboriginal race in Bengal, had long since arrived in the highlands to the south of the Rajmahal Hills, in Birbhum, Manbhum, and along the banks of their sacred river, the Damuda. Time after time they had given up their lands and moved on to escape the tyranny of Hindu zemindar and mahajan, until pressing northward they reached at last the Skirts of the Hills. The fertile lowlands that the Paharias scorned were to them as a promised land where the oppressor before whom they had so often fled could not follow. They hailed it with delight, and Government, glad that this wandering tribe should find a home and recognising the hopelessness of expecting the Paharias to settle in the plains, threw open to them the Daman-i-koh, and the next chapter in the history of this hill tract is the peaceful invasion of the Santals. The Paharias offered no resistance. Rather they welcomed the settlement of this aboriginal race on the lands they did not want as a safe and permanent barrier between themselves and the foreigner beyond. Henceforward the Paharias suffer eclipse, wellnigh passing out of the annals of their own district altogether. Cut off from the plains by the most permanent of barriers, they have continued their primitive existence in their secluded hills almost as undisturbed and unchanged as in the days before their first entry into the annals of British history in Bengal more than a century ago.

THE DAMUDA: THE SACRED RIVER OF THE SANTALS

CHAPTER VI

THE COMING OF THE SANTALS

EVEN in the annals of India, where events move fast, so sudden a change as that which transformed the Daman-i-koh at the coming of the Santals is almost without a parallel. A nomadic people, forced by new conditions to seek a more permanent home, they seized eagerly upon this land of promise, and forest, shrub, and jungle went down before them like saplings before the storm. Once admitted within the charmed circle of the white stone pillars they overran the low-lying lands like locusts, sweeping them bare of nature's handiwork and forcing them, plotted out into trim brown cultivated fields, to yield them sustenance. Whence this industrious, indefatigable race came is almost as forgotten as the beginnings of the Paharias themselves. But the Santal, though he can give no clear narrative of his wanderings, has preserved innumerable traditions of the origin and early doings of his race. Steeped in myth and legendary lore, he has obviously invented many stories to account for those things which his limited intelligence is not able to grasp. Groping in the dark in his inquiry into things past, he has fashioned a legend of his own as best he can when met by the blank wall of ignorance. Being, unlike the Paharia, of an inquiring turn of mind, but unable to account for the beginnings of his race, he has invented a story of his genesis that has been handed down through countless generations, until it has become implicitly accepted and unquestioningly believed. It is a quaint story of primitive folklore, but of much value in itself as revealing something of the character and habits of life of the interesting race that fabricated it.

In the beginning, runs the Santal tradition of the origin of the race, the world was a waste of waters and there was no dry land. Only Thakur, the Supreme Being, and Marang Buru, the Great Spirit, with the Munds, their Council of attendant Spirits, reigned over this desolate kingdom. Suddenly it occurred to one of the lesser divinities that it would be well to create human beings, and he proposed the plan to Thakur. The Supreme Being consented, and one of the attendant spirits, known as Malin Budhi, was chosen to prepare suitable bodies into which when ready he might breathe the breath of life. Malin Budhi at once set to work, and, labouring all the day, finished her task towards sunset. The two forms that she had made out of the froth that floated on the face of the waters, being not yet dry, were laid out to catch the warmth of the last rays of the setting sun. But at that time came down Sing Sadom, the Dayhorse, to drink, and he, not noticing, trampled the new-made bodies under foot, utterly destroying their shape and symmetry. Malin Budhi, in great distress at the ruin of her handiwork, hastened to Thakur, bitterly complaining of what Sing Sadom had done and accusing him not only of carelessness, but of actual malice and ill-will. He was jealous, she said, that to her had been given the honourable task of making the bodies of the first human beings. Thakur, however, succeeded in pacifying her, and ordered her to remodel them, severely reprimanding Sing Sadom and commanding him to interfere no more with the fulfilment of his orders. Malin Budhi, thus assured, again set to work, and this time the forms that she had made dried undisturbed in the sun. When at last they were ready she went to Thakur and besought him to come and put the crowning touch to her handiwork by giving them the gift of life. Then Thakur and his attendant deities proceeded to the scene of her labours and looking upon the forms that she had made pronounced them to be good. Whereupon the Supreme Being ordered Malin Budhi to return to his house and bring the spirit of life that they might live. Before she started he strictly enjoined her to remember his directions, or dire results might follow. Above the door-frame of his house was the Bird Spirit: that she was not to touch. Higher up among the rafters was the Human Spirit: that she was to take and carefully bring to him. But unfortunately Malin Budhi was short of stature, and when she arrived at Thakur's house she found she could not reach up as high as the rafters. There was none near to help her, and she was at a loss what to do. Then temptation came to her and she fell. She took the Bird Spirit from above the door, disobeying the strict injunctions of the Supreme Being, but thinking to deceive him. So she returned to the place where the gods awaited her, and, saying nothing, handed the Bird Spirit to Thakur, who apparently did not recognise the deception that had been practised upon him. He solemnly imparted it to the two lifeless forms, and they straightway became birds, and flying away into the air disappeared over the waste of waters. The punishment of Malin Budhi was swift. The Supreme Being turned upon her in wrath and condemned her for her faithlessness to become a Bhut (evil spirit) and to have her dwelling only in the loneliest of rocks and caves in the forest.

After a period of twelve months, or it may have

been twelve years—time is of no account among the Santals—the birds flew back to Thakur with the request that he would give them a place wherein to build their nest. This was a difficulty that had not previously occurred to the assembled divinities, and they gathered together to take council how best to meet it. The discussion was long and wordy, as in many a Santal council since. Each divinity had original ideas of his own and clamoured to be allowed to put them to the test. Sole Hako, a fish, was the first to be called upon to try his plan. But, work as he might, all his efforts to raise up dry land above the waste of waters were in vain, and he was finally forced to acknowledge that the task was beyond his power. Then Kaskom, the crab, tried, with only a slighter degree of success. Occasionally he succeeded in throwing up earth on to the surface of the water, but the stream quickly swept it away. Next the Earthworm took up the task. He placed himself with his head resting on the land at the bottom of the water, so that the earth which he ate might pass through him and fall on the surface, thus forming dry land. But as fast as he threw up the earth it subsided again into the water, and no sign remained of all the Earthworm's labour. He, too, was fain at last to admit that the work was greater than he could accomplish.

The assembled divinities were at the extremity of despair. But at that moment up rose the Centipede with a proposal that inspired fresh hope. In the water there lived the Tortoise, and his back was broad and strong. By chaining him to the bottom of the water it might be possible to heap earth upon his back until dry ground appeared. The legend does not state whether the Tortoise nobly sacrificed himself for the public good or whether his feelings were disregarded in the matter, his interests being subordinated to the greatest good of the greatest number. Be that as it may, he was promptly chained with four iron chains to a certain spot, and the Centipede and the Earthworm, to the great delight of all the divinities, finally succeeded in raising the earth so high upon his back that dry land at last appeared. On the island thus formed, and gradually increasing in size, the Supreme Being caused a tree to grow and planted grass beneath its shade. It is on this same island, built up on the back of a tortoise, that the Santals say that they live to-day. Earthquakes they attribute to the Tortoise shaking himself from time to time in his endeavours to be free. The end of the world will come at last when the Tortoise finally shifts the burden from his back, and the land sinks again beneath the waste of waters.

On the first land thus formed the two birds,

whom the Santals call Has and Hasin, made their home. Building a nest among the *sirom*, the coarse grass that quickly sprang up everywhere, the female bird laid two eggs. In the fulness of time from these eggs were born the first two human beings—a boy and a girl—the progenitors of the human race. They are known among the Santals as Pilchu Haram and Pilchu Budhi. As soon as Thakur heard that they were born, he sent Marang Buru to bring them before him. When they appeared he saw that they were giants, but that as yet they had no clothes. Hastily sending for some cloth, he gave them each a piece. The boy's was ten cubits long, and Marang Buru showed him how to tie it round his loins. The girl's was of twelve cubits' length, and so it partly covered her head also. But the gods thought that this was sufficient—so the Santals say—and omitted to teach them how to make other clothes of any kind, wherefore they wear but a single strip of cloth for garment until this day.

Thus provided with one of the first requisites of life they were given over into the care of Marang Buru, who was ordered to see that they were brought up as human beings should be. For their use Thakur created the Kapil cows. These in course of time had two bull calves with which, when they had grown sufficiently, Marang Buru taught Pilchu Haram how to plough the land. Then supplying the seed he helped him with every stage of cultivation until the harvest yielded its bountiful return and the first human beings saw that reward followed labour. 'Now that your work in the fields is done,' said Marang Buru as Pilchu and Budhi contemplated their well-stocked barn, 'it is right that you should turn aside for a while and indulge in pleasure.' Thereupon he proceeded to teach them how to make rice beer. Giving them leaven he showed them how it should be prepared, and then told them to leave it to ferment for four days. Pilchu and Budhi obeyed his instructions, wondering what new experience was in store for them. Then at the close of the fourth day Marang Buru came to them and looking at the *haria* informed them that it was ready for their use. First of all he showed them how to pour out a libation to the gods, and then making cups for them out of the leaves of the banyan tree he left them with his blessing, telling them that they might drink. So Pilchu and Budhi drank of the liquor, and finding that it was good they imbibed large quantities. Soon they became intoxicated, and then for the first time Pilchu saw that Budhi was fair. From that time they lived together as husband and wife. To this legendary divine origin of the much-loved *haria* the Santal still points to-day in mitigation of all the excesses and orgies that are due to his too great fondness for it. It is the gift of the gods, he says, and he never fails to honour it by enjoying it to the full.

To Pilchu and Budhi were born seven sons and seven daughters—the sons strong and lithe and skilful with the bow, and the daughters fair and comely to look upon. But, unfortunately, while these children were quite young the peace of the family was broken by the quarrels of the parents, who were old enough to have known better and to have set a more fitting example. Finally, in a fit of temper, they separated. Pilchu Budhi, gathering her daughters around her, went off into the forest; while Pilchu Haram with his sons took the opposite direction, and it was not until after many years that they met again.

Meanwhile the seven sons grew to manhood and fulfilled the promise of their youth, becoming mighty warriors and tireless in the chase. Far afield they wandered in search of game, until one day, in the innermost recesses of the forest where they had not hitherto penetrated, an adventure befell them that altered the course of their lives. The seven daughters of the family had meanwhile grown up under their mother's care, learning all that it was right and proper that a Santal maiden should. Every day they went to the jungle collecting herbs which Pilchu Budhi showed them how to prepare for food and medicine. On one occasion these maidens, having gathered their store of herbs, were amusing themselves by swinging on the branches of a pepul tree, singing the songs of the forest that their mother had taught them. It was thus that the seven brothers, pursuing the chase, came suddenly upon them. The first natural shyness of the maidens, who had never as yet beheld a man, having worn off, they quickly succumbed to the advances of the gallant hunters, and dancing, singing, and merrymaking marked the beginning of their acquaintance. Pairing off in couples according to their ages they decided to quit their old homes, and clearing the jungle make for themselves a new abode. Each couple henceforward lived together as man and wife, knowing nothing of the relationship that already existed between them.

The first parents, Pilchu Haram and Pilchu Budhi, were thus left deserted in their respective dwellings. After waiting long for his sons' return Pilchu Haram set out in search of them. For many days he wandered hither and thither, finding no trace, until at last he came to a clearing in the forest where an old woman sat spinning at the door of her house. Going up to her he asked her for fire to cook his food. This she gave him, and entering into conversation they quickly recognised

A SANTAL YOUTH FULLY EQUIPPED FOR THE DANCE

each other, and making up the quarrel that had separated them for so many years they settled down again together.

Such is the legend of the Santals to account for the origin of their race, told with many variations and additions, excusable among a people of vivid imagination and unblessed with a written history, but always faithfully adhering to the main points of interest, whether it be told on the banks of the Ganges in the north or in the jungles of Orissa in the south. One version, for instance, varies the episode of the creation of the bird spirits, assigning the origin of the race to two feathers that fell from Marang Buru as he flew over the waste of waters, while in another it is the Lende—earthworm—who finally succeeded in lifting the earth upon the leaf of a white lily that grew on the surface of the water. There is also another and more detailed version of the reunion of Pilchu Haram and Pilchu Budhi and the ending of the story. Deserted by her daughters, Pilchu Budhi passed many days of anxious waiting, weeping bitterly at the thought of the harm that had probably come to them. Suddenly Marang Buru appeared before her and inquired the cause of her grief. She told him of the disappearance of her daughters and her fears on their behalf. He assured her that they were safe and happy, adding, 'You have been too long at variance with your husband. Come, I will lead you to him and you shall make up the quarrel that has so long separated you.' So saying, he led her to where Pilchu Haram lived, and the old couple, rejoiced at meeting again, forgot their differences and settled down together. Afterwards Marang Buru told them what had happened to their children, leading them to the place where they had made their home. But when the seven brothers learned that they had married their sisters they were very angry with their parents for not having informed them of each other's existence. So great was their wrath that they would have killed the old couple had not Marang Buru once more come to their help and hidden them in a cave. Here after their many vicissitudes ends the story of the first two human beings, for from that cave they were never known to emerge.

In a legend so vague and mythical there is little idea of locality. Where these earliest ancestors of their race first made their home the Santals have no knowledge. The earliest place of residence of which the name survives in their traditions is Hihiri Pipihri in the Siri Forest. One of their rhyming legends runs :—

> In Hihiri, mother, I was born ;
> In Pipihri, mother, I saw the light ;
> In Haradata, mother, I grew up ;
> In Khojkaman, mother, I was sought for.

Many attempts have been made to identify this earliest geographical name known to the Santals. It may be, as some suppose, identical with Pargana Ahuri in Hazaribagh; but if so, it is connected with a comparatively recent period of Santal history, unless, indeed, these are no new names, but old ones brought from their far-off camping-grounds, as yet unidentified. There is also the theory that it is no geographical designation at all, but merely a rendering of the word 'hir' (origin), used by the Santals in referring to their original home. No legend attaches to their stay at Hihiri Pipihri, wherever it may have been, except that here the descendants of Pilchu Haram and Pilchu Budhi grew and multiplied, and were known as Kharwars. From this place they removed to Khairagarh and Haradata, and thence to Khojkaman, where they apparently made a protracted stay. It was here, according to tradition, that they first became divided into groups or tribes, named after the seven sons of the first parents—Kisku, Murmu, Hembrom, Soren, Hasdak, Marudi, and Tudu. Many of their legends, such as those relating to the origin of the Chilbundhu sub-caste and the Murmu tribe, are supposed to date from the residence of the Santals in Khojkaman.

So far all the geographical names in the legend of their race wanderings are impossible of certain identification. But the next move of the tribe, according to tradition, brings the story within the range of possible verification. From Khojkaman they moved to Chae, and thence to Champa, both situated in the north-west corner of the Hazaribagh district. No Santals remain in that locality at the present time, but they have left behind them traces to show that they once passed that way. At Chae an old fort still survives, its ruined walls of earth and stones enclosing a space something like five acres in extent. At one time, so runs the legend, it was in possession of one Jaura, a Santal Raja, who, distrustful of being able to hold it against an advancing Musulman army, destroyed himself and his family rather than fall into the enemy's hands. The victorious troops are said to have been commanded by one Sayyed Ibrahim Ali, known also as Malik Baza. This first mention of a name known to history is of importance as giving the first clue to any definite time or period to which the Santal legends relate. Sayyed Ibrahim Ali was a general of Mahommed Tughluk, and he died in the second year of the reign of Firoz Shah on January 25, 1353 A.D. A Mahommedan officer, Hazrat Fathi Khan Duala, was placed in charge of the fort, and on his death a *darga*, or mosque, was erected near his grave. Four miles from Chae, at Mangarh, are the remains of another fort, which presumably is of the same period and which Santal tradition ascribes to a chief of their race called Man Singh, who, unlike Jaura, fled at the approach of the Musulman army.

Champa seems to have been the name vaguely given to a stretch of country in the north-west corner of Hazaribagh. Their stay here was the time of the Santals' greatest prosperity, which their descendants still love to recall to-day. Tradition fondly reverts again and again to these years at Champa as the good old times when the tribe lived at peace, with broad lands at their disposal and with no hated 'foreigner' to interfere. It was the golden age when for the Santal there was no law save the rules and precepts of the tribe, which it was his nature by custom and tradition to reverence and obey. The land was his for the taking. Rent, with all the means of oppression it still implies to the Santal of to-day, was as yet unknown. No forest laws to prevent his cutting as much of the jungle as he pleased had yet been framed. These days of freedom in Champa and elsewhere have so indelibly impressed themselves upon the Santal mind that even to-day he fails to understand how any power, any law, or any authority can rob him of his immemorial right to the land and to cut as much timber as he desires. Even repeated convictions in the courts have failed to impress the

Santal with the fact that the jungle is no longer his to destroy at will. Consequently to the Santal of the present day, bound down by laws, the necessity of which he sometimes fails to see, the memory of the time of untrammeled freedom at Champa appeals with special force, surrounded as it is with the halo of independence and prosperity.

But even into the peaceful land of Champa the oppressor came, and the Santal preferred to pack up his goods and chattels and trek for pastures new rather than submit to the slightest sign of domination from the foreigner. No tradition of warlike deeds and spirited resistance lingers round the Santals such as is associated with the Paharias from their earliest days. The Santal was no warrior. Being of a roving disposition, he knew nothing, in his earlier days, of that passionate attachment to his home that animated the Paharias in their magnificent defence, causing them to resist successfully every attack from without until the coming of the British. Ever present deep down in the Santal mind has been a spirit of unrest. No sooner in the old days had he cleared the jungle and tilled the lands, subduing Nature in a hard-fought fight, than the easy daily labour of the fields palled, and the passionate love of intake seized him again, leading him to move on to lands as yet untouched to commence again his strenuous toil.

But in Champa, from the remains that they have left behind, it appears that they made their longest stay. Here they built their forts and grew rich and multiplied. Fort Koendi was the residence of the royal house of Kisku, the first and greatest of the twelve Santal tribes. Fort Champa itself was the stronghold of the second tribe, the Murmus, princes in the land. Fort Kaira owed its existence to the noble house of Hembrom, while Fort Badodi was the treasure-house of Marudi, the traditional stewards to all the kings, princes, and nobles of the Santal race.

But the days of their prosperity came to an end even in Chae Champa. In this wise it was that their exodus took place. In that country were many Birhors—so runs the legend, and this is an interesting point, as it is still the home of that tribe to-day—and they were in the service of the royal house of Kisku. To them fell the duty of providing ropes with which to tether the elephants and cattle belonging to the king. Now on one occasion they neglected their duty, and no new ropes being supplied the elephants and cattle broke loose during the night, working havoc among the crops and neighbouring villages. The Birhors, hearing what had happened as a result of their neglect of duty, were overcome with fear at the thought of the swift punishment that would assuredly overtake them.

Hastily gathering together their few personal belongings, they fled away in a body into the jungle. The news of the damage done to his lands and the flight of the Birhors was brought simultaneously to the lord of the Kiskus. His anger knew no bounds, and buckling on his sword he ordered his retainers to follow him in pursuing the fugitives. The Birhors were at first hard pressed, and during the flight one of their women gave birth to a child; but such was their fear of their lord's vengeance that, unwilling to be further encumbered even to so slight an extent, they left the new-born infant on the road, hastily covering it with a few large leaves. As the pursuers passed by they heard its cries, and the king stopping to inquire what it was, the child was found and brought before him. Now the infant was a male child, exceedingly strong and well favoured, and the king took compassion upon its helpless state. The day was already drawing to a close, and abandoning the chase he returned home, taking the foundling with him. The child was reared in the king's house, almost as the king's son, and the name given to him was Madho Singh.

Even in his earliest years it was seen that he was endowed with abilities beyond the common, and when he grew to years of discretion the king appointed him to collect the revenue. But, thus marked out for distinction, Madho Singh became presumptuous and forgot that he was sprung only from the Birhor race, who were but the servants of the Santals, who of their favour had preserved his life. Many things, however, were forgiven him until at last he announced his desire to marry one of the ladies of the Raja's family, when every Santal felt that the limits of forbearance had been reached. Assured that his suit could not be entertained—for the Santal marriage law is strict that none may marry or be given in marriage to one of another race—Madho Singh threatened to avail himself of the form of marriage known as *itut*, by which a rejected lover may marry the lady of his choice, even against her will, by simply marking her on the forehead with vermilion (*sindur*). This threat so enraged the Santals that a durbar was held to devise means to prevent such an outrage on their institutions and traditions. The assembly of the wise men consulted long together, for it was a difficult point which in the whole course of their history had never before arisen. There was no question but that *itut* was a legal form of marriage according to their law, yet that law was equally emphatic in forbidding marriage with any one outside their own race. Hitherto none of another race had presumed to aspire to the hand of a Santal maiden: Madho

Singh was the first to attempt to take advantage of a Santal custom to outrage a Santal law. Either the tribe must alter the marriage law or abolish the *itut* form of marriage if men of another race were not to be admitted within its limits. But either of these things the Santal was loth to do, for both were sanctioned by custom and tradition. But to admit a stranger within the tribe was altogether repugnant to the first principles of their tribal organisation and was not for a moment to be considered. There was thus nothing to be done, so decided the assembly of the wise, but to flee from the evil, which consisted in the designs of a single Birhor. Rather than suffer disgrace through the breaking of their sacred traditions, they were ready to leave the prosperous land of Champa and seek for themselves a new home, where they might safely maintain the integrity of the immemorial customs of their tribe. The whole story with its obvious improbability of the entire Santal race fleeing before the machinations of a single Birhor, is evidently only a legend invented to account for the removal of the Santals from Champa, the real reason of which they have long since forgotten.

The hasty and secret flight from Champa is graphically described in the legend. Unknown to Madho Singh the Santals decamped by night, leaving him in possession of their forts and taking with them only such of their belongings as would not greatly impede their flight. But after they had gone some distance they met with a sudden check. It was the Singh door, by which they found the road obstructed—a solid mass of stone covering the whole face of the hillside. Try as they might they could find no way over, round, or through it, and the few implements that they carried made no impression upon its hard rocky surface. In despair they sat down before it and wept. Then suddenly before them appeared two unknown men whose names they afterwards knew as Jahan Paika and Kapi Karan. Learning the reason of the Santals' distress, they said to them, 'Call upon our gods, the Bongas, and they will enable us to clear a path for you with our bows and arrows.' The Santals at first demurred, refusing to call upon strange gods; but the fear of being overtaken by Madho Singh at last prevailed, and lifting up their voices on the hillside they besought the help of the Bongas. Then Jahan Paika and Kapi Karan struck the stone door with their arrows, and it shivered at their touch, falling into a thousand fragments. The Santals, strongly impressed with the power of these strange gods, hastily crowded through the opening thus made and pursued their way.

But further on they were again brought to a standstill by another mass of stone—the Bahi door. Like the Singh door it proved impregnable, and all their efforts were again of no avail. But as before, just when despair had come upon them, two strangers appeared to offer their advice and help. These men were Ulum Paika and Bhalwai Bijai, and they also told the Santals to call upon the Bongas, who would not fail to help them once again. With the strong proof that they already possessed of the power of these strange gods, it would have been the height of folly and ingratitude not to implore their assistance in this new difficulty. So the Santals called upon the Bongas, and Ulum Paika and Bhalwai Bijai struck with their bows upon the rock, which crumbled at their touch. But this time the gods demanded some acknowledgment of their favours, and Ulum Paika and Bhalwai Bijai initiated the Santals into the mysteries of their worship. Sacrifices were offered by the wayside—a black cock for one spirit and a brown one for another, while strips of ox-hides were hung on the bushes, and *sindur* placed upon the stones at various stages along their line of march as a sign of their reverence for the new gods.

Meanwhile, in Champa, Madho Singh had discovered their flight, and, furious at being thus baffled in his designs, he set out in hot pursuit.

Passing through the Singh door and the Bahi door, which no longer offered any obstruction, he saw the places where the Santals had sacrificed, and the ox-hide strips on the bushes, and the *sindur* on the stones, and by these signs he knew that they had deserted the old worship and adopted a new faith. Disgusted at their treatment of him and their abandonment of their ancient gods, he returned home and set up his Birhor kingdom in the land they had deserted. So the Santals pursued their way to a new country unmolested, and followed after the strange gods who had so miraculously assisted their escape.

Their flight, according to the legend, was in the direction of Chota Nagpore. Here the Mundas were already in possession, but seeing that the Santals worshipped their own deities, the Bongas, they received them hospitably. But a country where the jungle had been cleared and the land cultivated failed to appeal to the Santals, and they made no long stay in Chota Nagpore. Pursuing their way to the south-east they came to Jhalda, which the Mundas also held. Thence, still moving on in search of pastures new, they arrived at Patkum; but here the Bhumij Kols had been before them, and this land, too, was occupied. Thence, under a Raja known as Hambir Singh, they pushed on across Manbhum to Pachet. Here for a time they remained, and their Rajas, influenced by continual intercourse with the Hindus, gradually adopted their religion and arrogated to themselves the name of Rajputs. But the mass of the people refused to forsake their old gods, and preferred once more to set out in search of a new home where they might worship their Bongas undisturbed. Travelling again in a south-westerly direction they came to Saont, which, according to them, marks an important stage in their history, since it was here that they first acquired the name of Santals—a designation, however, they never use, 'Hor' (a man) being the usual name by which a Santal calls himself. This would seem to point to the fact that the name of Saont had been given to the place before their arrival, and that from it they derived their name. No other derivation of the word Santal has been suggested. Saont has been identified by some with Silda in the Midnapore district, which still contains within its borders large numbers of the tribe.

Here the Santal traditions of their wanderings practically cease. They left Saont, they state, because the Raja of that place, watching the Santal maidens as they danced, saw that they were fair and wished to make one of them his wife. Thus the same danger threatened that had once before driven them out of Champa, and again they preferred flight to any interference with their strict caste system. But already the tribe had grown to such proportions that it was impossible for them to move in one united body as of old. It is probable that ere this the tribe had already split up, some of its members remaining along the route trodden by the main body. Some settled in Southern Manbhum, others in Hazaribagh along the banks of their sacred river the Damuda, while the largest body of all went northwards and finally made its home in the land that is now known by their name —the Santal Parganas.

The first mention of the Santals in English records is to be found in Mr. Sutherland's report after his inquiry into the state of the Daman-i-koh in 1818. None of them had as yet entered within that charmed circle which was still strictly preserved for the Paharias, and Mr. Sutherland only mentions having met on the extreme southern edge of the district a few members of the tribe whom he calls Sontars, noting their reputation as industrious tillers of the soil. Ten years later, from Mr. Ward's report, they appear to have greatly increased in numbers on the south-west borders of the Daman-i-koh; and four years later, in 1832, they made their first entry into the promised land under Mr. Ward's superintendence, though in direct opposition to the orders of government. But when, within the next few years, it became evident that the Paharias would never descend from their hills and undertake the cultivation of the fertile fields that lay at their feet Government adopted another course. Anxious alike to see a restless wandering tribe permanently settled, and the land that they had spent so much time and money in demarcating brought under cultivation, those in authority at last gave the order for the admission of the Santals within the charmed circle. In 1836 Mr. James Pontet, the Senior Deputy Collector in Bengal, with the express object of settling the newcomers, was appointed Superintendent of the Daman-i-koh. After many wanderings the main body of the Santals seemed to have reached its final goal.

CHAPTER VII

THE SANTAL REBELLION

THE first few years in the Daman-i-koh were years of strange peace and quiet. The Santal, a very Ishmaelite even among wandering tribes, had found a home at last. Here for the first time in all the history of his race he felt secure. The great white pillars that the British Government had built formed a more impregnable defence than any barrier that Nature could devise. The land within was to him a haven of rest such as he had never known, whence Hindu and mahajan, Musulman and zemindar, might no longer oust him at their will. So long as the Santal kept the peace the land was his. Government had proclaimed itself proprietor, and even the wildest among all the aborigines of Bengal had learned long since the magic power of the British name. The Skirts of the Hills was a land such as the Santals loved. Eight hundred and sixty-six square miles of highland and five hundred of lowland soil, it offered to them the labour and the recreation that centuries of custom had made characteristic of their race. In their many wanderings through wild untouched jungle they had learned perforce the strenuous toil of pioneers. To settle on some tract of land whereon the foot of man had never yet trod and fell the mighty monarchs of the forest that had hitherto reigned supreme, to turn the virgin soil and force subsistence from a hitherto unproductive land—this was the labour that appealed to them above the milder labour of the long-tilled fields in the rice plains of Bengal.

Here, too—what the Santals perhaps valued most of all—they could still preserve their nationality intact. With jealous exclusiveness they had shrunk from mixing with men of another race. Time and again, as their legends have recorded, this passionate desire to preserve the tribe from contamination had led them to forsake their homes and wander forth in search of new lands rather than admit a stranger within their ranks. It was this national spirit, this clannish sentiment, that united the Santals in one unbroken front against the foreigner, that enabled them to stem the tide of every conquest that engulfed their less united neighbours of the plains, and enabled them finally to wring practically their own terms from the last and greatest conqueror of all. But they had long since learned the danger that beset the integrity of the tribe from constant intercourse with the stranger at their gates. There were not wanting instances of aboriginal tribes which had fallen from their first traditions, and from close contact with a higher civilisation were rapidly becoming Hinduised. Such a fate the Santals had strenuously resisted, as when the danger threatened at Pachet; but the times had changed since they could wander on as in their legends they wandered from Chae Champa to Chota Nagpore, from Patkum to Jhalda, along the banks of the Damuda to Saont, ever finding fresh lands to be reclaimed. The old conditions of movement and unrest were coming to an end and order and stability were the watchwords of the new power. The race had already multiplied and grown beyond its old tribal limits: it was no longer possible for it to move as the one united family of former patriarchal days. There was a very real danger that it might split up into small scattered communities gradually losing their nationality and becoming absorbed in the lowest classes among the Hindus. Against such a fate the whole Santal nature rebelled. Suspicious of interference and restless of control, the Santals have always entertained a peculiar aversion to the entire Hindu race. The hatred and contempt on either side have been equal. The Hindus regarded the aboriginal tribes as outside the pale, below even the very meanest of their own race—Mehtas and Domes, Haris and Bhowris, sweepers and scavengers and buriers of the dead. The Santals, in their turn contemptuously assigning the Hindus a low place in the distribution of the human race, looked upon them as a weak-kneed people who fed only on vegetables and rice because at the beginning they had been unable to secure the strong meat fit food for the sons of men. Thus for the Santals life among the Hindus was doubly galling. They had the humiliation of being despised and oppressed by a race for which they themselves had nothing but contempt.

The Daman-i-koh, offering an escape from contact with the hated race, was thus to them a veritable land of Canaan. Here, without fear of being merged in a higher but repugnant civilisation, they could maintain their old tribal life and time-honoured customs intact. Here the traditions faithfully handed down through long periods of time might be passed on in unbroken succession to their children's children, and their worship, festivals, and ceremonies might be preserved under all their primitive conditions. So from every direction where they had made their temporary homes, from the banks of their sacred river the Damuda, from Hazaribagh, Manbhum, and Midnapore, the Santals came with their flocks and their herds, their families and household belongings and all that they had, to this promised land in the Skirts of the Hills. Here they foresaw a period of prosperity that brought back to memory the days in Chae Champa, round which a halo of recollection has always hung. It seemed as if at length the halcyon days known only from tradition had indeed returned. Free and untrammeled, they might pursue their peaceful lives in the same simple daily round that from time immemorial had been the custom of the tribe. Their village system was intact—the Manjhi and the Pahn, the Ojha and the Sardar, fulfilled their appointed functions without fear of molestation in peace and plenty, performing all that rigid custom demanded. Here at last they seemed to have found a home where change need never come. So in a great content and fancied security the Santal tilled the rich soil and gathered in his first abundant crops, little dreaming in his new-found joy of the dark days that were so soon to follow.

It was largely owing to the unfortunate omission to extend to the newcomers the special privileges already granted to the Paharias in the Daman-i-koh that the promise of the first years of Santal prosperity were not fulfilled. Mr. James Pontet had been appointed Superintendent of the Daman-i-koh at the instance of the Collector of Bhagalpur, with the express object of effecting a peaceful and orderly settlement. But his powers were of the most limited description. He had no criminal authority, and his jurisdiction did not extend to the Paharias in the Daman-i-koh or to the working of Regulation I. of 1827 which had been passed expressly for their benefit. Consequently the Santals, though admitted within the pillars, were not admitted to the special privileges which had been conferred upon the Paharias, and it was this which eventually left them once more a prey to their Hindu and Musulman enemies, and was mainly responsible for the evils that led to their rebellion twenty years later. It was not understood, in the first years of prosperity that followed their admission into the Daman-i-koh, that the Santal was as unfit as the Paharia to cope with the craft and wiles of a more highly civilised race, and that protection from without was as necessary for the one as for the other. Government, congratulating itself on the rush of Santal immigrants and the rapid changing of the untouched wastes in the Skirts of the Hills into fertilised fields, failed to discern the underlying danger that threatened the simple untutored settler almost from the first day of his arrival in the land.

All that could be done with the limited powers at his disposal Mr. Pontet did. Disobeyed and harassed by the police, who had no respect for a magistrate with neither criminal nor civil powers, his opinions and advice ostentatiously neglected

THE OJHA

by successive magistrates at Bhagalpur, the only measure of support that made his position tenable came from the Board of Revenue. From one unfortunate occurrence directly after he had entered upon the Superintendentship, his action in which his superior officers chose to regard in the light of an impertinence, he never wholly recovered. In ascertaining Mr. Ward's roughly defined boundaries he discovered that the Resumption Commissioner had decreed to Pargana Ambar the whole of *tappa* Sumarpal which Cleveland had expressly taken from it to form his Daman-i-koh in 1781. Indignant at this unjustifiable resumption, he at once wrote to the Commissioner a letter of protest, stronger unfortunately in language than in grammar, pointing out what he considered to be the obvious injustice involved. The tone of the protest from a Deputy Collector to a Commissioner was considered highly presumptuous, and official rebukes fell upon the unfortunate writer from all sides. Throughout the rest of his career he met with little sympathy and support from his immediate superiors. But, on the other hand, he gained the complete confidence of the Santals themselves, and his actual settlement of the newcomers in the Daman-i-koh was marked by conspicuous success for which he appears to have gained little of the credit due. From a minus quantity he raised the revenue of the Daman-i-koh to eighty thousand rupees, and without the aid of a map or any of the means of survey he performed the difficult task of dividing it into Mauzas and fiscal areas, corresponding with Parganas, and called by him 'bungalows.' But beyond this his authority did not extend, and the great evils that he saw rapidly closing round the fair land which he had so admirably settled he was powerless to counteract. For, from the very first, covetous eyes were fixed upon the Santals' growing prosperity, and their deadly enemies the mahajan and the zemindar were but waiting until the time was ripe to step in and reap the harvest that they had not sown.

Out beyond the pillars that marked off the Daman-i-koh a new impetus had been given to cultivation. For the first time in their history the lands at the foot of the Rajmahal Hills ceased to be the prey of raid and foray. No longer armed bands sallied forth from their hiding places in the hills to work wanton havoc on the crops and herds. The Santals, content to have found a spot where they believed that they might rest in peace, had as yet no cause of complaint to lead them to the old restless habits that they had learned in less prosperous days. They were too busy bringing their new lands under cultivation to pay any heed to what went on outside. The new home that they had found sufficed: they desired neither to see nor to know what happened beyond its limits. Even the Paharias had learned that the old days of unbridled licence were over, and the low-lying lands of the Daman-i-koh that they had scorned to occupy effectively cut them off from the scenes of their old plundering exploits.

The zemindars were not slow to take advantage of these peaceful conditions Following quickly in the wake of the Santals they pushed their cultivation to the utmost limits, right up to the stone pillars that marked the boundary of the Daman-i-koh. Quickly, while the Santal was busy at his labours, the hated foreigner approached even to his very gates. Once more history was repeating itself with strange reiteration. The Santal had gone ahead to prepare the way, and a keener-witted, more astute race was following close upon his heels to reap the benefit. Trusting blindly in his present possession of the land, the Santal was ignorant as yet that there were other and more subtle methods of oppression than being rudely driven from the soil. But it was soon to be borne in upon him that, though the foreigner might not get his land, he had the skill and the cunning to wrench from him all else that he possessed, even his freedom and the freedom of his wife and of his children even unto the third generation.

The Santal is of a happy-go-lucky disposition, the most improvident of men. The soil furnishes all that he asks of life, and yearly he looks to it to perform its allotted task. To save against a rainy day makes no appeal to him. Though all else may go, the land still remains a secure safeguard between himself and starvation. Consequently when the rich hitherto untouched soil in the Daman-i-koh under his exertions began to yield a hundredfold, and his barns and granaries grew full as they had never been before, no thought of future need tempted him to guard this new-found wealth. Rather he revelled in the unaccustomed plenty, growing reckless in the enjoyment of the present, with no thought of days to come.

Here was a field ready to hand for the rapacious zemindar and mahajan. A smiling prosperous land and a simple artless people offered fair ground for their keener worldliness and cunning. As the Santal gathered in his harvest, they crossed the border into the Daman-i-koh with their eyes upon the well-filled barns. Even legitimate trade paid cent. per cent. The Santal, carried away by this wondrous fertility, which to his limited imagination promised unlimited supplies, was willing to sell his stores of grain for the smallest sums of cash. But the astute trader, not content with legitimate trade, was not above resorting to deceit and fraud. False weights and measures were freely used, and the guileless Santal, ignorant and at first unsuspicious, failed to detect the sharp practice. It was a contest about to be fought out on the most unequal lines. Here it was no question of physical prowess, of the old wild onslaught of unsettled days, victorious by reason of its breathless courage and rash fearlessness of danger. Had it been such a contest, the Santal might not have feared defeat. But this was a fight on far different lines, wherein the other side held all the weapons of attack and the Santal was unskilled in the method of defence. Intellect against intellect, there was no question on which side the superiority lay. In skill and cunning, in the tortuous ways of the mahajan and the art of buying and selling, learned in the crowded mart and the daily traffic of the bazaar, the Hindu stood supreme. In all these things the Santal was but a child. Ignorant of the art of writing, even of counting beyond the fingers of his hands, and with none but the most rudimentary notions of keeping accounts, he lay completely at the mercy of his old enemy who had pursued him so relentlessly throughout his wanderings.

The trader, by fair means and foul, having fleeced the Santal of his stock of grain, it was time for the mahajan to step in. Did the simple villager, his last piece of ready money recklessly spent, desire to celebrate his son's marriage? He was at hand to proffer an advance with fair words and seeming generosity. Had the villager exhausted all his stock of corn before the next harvest had fully ripened? The usurer was at hand to tide over the evil days and supply his needs. The Santal, dazzled by this his first experience of a loan, took the proffered advance with alacrity, executing a bond of whose contents he was blissfully ignorant. One advance but led to another, with that strange fatality such transactions have the world over, and the Santal, making no count, fell deeper and deeper into debt. Interest, the very nature of which he failed to grasp, mounted up with outrageous rapidity, and the mahajan, responding willingly to the call for another advance, bided his time until the measure of indebtedness grew full.

Then, when at last the Santal was safely in his power, the mahajan began to reap the fruits of his well-laid plan. First the debtor's flocks and herds were taken from him, merely to pay the interest of the debt, only the oxen that drew the plough being 'lent' back to him to enable cultivation to proceed. Slowly the unfortunate peasant, held fast in the grip of his inexorable creditor, saw his treasured possessions go one by one. Almost before he had realised that the first days of his prosperity were past, ruin stared him in the face. How the change had come about he scarce understood. He only realised that it was due to the mahajan and the zemindar at his gates, and that he was gradually slipping more and more into their power with no loophole of escape. Anxiety and despair succeeded peace and plenty, and the sound of joy was no more heard in the land. Then the festivals were shorn of all their late splendour, and the Santals celebrated them as those who had hung their harps upon the willows. The oppressor had once more gained the upper hand, and there was none to help them.

When the mahajan at length seized the crops, as soon as they had ripened in the fields, the end had almost come. Starvation looked the helpless peasant in the face, and the terrors of the law, as exemplified in the mahajan's threats, loomed over him for the hopeless debt that had mounted up against his name. Then he learned the awful truth that, once he had fallen into the clutches of the moneylender, there was no escape. Conditions had changed since the days when he had sought refuge from the oppressor in flight, and a wholesale movement of the tribe was no longer possible. Flight in any case was but a courting of the perils of the unknown. Here, at least, miserable and helpless as he was, he still had the bare necessaries of life—the mahajan saw to that. The labourer is worthy of his food lest he become too feeble to labour, and the master's source of gain be gone. Yet to such an extent did the oppression come that many of them did prefer flight to the indignities they suffered under the hated yoke of the foreigner. In one year three whole townships suddenly disappeared, their inhabitants taking with them the few household gods that had escaped the mahajan's claims, and passing out to seek the inhospitable recesses of the jungle rather than remain as the slaves of the taskmaster.

But there was one last depth of degradation to be reached before the peaceful Santal rose in revolt against his fate. The day came in but too many cases when his land, the last thing to which the Santal clung, followed the rest of his possessions and fell into the mahajan's hands. Often the latter never even troubled to get a decree from the Courts: a forged one was good enough to deceive the Santal, ignorant of all forms of law and procedure. Or, if he preferred to proceed on legal lines, his success was no less assured. To the unfortunate peasant the far-off courts were often but a name, and no notice ever reaching him in his distant village, he knew nothing of the suit and decree until the subordinate officers of the law, the

Daroga and the Civil Court peon, came to dispossess him and sever his connection with the land which he had cleared and tilled and sown, and which he regarded with that passionate attachment that lies deep down in the primitive heart of man.

It was this attachment that made the dispossessed ryot still linger on, that took the heart out of him to leave friends and kindred and start life again alone in some distant and unknown spot. This was a different thing from the old days when all had moved in company. Now in his despair it was difficult even to bring home to him that his land was indeed gone, and to remain on as the labourer of the oppressor on the land he had once owned seemed a better fate than to tear himself away from it for ever. It was then that the last degradation was reached. For this the mahajan had been scheming through all the tortuous course of his dealings with the ryot. Of what use was the land to him if he had none to cultivate? It was to this reluctance of the Santal to quit the land, even though it might no longer be his, that the oppressor had trusted from the first. Now, entirely in the hands of the hardest of taskmasters, the wretched Santal had to accept what was given him, and the mahajan gave only what was necessary to keep his workmen fit for their work. He fed them on the same principle that he fed his oxen, that they might be strong to labour.

But in spite of his misfortunes the Santal was still intensely human, still a member of an organised community that demanded much of the individual. There were festivals to be celebrated now as always, prayers to be performed, and marriages to be arranged, and for all these things ready money or wealth in kind was essential. Bound down by custom and tradition and careless of the future, the Santal thought only how to celebrate each event as it occurred. Yet again he found the mahajan near at hand, complacent still and ready to lend, for there was one thing more the Santal had that the mahajan coveted. His land and all his possessions gone, the wretched peasant divined no further degree of degradation to which he might fall; but the mahajan, with his keener instinct, saw into the future, perchance foresaw the changes that were about to take place in Bengal, and he demanded of the Santal the last thing that he had to give—himself. Degraded, landless, and penniless as he was, the ryot was still a free agent. He might decamp and there was nothing to prevent him. A wave of feeling, sudden and mysterious, might sweep through this strange people as it had done on occasions before, moving them to set out again blindly in search of a new land. That would mean the undoing of all the mahajan's work. If the Santal left, there would be none to cultivate, and so for this end the mahajan worked that the Santal might lose his right to go away. It was this that explained the moneylender's willingness to lend, even when the ryot had parted with the last of his possessions. Having nothing tangible to give, the Santal pledged himself to work off the debt, little dreaming even then in his simplicity and guilelessness to what a life of slavery he was dooming himself and his family. As the Hindu counted out the scanty stock of money of this his last loan into the Santal's hand, bargaining afresh at every coin, he foresaw the rich harvest that it would bring. Work as the Santal might, he could never even so much as pay off the exorbitant interest that would mount up by leaps and bounds until the original sum was but a trifle in the huge burden of indebtedness. The mahajan took care that the Santal had no time to work elsewhere, no leisure from his slavery to earn the wherewithal to pay off his debt. Actual money repayment was the last thing the usurer desired. The Santal and his family were much more useful to him as slaves, as dependent on him for maintenance as the cattle that ploughed his land or the oxen that trod out his corn. Did the Santal refuse to work, his master stopped his food, and the end of the short struggle was a foregone conclusion—the slave submitted and took up again the burden of his hopeless existence.

Against this condition of rank slavery the law, never foreseeing the need, had made no provision. Unfortunately, on the contrary, it was his ultimate recourse to the law that made the usurer's position secure. The bonds executed by the ignorant ryots were held good by the courts, and civil suits were decreed in the mahajan's favour. 'In consideration of having received twenty-five rupees,' ran the bond, 'I undertake to work out at any time I may be called upon to do so this debt with interest at 50 per cent.' It bore the signature of the ryot, the mere scratch of an arrow-head, but duly attested by witnesses. It was more than probable that the unhappy ryot knew nothing of the contents of the bond he was signing, but once his mark was affixed the courts held him bound by its terms. To such a climax did this evil reach that it was no uncommon thing for a decree to be given against a son and even a grandson of the original debtor, ordering him to give personal service in liquidation of the debt from which he had received no personal benefit, and of the very existence of which he was probably in entire ignorance. There is an instance of a bond of this nature, originally for twenty-five rupees at 75 per cent., for payment of which the debtor worked out his lifetime, his son succeeding him in the hopeless task, while his grandson was only released in the better days that followed the rebellion—just thirty years after the debt of twenty-five rupees had been first contracted.

Look where he might, the Santal could find no escape from the oppressor. The daroga, ill paid and in close touch with the mahajan, was not the man to whom to appeal. Conscious of his own misdoings, it was his object to prevent the Santal from taking his complaint to the courts, though even there a bribe to the clerks and amlahs was sufficient to secure his safety. The burkundazes, or constables, under the daroga reaped a fine harvest of illicit gain, and for a small fee were ready to carry out the mahajan's orders, whether he had gained a decree or not being a matter of pure indifference. Did one Santal prove less easy to oppress than his neighbours, the chances were small that he would ever obtain redress. The courts were a long distance off, outside the limits of the Daman-i-koh, and necessitated a weary tramp by unknown roads to Bhagalpur or Deoghar. Arrived there none of the swift justice he had fondly hoped for met the unfortunate petitioner. To file his complaint even was a work of difficulty. His enemy the mahajan or the police may have been before him and bribed the amlahs to keep back his petition; in any case he himself must pay a fee before it would be allowed to be put up. Then, ignorant and dazed amidst all this show of legal form, it was necessary for him to pay again to engage a mooktear if his case was to be presented in an intelligent way. So at last the petition came before the Collector; but from this hard-worked official no other order was possible than a direction to the local daroga to inquire. The ryot lived possibly fifty or even a hundred miles away, and time must elapse before witnesses could be produced and the case proceeded with at headquarters. The daroga had every inducement to report against the petitioner. Anxious to escape all inquiry on his own account, a bribe from the mahajan secured the desired report. Even if the case were not thrown out on the daroga's report, the Santal had endless difficulties still to surmount. It was to the mahajan's interest to invent delays, and the Santal, passing on his weary way to and fro, often ignorant or forgetful of the days fixed for hearing, and ruined by the expense, grew at length disheartened and gave up the hopeless case. He had gained nothing, and was even in worse case than his neighbour who had made no protest and taken resignedly what the gods had sent.

It was not altogether surprising that the

English officials at the head of the district were meanwhile in absolute ignorance of the Santals' distress. Ever since Cleveland's day the Daman-i-koh had come in for but fitful attention from the authorities at Bhagalpur, busy as they were with a large area more directly under their control. The Santals were practically an unknown people. Shunning the law courts, with an ineradicable aversion to towns and town life, they seldom stirred far from their own homes, and all personal knowledge the Collector had of them was gained during an occasional hasty camping tour through the most accessible parts of the Daman-i-koh. Of these rare opportunities to air their grievances the Santals, the most silent and uncommunicative of men, never made use. The Great White Saheb was altogether too far removed and his powers too vague in their imagination for them to appeal to him direct. Throughout they regarded the contest as one against the Hindu, the zemindar, and the mahajan. Against the British Government, of which they knew so little, they bore no ill-will.

So far from being aware of the existence of the evils that cried aloud for redress, Government, even within a few years of the outbreak of rebellion, was congratulating itself on the successful solution of the difficulty of peopling the Daman-i-koh, and on its generosity in giving this land of promise to the Santals. Its grievances thus unsuspected, no further reason was apparent for obtaining a more intimate knowledge of this backward aboriginal race. Speaking an unknown tongue which the British officials in charge had not the time, even if they had the inclination, to learn, the Santal and all his ways were a sealed book, the only insight into which could be gained through a crowd of subordinate officials, almost all of them Hindus, who naturally sided with their own race in the struggle, and against the unclean Santal, whom they despised. It was not to be expected that the story of oppression would filter through this source to the ears of the officials at headquarters. So it came to pass that those in authority, viewing with complacency the vast increase in the revenue and the apparently peaceful conditions of this once distracted land, saw nothing of the coming storm, while the Santal still bore his lot in silence, awaiting the chance of escape that should awaken in him again the desire of better things and the consequent spirit of revolt.

It was the advance of civilisation outside the Daman-i-koh that finally stirred the longsuffering Santal to deeds of violence to vindicate his rights. The marvellous change that was passing over the face of India in the middle of the nineteenth century had reached at last the outskirts even of the

A GROUP OF SANTAL MANJHIS

Daman-i-koh, and the first great westernising influence was forcing its way into the hitherto untouched country of the Santals. Suddenly where there had been an excess of labour arose a great and unexpected demand that far exceeded the supply. For two hundred miles along the edge of the district a scene of vast activity had suddenly sprung into existence. In a brief space—it seemed to the astonished Santal almost in a day—the whole aspect of that long strip of land was changed. With rapid strides the railway that was soon to link the most distant parts of the Indian Empire ran along the western and northern limits of the Daman-i-koh. Crowds of workmen, busy with the pick and spade, were throwing up one long straight line of earthwork, levelling here, bridging an impassable gully there, piercing a high-banked cutting or circumventing a group of rocks, but always pressing on to reach their goal by the most direct route that they could find. The Santals regarded the work with unconcealed wonder, knowing as yet nothing of the use to which it should be put. Only the vaguest rumour of the iron horse, that new invention of the Sahebs, had reached them. But be what it might, it offered them a field of labour where their services were in great demand and wages high. Instead of a bitter struggle for bare existence, instead of an enormous excess of labour over capital, came suddenly an influx of wealth and a practically inexhaustible demand for their services. Here on the line of rail there was work enough, laborious indeed, but highly paid, for the whole Santal population had they been free to accept it. It was this fact, the fact that they were not free to take this great chance, this god-sent opportunity to restore their fortunes, that stirred the Santal at last to a full and deep sense of his many wrongs. Those who were yet free to go where they would, though deprived of lands and homes and all that they possessed, hurried to this new scene of labour. Here they were welcomed with open arms, and the railway officials soon learned that there was no better workman than the Santal. No labour is harder than the ceaseless struggle against nature for existence and the labour of the intake, and it was in this school that the Santal had long learned. Wages were high, and to the Santal, unaccustomed to wealth in any form, least of all in hard coin of the realm, they appeared high beyond the dream of his wildest desire. Not only himself, but his wife and his children, even to the youngest, found work here, no child being found too small to carry its basket of earth and help to swell the earnings of the day.

To those who perforce remained behind—and they formed the majority—the rumours of this paradise of labour but accentuated the misery of their condition. To see their more fortunate neighbours return after a brief spell of work, their waist-cloths heavy with rupees and their wives and children gay with ornaments, well fed, well satisfied, made them realise their helplessness as they had never done before. It was no longer a solace to them, as it had been in the past, that serfdom gave them at least the means of subsistence. Here was labour, far less exacting, that gave a return in coin capable of restoring to them their lands and permitting them to infuse new life and vigour into their tribal customs and festivals as of old. But escape there was none. As labour grew dearer and the serf became more valuable the clutch of the mahajan tightened. Even flight was impossible, for the taskmaster was vigilant, and he held the serf's wife and children as hostages. Maddened by the sharp contrast between his lot and that of the free man, a wild desire for release from the oppressor's yoke sprang up in the Santal's mind, and grew until it became stronger than his hereditary instinct to suffer in silence, conquering even his habitual apathy and slowness to resolve. And so at last the end came.

The winter of the year 1854 in the Daman-i-koh was a time of unrest fraught with moment, but as yet hidden from the eyes of those in authority whom it most concerned. All through the tribe, beyond even the limits of the Skirts of the Hills, passed one of those strange waves of feeling, deep, mysterious, with no ruffle on the surface, yet real and intense, that from time to time have moved the slow-going Santal to the very centre of his being. From one end of the land to the other, into the remotest villages far off in the recesses of the jungle, the spirit of unrest passed unseen, like the wind that yet stirs the old and knotted monarchs of the forest from their wonted calm. That marvellous sense which is neither sight nor touch nor hearing, the gift only of primitive man, has been given in special measure to the Santal race. To none but to those who have lived close to the beginnings of things, one with Nature in the depths of the primæval forest, is this subtle sense known, the sense of instinct acutely developed—the power of knowing before any appeal has been made to the other five senses. So it was that throughout the winter of 1854–5, while as yet the idea of open rebellion was scarcely in the germ, the spirit of unrest—the foreknowledge of impending events—passed to and fro among the tribe. In every village, after the day's toil was done, the Santal met his neighbours at the Manjhi Than and in whispers, as if the spirit of the taskmaster oppressed him even there, passed his grievances from mouth to mouth, or waited in a silence broken only by the weighty words of his chief the coming of events foreshadowed. To fan this half-articulate murmur of protest into wild uncontrollable revolt, all the more wild and uncontrollable by reason of its long suppression, there was needed but the smallest spark.

To this waiting people, mystic and superstitious, came the news that had most power to stir their imagination—the news of a sign from heaven. Marang Buru, the Great Spirit, had appeared and spoken, and a thrill of awe passed through the race as the rumour spread. For the gods of the Santals are invisible, and in all their mythology no revelation of the divine had ever before been vouchsafed to human eye. With unquestioning faith they accepted the rumour. None would dare to take in vain the name of Marang Buru, the Great Spirit. To four brothers, Sidhu, Kanhu, Chand, and Bairat, sons of one Chunar of Bagnadihi, it was that Marang Buru had appeared, not once but seven times, and each time in a different guise. First he came in the form of a cloud descending from the skies, then as a tongue of fire, thirdly as a hooded figure the face veiled in mist, fourthly as a shadow in the full sunlight where no earthly shadow fell, fifthly as a mountain rising suddenly out of the earth, sixthly as a sal tree springing up where no trees grew, and lastly as a white man clothed like a Santal, with but a cloth about his loins. At his last appearance the divinity gave the brothers a sacred book wherein no words were written, but the pages of which they were enjoined to distribute far and wide throughout the Santal country as a sign to prepare for the great events to come, by which all their wrongs should be redressed and the Santals become once more a free people. So from hand to hand and from village to village passed these slips of paper, apparently meaningless and vague, yet stirring the race to its depths, by their very mysteriousness appealing with supreme force to the Santal mind.

Even at this the eleventh hour no sense of impending danger disturbed the complacent satisfaction of those in authority. The late crop had been unusually good, and from official reports even down to February 1855 there is no hint to be gleaned of any apprehension of the coming storm. Everything was considered to be satisfactory. To the official, busy at headquarters, the winter of 1854–5 represented only an exceptionally good harvest, and consequently an easy collection of the revenue, the deep-seated discontent and all its causes remaining below the surface deep hidden in the long-enduring Santal's heart. How far the people did actually attempt to bring their grievances to the notice of the magistrate and the Government at the last moment it is not easy now to discover. It is stated that they petitioned both the Collector and the Commissioner as well as Government at head-quarters, setting forth their needs and praying for the regulation of usury and the expulsion of the hated foreigner from their land. But whether these petitions if sent ever reached those for whom they were intended there is no record to show. It is quite possible that they may have done, and yet, in the general sense of security and prosperity that prevailed, have been disregarded or laid aside for subsequent inquiry, or, more probable still, they may have been intercepted on the way by the subordinate officials of the same race as the hated usurer and zemindar. In any case, if the warning came, it was not understood, and passed unheeded until too late.

So it happened at length after years of patient endurance that the final outbreak came. The Santals knew that there was none to help them, and that their salvation must be the work of their own hands. Their gods, perforce gone empty of their sacrifices during the years of poverty and distress, were offended and vouchsafed no answer to their prayers. To be able to worship them again as they demanded to be worshipped played no small part in stirring them to final action. The sal branch, the Santal national emblem of war, was sent like the fiery cross through every village in the land, speaking its eloquent message of revolt, and from every hill and valley where the race had made its home came the flower of its youth unquestioningly obedient to its call.

It was a vast assembly that collected near Barhait—the only place of any size in the Daman-i-koh. Practically the whole fighting population within the pillars answered the summons of the sal branch, and the gathering was augmented by many from beyond towards Birbhum whose grievances were no less great. Two of the four brothers Sidhu and Kanhu to whom Marang Buru had appeared were the recognised leaders, and for some days while detachment after detachment came in from the outlying districts the immense gathering halted, uncertain of its next move. Day and night they sat and talked, as the Santals love to do, discussing their grievances and fixing their determination, now that they had come together, to be content with no half-measures, but to sweep the hated usurer and all his satellites from the land. Among them passed the bolder spirits, dwelling in eloquent words upon their wrongs and inflaming the passions of retaliation and revenge. It was not long before one unanimous deep-voiced cry rose from all the vast assembly, and the cry was death to the mahajan, the zemindar, the police, and all who had taken part or share in the long years of their oppression. Against the British Raj and its representatives there was no thought of animosity. The leaders, it is said, even went so far as to assure the ignorant people that the Sahebs would approve of their action in bringing to justice those who had done so great a wrong. So in exhortation and endless discussion the days passed until want of provisions rendered action imperative. The supplies they had carried with them from their own homes were exhausted, and for so huge a gathering the surrounding country could not provide. It was the end of June, and the worst time in all the year to be dependent on the jungles for subsistence. But even now the Santal with his fatal propensity for procrastination only moved because he needs must, and the great army set out at last, vague in intention and design, determined only as to one thing—to right the wrong and bear the oppression no longer. What actual plan, if any, was in the leaders' mind it is impossible to say. It was supposed at the time that the intention was to march direct to Calcutta to lay their grievances before the highest authority of all. But whatever the leaders may have intended there was no concerted plan of action, no definite idea of the way in which their wrongs were to be redressed.

All was vague, as it is the Santal's nature to be, and things were allowed to take their course.

Chance threw them in the way of their first act of violence. Moving on in one vast irregular mass towards the south-east in search of provisions and plundering as they went, they roused the Hindus at last to a sense of their danger. The Inspector of Police, already in their pay, was prevailed upon to go out with all the forces of law at his command and arrest the leaders on a trumped-up charge. The Inspector, little realising what the vast gathering meant and relying on the peaceable nature of the Santals, went out to do their bidding. But he soon found that there was a spirit abroad among them which transformed them from the dull listless men he had been accustomed to oppress with such impunity. Taking him by force, the leaders extorted a promise from him, as the only condition of his being allowed to return, that he would levy a tax of twenty rupees on every Hindu household in his jurisdiction to provide the Santal army with supplies. The Inspector, glad to escape with his life at the cost of a mere promise easily broken, prepared to set out on his return. But there were those in the Santal army who had experienced the oppression of this particular police officer, and the rumour that he had come out to arrest their leaders on a false charge was eagerly believed, and quickly spread until it reached the ears of Sidhu and Kanhu. Recalling the Inspector they faced him with apparent simplicity and guilelessness. 'If we have broken the law,' they said, 'and you have proof against us, take us and we will stand our trial.' The Inspector, taken by surprise and fatuously thinking that they were actually willing to give themselves up, ordered his constables to take them into custody. It was the signal for the breaking of the storm. Maddened by the insult to their divinely directed chiefs, the Santal host suddenly broke bounds and fell upon the offenders. Sidhu slew the Inspector with his own hands with one stroke of his *balua*, and of those with him none escaped. The rebellion had at length begun: with this first shedding of blood all the old barbarian instincts, long suppressed, seem to have returned, and their wild passions once let loose there was no restraint until the revolt was finally crushed out by the sheer weight of superior military organisation and force.

For more than a fortnight the Santals moved slowly on unchecked, plundering and murdering by the way. Knowing that as yet they had no opposition to fear, they broke up carelessly into small companies, each intent upon its own plan of campaign, looting and burning without mercy the property that the Hindus had left behind them in their flight. It was one of these small companies in advance of the main body that Mr. Pontet met as he hastened to the scene of action on receipt of the news of the murder of the Inspector and the police. Fortunately for him it contained many of the older and steadier spirits of the revolt who knew and revered 'Ponteen.' Some of them had had dealings with him, and had experienced his fairness, uprightness, and honesty of purpose. It was not he who had oppressed them, and they gave a striking proof of their belief in him. Behind them was advancing an unruly rabble, the young men drunk already with the lust of robbery and murder, and the older and wiser men felt that they could not answer for 'Ponteen's' safety if he advanced to meet them as he now proposed to do. Who could say but that one in all that huge crowd might not draw a bow and take the life of the man against whom they had no just cause of complaint? Yet Mr. Pontet was not to be persuaded, and was for moving on at once to confront the ringleaders and the main body. So the old men felt that they must save 'Ponteen' against his will, and taking him by force they removed him to a place of safety in the hills until the mad passion of revolt should have died away. It was a touching proof of their honesty of purpose and respect for the man, given in the first heat of rebellion, when the wild spirit of lawlessness and revenge, long held in check, had been but just released.

At headquarters, though rumour after rumour came in, there was still the greatest reluctance to admit that anything was wrong. To do so meant to go back upon recent reports that all was well and to acknowledge the mistake that had been made—never at any time an easy task to the official mind. Mr. Pontet in the hands of the Santals was unable to report, and until news came from him it seemed possible to hope for the best. But when men came in who had fled before the Santals' wrath, telling how village after village had been burned to the ground, the young crops destroyed, mahajans and zemindars put to the sword, and even English men and women murdered, the gravity of the situation could no longer be ignored. Then with a swift change of feeling panic spread among the officials and through all the country that lay within the Santals' line of march. Government at last awoke to the fact that an actual rebellion was in progress, and disquiet spread even to Calcutta, where exaggerated rumours of large bodies of 'barbarians' scarcely seventy miles distant, drunk with blood and plunder, gradually filtered in. A body of troops under Major Vincent Jarvis was hastily despatched by the new railway as far as Burdwan, whence they had to make their way through the pouring rain towards the scene of revolt. Suri in Birbhum was the point for which they made. Lying right in the Santals' line of march, its inhabitants had given way to the direst panic. The usurer and the zemindar, merciless in the day of their power, proved abject cowards when once the Santal had thrown off their yoke and made appeal to the most primitive of all arguments, and they hailed the company of sepoys, drenched to the skin and foot-weary after their two days' march, with exuberant protestations of delight. Suri was as if in a state of siege. The gaol had been hastily fortified, and a general stampede of the Hindus had been prevented only by the spirit shown by the European officials in charge. Unfortunately, however, Government, still adhering to the old plan of subordinating the military to the civil element, and expecting the most varied abilities from its civilian officers, had placed the troops under the civil authority. But the days when the Collector was as much soldier as civilian had already passed. The civilian of the eighteenth century was as a rule no lawyer, but he had proved himself a capable administrator, as ready, if need were, to suppress a revolt or lead an attack as to administer justice. The civilian of the nineteenth century, a better lawyer, perhaps a better judge, and certainly a more irreproachable

GOFUR KHAN, AN OLD SEPOY OF THE 41ST HINDUSTANI REGIMENT, WHO FOUGHT DURING THE SANTAL REBELLION AND SEPOY MUTINY

administrator, knew nothing of military tactics. Consequently his substitution for the legitimate military authority in this as in many similar instances led to constant dissensions and much ill-feeling. Prompt action towards suppressing the Santal revolt was greatly impeded, and at the end of July the Government, becoming alarmed at the reports that came in, hastily despatched General Lloyd with vague powers that practically placed in his hands the chief responsibility for the success of the campaign. But even then, lest this should be deemed an affront to the civil power, it was expressly ordered that the military should in no way act independently of the civil authorities, although military dispositions were to be always in the hands of military men. But thus curtailed as his powers were, the arrival of General Lloyd and his reinforcements put new heart into the terrified Hindu population. The zemindars, confident once again at the sight of English troops, were eager to offer their services and those of their retainers. The English planters, grateful for the succour that had saved them from the fate of their fellow-countrymen who had fallen victims at the beginning of the rebellion, supplied *rasad* (provisions) for the troops and volunteered for service. From the Maharaja of Murshedabad came a magnificent train of elephants that proved of the greatest service for transporting troops and arms over the marshy rain-sodden fields that lay between them and the enemy. In the face of this encouragement Suri recovered from its panic and watched with confidence the departure of the troops for the scene of action.

It was no campaign productive of military glory or regular strategic fighting. The Santals, without organisation and without weapons save their bows and arrows and *baluas*, could not hope to stand for a moment against the trained well-armed sepoy forces in open fight. They recognised at once that their only chance lay in their knowledge of the country, and that in ambush, sudden sorties, and surprises lay their strength. It was thus that on two occasions British detachments were overwhelmed and cut to pieces by the wild onslaughts of raw Santal levies. The difficulties of the march, through unknown country devoid of roads and furnishing abundant opportunities for ambush, the scarcity of provisions increasing as they advanced, and the inclemency of the weather all impeded the British troops and gave the rebels a temporary advantage. It was the same country that had so long protected the Paharias from attack, and for a time it stood the Santals in good stead. But unfortunately for the latter the Paharias were on this occasion arrayed against them, and they knew the country with all, and more than, the knowledge of the Santal himself. The Bhagalpur Hill Rangers, commanded by Captain Fagan, had been called out at the commencement of disturbances, and they won the earliest successes on the side of law and order while yet the regular troops were struggling with the difficulties of this irregular and unaccustomed warfare.

Many were the deeds of violence that marked the Santals' short hour of unbridled licence. Though against the white Sahebs, as they admitted, they had no grievance, there were several Europeans who fell victims to the indiscriminating passion of this outraged people. Factories were attacked and burned to the ground, and their occupants, Englishmen and Englishwomen, ruthlessly butchered. A planter, going out with his two sons to attempt to reason with a marauding band in his vicinity, was met with a volley of arrows and shot down as he approached. Another party of Europeans, surprised in their factory near the Ganges, barely escaped with their lives by boat amid a shower of arrows. For the hated Hindus the most terrible and barbarous of deaths were reserved. A zemindar, taking refuge in a tank, was shot at until his head was like a quiver full of arrows, when he was dragged out and his body cut into twenty-four pieces on a stone close by. For their old enemy, Sumar Singh of Sankara, they had designed the worst penalties of all, in revenge for the many acts of oppression they had suffered at his hands. But the old self-styled Raja outwitted them in the end, as he had so often done before, dying peacefully and full of years in the very nick of time, unpunished for his sins and in full possession of his unlawful gains. The zemindar of Narainpur was far less fortunate. Against him, too, the Santals had many old scores, and these they paid in full. Seizing him in his house near the Barakar River, they chopped off his legs at the knees, crying, 'Four annas!' meaning that a quarter of the debt had been thus paid. Then cutting off his legs at the thighs, they cried, 'Eight annas!' and again his arms, crying, 'Twelve annas!' Finally they cut off his head, exclaiming triumphantly, '*Farkatti!*' (Full quittance.)

But, as was inevitable, the first brief successes of the Santals were soon turned into utter and irretrievable defeat. These few months of actual fighting form a record pathetic yet unavoidable over which one would fain draw a veil. It was not warfare, as officers and men admitted in disgust at the work which yet had to be done. The Santals, driven to bay, but fighting to the last, were mown down like corn before the reaper's sickle. Yet of submission among them there was no thought.

Once fired after long years of oppression with the spirit of revolt, all their old savage instincts had returned, and even when the first enthusiasm of revenge, unbridled plunder and rapine was over, the dull dogged passion of resistance remained. The huge levies, split up into small groups, carried on the revolt with untiring determination, believing that for those who had done the deeds that they had done there could be no hope of reprieve. Marvellous stories of their courage and absolute insensibility to danger remain. Small bands of fifty or a hundred men again and again defied double the number of British troops, better armed, better disciplined, against whose compact concerted action they had not the smallest chance. When called on to surrender their only answer was a shower of arrows that compelled the British troops to advance against them. In the face of attack they stood firm, their drums beating with a note of determination and defiance. Maddened by the arrows poured into them at close quarters, the troops at last had the word to fire, and a volley thinned the crowded irregular Santal ranks, but had no effect upon the heroism of those who remained. The defiant challenge of the drums ceased only as the drummers fell at their posts and the music of the flutes ended only in the wail of death. Their last arrows gone, all that survived of the Santal band flung itself, axe in hand, against the steadily advancing wall of British infantry, hopeless but thoughtless of victory or defeat in the last mad passion of despair. None fled, and only the wounded fell into the hands of the conquerors. From them the English officers learned more than they had ever known before of the cause of the rebellion they had been sent to crush. It was not against the British Government, the wounded prisoners told them again and again, that they had set out to fight, and though some Englishmen had fallen that must be attributed only to the mad passion of the Santal youth. Against the English they bore no grudge. Had but one of them, they pathetically said, come among them and, understanding them, helped them to right their wrongs, there had been no rebellion of the Santal race.

A month of such irregular warfare vigorously undertaken was sufficient to clear the outlying districts. But in the uplands in the Daman-i-koh itself, where the rebellion had first begun, the spirit of revolt lingered. In the hope that, after the terrible losses they had already suffered, the remainder might submit, a proclamation was issued on August 15 offering pardon to all who would lay down their arms, the ringleaders of the rebellion only excepted. 'Inasmuch,' runs the official wording of the pardon which the local authorities were ordered to promulgate among the Santal population by every means in their power, 'inasmuch as it appears that amongst the Santals who have risen in rebellion against the Government, plundering and devastating the country and opposing the troops, there are many who see the folly and iniquity of their proceedings and are desirous of being pardoned and resuming their former quiet life, notice is hereby given that the Government, ever anxious for the welfare of its subjects, though led away by the counsels of bad men, will freely pardon all Santals who may within ten days appear before any constituted authority and tender their submission, always excepting those who shall be proved to have been principal instigators and leaders of the insurrection and those who shall be proved to have been principally concerned in the perpetration of any murder. As soon as complete submission is shown all well-grounded complaints preferred by the Santals will be fully inquired into. But, on the other hand, all insurgents remaining in opposition to Government after the issue of this proclamation will be visited with the promptest and severest punishment.'

But to make this promise of pardon known among the rebellious Santals was no easy task, and it is doubtful how far the purport of it ever reached the last strongholds of revolt. In any case they were even yet in no mood for submission. More than a month later the rebellion still dragged on, developing more and more into mere raids and forays—dacoities on a large scale. 'During the past fortnight,' wrote the magistrate of Birbhum on September 24, 'upwards of thirty villages have been plundered. The whole country to within a short distance of Deoghar is in their hands. The mails are stopped and the inhabitants have deserted their villages and fled. They are divided into two large bodies, and their numbers average, as nearly as we can ascertain, from 12,000 to 14,000, and are receiving augmentation from all quarters.' One of these bands of rebels, led by one Seru Manjhi, was encamped only six miles west of Suri itself. Here they had thrown up earthworks and entrenched themselves against attack, while, strangely enough, they were reported to be preparing to celebrate the Durga Puja festival. This being a purely Hindu festival, even now rarely celebrated by the Santals, it is probable that the rebel ranks had been recruited by an accession of low-caste Hindus, whose lot, little better than that of the Santals, had far less chance of eventual amelioration. To celebrate fittingly the Durga Puja they had carried off forcibly two Brahmins from one of the villages they had plundered, and wild rumours of the orgies with which they finally performed the festival reached Suri. It was believed there that the insurgents were only awaiting the arrival of the other big contingent from the north to attack Suri itself. Owing to the heavy rains and their strongly entrenched position, it was impossible to undertake a punitive expedition against them with the small force then available in Suri, and the town was consequently once more given over to panic. The alarm was increased in the last days of September by the receipt of a strange warning from the Santal camp. The dâk runner from Deoghar arrived in Suri, robbed of his mail bags and half dead with fright, carrying nothing but a three-leaved sal branch in his hand. Breathless, he repeated his story. Not six miles away he had been set upon by a band of Santals, who seized the dâk and only spared his life on condition that he carried this warning emblem to headquarters at Suri. The missive needed but little interpretation. The three leaves represented three days, and after their expiry the Santals would follow in their wake to raze Suri with the ground and spread fire and bloodshed over the land. Panic increased in the town and the adjacent countryside, and the craven and weak-kneed, who were many, stole away at night towards the east, carrying with them all that they could hastily collect of their belongings to await quieter times in some less dangerous locality. So in fear and trembling the three days dragged on and none doubted that the Santals would keep their word and descend upon them when the third day had passed. The English officials, anxious but still incredulous that a band of savages should attack a town defended by regular troops, tried to appease the panic by taking every possible precaution. The colonel commanding stationed picquets round the town to the north and west whence the attack, if it came, might be expected, while the gaol was once more fortified as a last resort in case of need.

But the attack so anxiously awaited never came. For once the Santal turned aside from his purpose of revenge, but only to face a greater danger. News of a great and crushing defeat of the other Santal host had come from the north, and the rebel hordes encamped near Suri turned from the town within their sight to face these new conquerors who had slain their fellow-men in thousands. At Sangrampur the main body of the rebels had come face to face with a wing of the Hill Rangers. Captain Fagan was in command, and the lessons of obedience, discipline, and concerted action that he and his predecessors for fifty years had taught the hillmen were turned to marvellous effect. It was the old story of the victory of well-drilled forces over raw levies, trusting all to individual prowess, and the result was never for a moment doubtful. The Paharias, though with little taste for the work —their sympathies were undoubtedly on the side of the Santals, with whom they had so long lived in close and amicable concert—behaved with exemplary loyalty. It was a marvellous exhibition of the influence that had been at work since Cleveland's day over this wild and barbaric tribe. They knew little of the Santals' grievances; they had none of their own—those had been long since obliterated on the most generous scale; they had lost much of the love of fighting for its own sake during more than half a century of peace and the Santals were their neighbours and friends. Yet none of these things had weight with them when the call of military duty came, and they loyally obeyed the orders of the British Government to which they had given their allegiance. The Santals, misunderstanding, bitterly resented the attitude of the Hill Rangers, but against them they had no chance and at Sangrampur they met with their most crushing defeat.

But this disaster, so far from striking fear into the Santals, only increased their determination and roused again the spirit of rebellion to its highest pitch. Bitter resentment for these disasters, added to their previous grievances, produced a dull passion of obstinacy and doggedness that nothing but complete conquest by the sword could ever wipe out. Government was at last convinced that the suppression of the rebellion must be taken in hand with greater vigour. In the early part of November, after the revolt had been dragging on for nearly five months, martial law was proclaimed, and the Santals soon found that they were met by a spirit of determination equal to their own. As many as fourteen thousand troops were now employed under General Lloyd and Brigadier-General Bird, and a cordon of outposts was formed that gradually closed in, driving the Santals back from all their outlying positions, until the last stand was made. Such tactics as these soon prevailed, and the Santal rebellion was at length crushed out. Sidhu, the eldest of the four brothers who had been the original ringleaders, was captured, and after a summary trial was hanged at Barhait by Mr. Pontet in the presence of a vast concourse of Santals, who watched the proceedings with the apathy born of defeat. No less than ten thousand Santals are said to have perished in the struggle, but their submission once accomplished was final, and the race, breathless and exhausted with the passion of the contest, sank back to await the fulfilment of the promises of redress that had been so freely made.

CHAPTER VIII

THE SANTAL PARGANAS OF TO-DAY

ONCE a full knowledge of the state of affairs had been gained, the British Government was not slow to institute reforms. A searching inquiry was made into the causes of the rebellion and the true facts of the Santals' grievances elicited. It was evident that these had arisen primarily not so much from defects in the law itself as from inefficiency in the local administration—an inefficiency for which government at headquarters, rather than the local authorities themselves, was most to blame. Government, always with a thought to the Board of Directors at home and bent upon a cheap system of administration, stood convicted of having saddled its officers with tasks which it was quite impossible for them adequately to perform. It had made the fatal mistake—a mistake made over and over again in our early dealings with native races—of accepting with confidence things as they appeared to be on the surface. Without inquiry it had contentedly looked upon appearances as existing facts, and spoken with certainty and satisfaction, where all was in reality in a state of ferment and unrest. It allowed nothing for the forceful undercurrent of thought and feeling hidden behind the impassive exterior of the Oriental, and it had yet to learn more fully from bitter experience that it is ignorance alone that ventures to speak with certainty of anything in connection with the native races of India. The Daman-i-koh, which it congratulated itself upon having settled in the cheapest possible way, and which showed no outward appearance of anything but quiet and content, it considered could be well neglected and left to itself. Other interests more absorbing and other questions more imperative demanded the attention of Government, and, lulled by a sense of false security, it had been content to leave practically the whole of what is now the Santal Parganas under the control of one man, and that man a Deputy Collector, not a civilian of the first rank.

The result of such a policy had been the recent rebellion, and though Government had sinned through ignorance, it is impossible to lay the blame elsewhere. Yet this is what unfortunately happened, and a man who had without doubt done his best under most adverse circumstances suffered. Mr. Pontet, who had been appointed to have charge of the Santals in the Daman-i-koh so long ago as 1836, had done nearly twenty years' work among them when the rebellion came. Though not a man of brilliant attainments, or even of good education, all the records go to show that he made a brave fight against innumerable difficulties, and in the face of continual snubbing and browbeating on the part of his superior officers. Just, considerate, and absolutely incorruptible, in spite of many and great temptations, he aroused a strong feeling of respect and personal devotion among the Santals, of which the striking instance of their care and solicitude for him at the commencement of the rebellion is sufficient proof. But these things weighed little with his immediate superiors, from whom he had never met with justice, much less with generosity, and Government, anxious to find a scapegoat for the blunders into which it had been led, fixed the blame upon the one man available. That he had lived among the Santals and had been in actual charge of them for nearly twenty years, and yet allowed their grievances to go unredressed and the rebellion to be sprung upon Government as an absolute surprise, did undoubtedly make out a *prima facie* case against him. But his anomalous position, practically without criminal or civil powers, and completely subordinate to a succession of unsympathetic officers at Bhagalpur, gave him little opportunity for independent action. Occupied primarily with the question of the revenue and the settlement of the Santals, to whom he was unable to extend the privileges granted to the Paharias, he had no concern with the civil courts, in whose action is to be found one of the chief causes of the rebellion. His reports and remonstrances time and again met with no response, or but the curtest notice from his superior officers, and yet, when events over which he had no control led to open revolt, the blame was thrown upon him. Shortly after the subdual of the rebellion and the inquiry into the Santals' grievances he was removed from the Superintendentship of the Daman-i-koh under a severe official censure. Two years later he died, brokenhearted at the treatment meted out to him by the Government he had so long served. But the name of 'Ponteen,' as the Santals called him, is still remembered among them to-day with affection and regard, even as the still greater name 'Chilmili' lives among their neighbours, the Paharias.

Government, anxious to repair the wrong done, determined that the Santals should never again have to complain of the difficulty of obtaining justice from the courts. No longer was a cheap administration to come before the interests of the people; the impossible was no longer to be expected of a single officer in charge of a huge district. By Regulation XXXVII. of 1855 the Santal Parganas was formed as a separate district, including a far wider area than the Daman-i-koh, and made up of portions of Bhagalpur and Birbhum. It was a strange medley of petty states and diverse peoples and interests welded into one. The meeting-place of Bengal and Hindustan, it had long been debatable ground where the lowest among the aborigines had stood face to face with the highest civilisation of the day, almost every race of Northern India being represented in the scale between them. Nowhere else can the linguistic and ethnic lines between Bengal and Hindustan be seen more rigidly drawn simply according to artificial and not according to natural boundaries, than here. Furthest north, bounded by the Ganges, lies the pargana of Tiliagarhia, famous for its mountain pass, the gateway of Bengal, and so long the home of the most turbulent among the Paharias. Once part of the Katauri chieftainship of Manihari it was cut off in later Musulman days to form a dependency for Roshan Bakt, a Hindu Teli by caste, who renounced his faith and embraced the creed of Islam to become chief of Tiliagarhia. Side by side, yet strangely separate in its history and interests, lay Rajmahal with its surrounding lands still held by the descendants of those Musulman

P 2

nobles who in the heyday of their power had peopled its palaces, now fallen to decay. Pargana Ambar, presenting the phenomenon of a Brahmin temporality peculiar to Lower Bengal, had once belonged to the Brahmin house of Pakur, its capital, while Pargana Sultanabad was ruled by a house of acknowledged Rajput purity. To these again was added the territory of the Pathan Raj of Kharakpur, including the Katauri chieftainship of Hendue and the Bhuiya pargana of Passi. The three remaining Katauri chiefships, Manihari, Barkop, and Patsanda, together with the five great tappas of the Pathan Raj of Birbhum, which include Deoghar with its Ghatwals and Belpatta, first transferred to Bhagalpur at Cleveland's request to complete his Daman-i-koh, make up the list of the petty states now known as the Santal Parganas. Brahmin and Rajput, Katauri and Musulman, Santal and Paharia, now live side by side in a condition of peace and amity hitherto unknown. Only the barriers of caste and language have as yet resisted strenuously the onrush of events.

The new district, still retained under the Bhagalpur Commissionership, was given a civilian officer of its own, his headquarters being fixed at Dumka as one of the most central and convenient spots available. The Hon. Ashley Eden, afterwards Lieutenant-Governor of Bengal, who had been especially deputed by Government to inquire into the causes of the rebellion, was appointed first Deputy Commissioner of the Santal Parganas, and his tact and ability did much to give the conquered people confidence in the new régime. Under him the district was further divided into subdistricts, each with its own officers and courts. The Santal need never again have cause to cry that justice was too far to seek. It was brought by these measures to the very gates of all, and men were appointed to administer it, such as Robinson, Yule, Braddon, and Money, to mention but a few whose names soon became household words among the Santals. It is a striking proof of their interest in and sympathy with the natives under them and evidence of the closer relations possible between ruler and ruled under the non-regulation system that these men were all known by name among the Santals. In the Regulation Provinces few natives except those immediately connected with the courts even so much as know the names of the officials at the head of the district. To them they are merely the 'Commissioner Saheb' or the 'Collector Saheb,' their personality often unknown or merged in their official position. Individuality perforce makes less impression where all is stereotyped as in the Regulation Provinces. But where, as in the Santal Parganas, owing to more primitive conditions, far greater scope has been left to the discretion of the officers in charge, it becomes a most important factor in the affairs of the district. Brought into nearer touch with the people and freed from many of the restrictions of the ordinary law, the officials wield an influence for good or evil that the Santal is quick to recognise and classify, though even their influence grows less under the levelling tendency of modern days which is rapidly bringing the various opposing elements, whether in regulation or non-regulation districts, once and for all into line.

In the years that immediately succeeded the rebellion prosperity returned to the long-suffering Santal. His old enemies, the police, met with short shrift from a government anxious to atone for past injustice. Throughout the new district the regular police force was entirely abolished. Even with the increased number of courts and European officials, it was not considered advisable to allow the police, who had so greatly abused their powers, to remain as intermediaries between justice and the Santal. Sweeping away the whole hierarchy of subordinate officials, Government made trial of a 'no police system.' The people were to be their own police. The village headman as the representative of his rural community was brought into direct communication with the

European executive officers. It was his duty and the duty of the whole village to aid him, by every means in its power, to report all crimes and misdemeanours committed within the limits of the community to the village chowkidar, who in turn took the information direct to the European officer in charge of the district. It was the most confiding and generous of police systems; with a people less honest and simple than the Santals it could hardly have been ventured upon. But to them it appealed with peculiar force after the ills they had but recently suffered at the hands of the regular police. The trust reposed in them met with immense appreciation, and cases of concealment of crime became rare. On the contrary so strongly did this confidence shown them appeal to their primitive sense of honour that there are many instances on record of men voluntarily giving themselves up to justice after the commission of a crime. One Santuk Manjhi, it is related, robbed of all that he possessed and driven to despair by the wiles of a mahajan, turned at last in a moment of passion and slew his oppressor. Fresh from the deed, he went to the village chowkidar and asked him to accompany him to the Magistrate Saheb, fifteen miles away. Together they went in to headquarters, and Santuk Manjhi told his tale before the Assistant Commissioner. 'I have killed a man,

Saheb,' he said simply. 'But what would you? He had wrung from me all that I possessed even unto my last plot of land. Yet I am guilty. Punish me as it seems right.' But this simple patriarchal 'no police system' has suffered like much else from the general levelling tendency, though the regular police, since reintroduced, are shorn of the vast opportunities of oppression that their predecessors possessed before the rebellion of 1855.

The other great enemies of the Santal—the mahajan and the zemindar—fared almost as badly as the police under the new administration, and for a time their flagrant exactions and extortions practically ceased in the light that the law, now rigorously enforced, shed upon them. No longer could they resort to their old devices of refusing receipts and weighing with false weights, and though the usurer might still charge his high interest, the courts and the police were no longer under his control, so that he might get as formerly what decisions he desired. Bound hand and foot to his master like a serf under the old system, the Santal, once tasting freedom, threw off the yoke in open defiance, and the courts were now on his side. Henceforward the law was construed so strictly that the master had no effective remedy if the slave fled or refused to work. Quickly the rumours of this new state of things spread among the Santals, and the spirit of the race revived. Mindful of the years of bondage and eager to recover lost ground, they were quick to take advantage of the wonderful opportunities that were opening out before them. The railway, stopped for a time by the rebellion, eagerly welcomed fresh recruits and furnished the Santal with the wherewithal to start life again in his own land after but a comparatively short spell of labour. Here even the landless homeless serf might quickly earn a good round sum, returning home perchance to buy back the very fields that he had lost. Beyond, for those ready to go still further afield, the tea industry in North-east Bengal, then in its infancy, awaited only a supply of labour to wake it into life. Emigration, that great outlet for surplus energy and safeguard against over-population, furnished the indigent with the hope of better days. Leaving home in large companies as the tea season in the Duars approached, they returned again, their waist-cloths heavy with rupees, in time to plough their fields for the next year's crop. That the emigrants experienced many hardships in the early days is true. Individuals suffered in the process as individuals must always suffer in every great movement. Much distress was felt at the outset when the means of communication were bad, and horrible stories survive of overcrowding on the river steamers when regulations were few and private contracting was subject to no authority. Now the Santal emigrates as far afield as to the tea gardens of Assam, protected in every way that a paternal government can devise. From the moment that he leaves his home until he reaches his destination, and afterwards throughout his service in the strange land, the law zealously watches over him, and though oppression and injustice, it is unavoidable, must occasionally creep in, such instances have happily become comparatively rare in recent years. The Santal has little cause to complain of emigration. Assam has offered him an immense field where his surplus labour is eagerly welcomed. His pay is good, and if he chooses he can return after the expiry of his contract with a sum of money that will make him a rich man in his own village and the envied of his neighbours. Unlike the Paharia, the Santal has shown no objection to go far afield in search of labour, though the opening of the huge coal fields at Girideh, at Jherria, and Ranigunj has given him vast opportunities of labour close at hand and largely obviated the need of emigration to more distant spheres of work. Nothing could be more convenient to the Santal than labour in the mines. No form of contract exists. He and his whole family can here find work that they may take up and drop at any moment that they please. Paid so much by the day or by results, they have the independence that they love, and a short spell of labour in the non-cultivating season of the year is undertaken with a lightness of heart and a profitableness of return wholly satisfactory and desirable. Among the coal fields no better and more cheerful worker is known than the Santal.

Yet this renewed prosperity has wrought little change in the Santal himself, in his thoughts and instincts and manner of life. It has raised him scarcely perceptibly in the scale of civilisation. Content with things as they are, he has made no attempt to attain a higher level. Education, compared with its results elsewhere, has made no rapid strides. But schools established all over the district in recent years give promise for future generations, and already, owing chiefly to the care and energy of the missionaries, many Santals have been enabled to go forth into the world as clerks, assessors, and accountants to compete on equal terms with their more favoured neighbours. The work of education carried on by the missionaries has been a conspicuous success. In the north of the district there are the Church Missionary Society's stations at Taljhari, Hiranpur, and Godda, while in the extreme south the Santal Home Mission, so long presided over by the Rev. Mr. Skrefsrud, has its headquarters at Benagaria. Great progress has been made by both, and whereas thirty years ago the Santal Christians numbered scarcely more than three hundred, they now number something like fifty thousand all told. Like most aboriginal tribes they have shown themselves far more fertile soil for mission enterprise than any section of the Hindu community, though the penalties for embracing Christianity are no less severe among the Santals than among the higher race where the caste system is rigidly enforced. No Santal will take food or water from a Christian, and the adoption of the new faith at once involves the extreme penalty—that of being outcast from the tribe and a loss of all privileges as a member of the race community. For a Santal to face so great a penalty requires much courage and belief.

Absolutely undisturbed by passing events, by cruel oppression, by the wild passion of rebellion, or the ease of prosperity, the round of Santal life moves on. The old customs long handed down from father to son are still religiously observed: if with a touch of growing scepticism, still as yet with no thought of omission. The patriarchal mode of life, with its perfect organisation, still survives in every Santal village. The Manjhi, as his fathers did before him, presides over all the social affairs of the village and settles domestic disputes, being learned in all questions that concern the land, and well acquainted with each man's holding and its boundaries, about which quarrels never fail. The Paramanik is his assistant and deputy, acting for him in case of need. The Naeke is the village priest, and the Kudam Naeke is the inferior priest whose duty it is to draw the blood from his own veins at the time of sacrifice in the Sacred Grove. The Jogmanjhi has charge of the morals of the village, shutting his eyes only at the time of the great festival of the Sohrae, when especial licence is allowed. The district organisation is as perfect as that of the village, at the head being the Parganait to whom reference is made on all important questions that cannot be settled locally. The Des Manjhi acts as his assistant.

Primitive justice is still administered by the Manjhi and the Panchayats, councils of wise men, and many are the local disputes that are settled by them without the bother and expense of a reference to the courts of law. Though litigation, which exercises so great a fascination for Indian peoples, has begun at last to draw the Santal within its clutches, he carries his grievance first to the Manjhi and the Panchayat, assembled in solemn conclave at the Manjhi Than. Failing to find what he considers justice there, he carries his case to the Parganait, and then in case of need to a higher and more formal court.

But it is upon all matters connected with Santal law and custom which the ordinary courts do not recognise that the Panchayat is chiefly called to speak. Even now, superstitious as in earlier days, the Santal lives continually in fear of witchcraft and the evil eye. The law makes no provision for such things as these, therefore the man aggrieved must seek redress among his own kindred at the Manjhi Than. If a man's cattle die mysteriously or his crops wither without apparent cause, or his wife or children fall sick and he has reason to suspect the evil eye, he calls together the village, submitting the facts and his suspicions for their consideration and decision. The Ojha, the village witchfinder, is called into request, and by means of the ordeal or many incantations he discovers the guilty person with whom is the power of the evil eye. Then the Panchayat deliberates. In past days terrible scenes disgraced the Santal judgment hall. The witch, in many cases, strangely enough, a young and comely girl, quite unlike the ancient hag of Western fancy, but too often suffered brutal treatment at the hands of her accuser and the terrified villagers. Scared beyond measure at the supernatural, they were often not content until they had beaten the unfortunate

AN OJHA DIVINING BY MEANS OF SAL LEAVES

victim to death and put themselves beyond the influence of the evil eye. Outcasting and exile from the village were comparatively mild punishments with which the supposed witch was lucky to escape. Occasionally even in these days a woman is beaten to death by the villagers on conviction of the sin of witchcraft, but seldom now does the Panchayat venture on any more drastic measure than driving the obnoxious individual from the village.

Yet peaceful in outward appearance as the years have been that have followed the Rebellion of 1855, they have not been without their periods of anxiety and disquiet. Among this strange people, hidden deep down under the most stolid and reserved exterior, it would seem that there must always be an undercurrent of unrest. Waves of excitement charged with danger have from time to time passed through the tribe, sometimes attributable to known causes, oftener due to some mysterious upheaval which baffles inquiry, the secret whereof the Santal zealously guards in the intricate recesses of his own heart. But it is not a wide range of things that has power to move this simple people. Every question and every movement traced back to its source is found to emanate either from their passion for the land or their fear and reverence for the spirits of the unseen world.

The land they consider theirs by an inalienable right. Anything that to them appeared an attempt to defraud them of it would have the same power to rouse them to resistance as in 1855. To the invisible spirits they owe unquestioning obedience and the sacrifices of propitiation. These two deep-rooted instincts make up the Santal's simple creed.

Only at rare intervals since 1855 has the first of these instincts threatened to disturb the peace. It was towards the middle of 1871 that the officials in charge first became aware that a vague spirit of disquiet was again at work among the Santals. They had proved themselves years before not to be men given to loud complaints, but they had shown at the same time that they were men swift to strike when the time came and, once aroused, difficult to subdue. Again they were slow in bringing their grievances to light in the proper quarter, and but for the prompt action of the officials serious disturbances might have taken place. Wild rumours flew from end to end of the district. A large body of Santals was reported to be advancing on Dumka, while whole villages were deserted, their inhabitants gathering together in the jungle and, with the vague mysticism characteristic of their race, awaiting the turn of events. By his prompt action, however, in going to the seat of the disturbance at Moraroi, where the largest band had collected, the Deputy Commissioner succeeded in bringing them to reason, and having at length learned their grievances he persuaded them to return to their homes, promising them redress. Their chief complaint was that on the expiry of their leases fixed in 1855 many of their Manjhis had been ousted from their villages because they had refused to submit to a large enhancement of their rents. Their places were promptly taken by outsiders, who agreed to pay the increased rents and were consequently forced to rackrent their ryots in order to meet their obligations. Moreover the strangers absolutely disregarded the time-honoured and custom-sanctioned rights of the ryots. For the mahua trees of the village the tenants had paid no rent, and to an improvident people the mahua crop, ripening at the beginning of the hot weather, had formed a necessary asset to tide them over the most critical season of the year. The new landlord, anxious only to get as much as he could from the land and with none of the kindly patriarchal interest in the tenants that his predecessors had, demanded rent for these trees, and when the ryots refused ruthlessly cut them down and sold the timber. This in the eyes of all good Santals was a criminal offence, not only interfering with their immemorial rights and customs, but seriously imperilling their means of subsistence. So strongly were they moved by this and other similar acts of injustice that a second rebellion was narrowly averted.

Sir George Campbell, who had but recently assumed the Lieutenant-Governorship, at once made a close inquiry into the condition of affairs reported by the local authorities. It was seen that, although the Santal Parganas had been made a non-regulation district in 1855, it had since been gradually drifting into line with the rest of the province, some acts being practically enforced there which the non-regulation system had been specially adopted to exclude. Sir George Campbell, recognising that the backward condition of the Santals did not fit them to cope on equal terms with their neighbours in Bengal, succeeded in passing a regulation placing things on a more definite footing. It clearly laid down what laws were in force in the Parganas, leaving to Government the option of enforcing any further existing law as it might at any time deem fit. The two questions that had always formed the chief grievances of the Santals—the payment of rent and the exactions of the usurers—were vigorously dealt with. The accumulation of interest on debts was limited, and a Grain Bank scheme was afterwards started whereby Government attempts to take the place of the mahajan to the great advantage of the ryot. Further a system of land settlements was inaugurated that clearly defined once and for all the rights and liabilities of the parties concerned. One of the most beneficent clauses, which has tended greatly to induce content among the Santals, prevented the permanent alienation of his holding by a ryot. The unfortunate cultivator might still get hopelessly into debt and see his holding sold for arrears of rent; but he had the satisfaction of knowing that he could not be permanently robbed of the land to which he was so passionately attached. The purchaser or moneylender could only deprive him of it until the time of the next settlement came. Then the land must revert to him free and unencumbered, and he was thus enabled periodically to start life afresh with a clean sheet. But such immunity from the ordinary course of law was not gained all at once, and the practice of the neighbouring Civil Courts at Suri, where permanent alienation was sanctioned, was often followed, confirming the moneylender in the lands he had seized. It was the time of the passing of the Bengal Tenancy Act, and the Santal Parganas, where transferability was obviously proving a serious evil, was an awkward exception to the law then about to be enforced. But that it was a necessary exception was forced upon the notice of Government, and the sale of holdings was finally interdicted throughout the Parganas. The penalty is eviction for both the alienee and the alienor, and thus the work of restoration goes on daily whenever any illegal transference is brought to light, the general time of reckoning coming at stated intervals, when officers especially deputed by Government make full inquiry into all the conditions of tenure. This periodical settlement of rents and recording of customs and rights by officers especially deputed for the purpose by Government has finally settled the question of the land on a clear and definite footing and prevented for all time a recurrence of any of the grievances of which the Santals have justly complained in the past.

The land question thus set at rest, the subsequent disturbances that have agitated the tribe have emanated solely from the ignorance and superstition under which the Santal still labours. It was the first census of 1872 that created the greatest commotion, threatening to break out into open acts of hostility. To the suspicious Santal, fearful of the unknown or of anything beyond his powers of comprehension, the numbering of the tribe assumed an aspect fraught with omens of evil and disaster. Yet at the outset every precaution had been taken not to arouse alarm, and in order to inspire confidence their own primitive methods of counting had been resorted to. The headman of each village was deputed to enumerate its inhabitants, and distribution was made among them of coloured strings in which a knot was to be tied for each man, woman, and child within his jurisdiction. Black strings were given to enumerate the men, red for the women, white for boys, and yellow for girls, thus reducing the numbering of the people to the greatest possible simplicity. But the Santal looked upon it with the deepest suspicion and refused to be counted. Why, he asked, should the numbers of the tribe be required? Surely it must be with some sinister motive. Rapidly from village to village wild rumours flew, first that the children were to be carried away to be brought up among the Hindus to learn their religion and beliefs, then that the whole tribe was to be forced to embrace Christianity, or, again, that a large number of the flower of the Santal youth was to be drafted off to supply labour for the tea gardens of Assam. In many villages where the Manjhis attempted to commence the enumeration the people rose up and refused to submit, destroying the strings that Government had supplied. For a time serious disturbances threatened, but the presence of the local European officers, who moved rapidly about among the people, soon inspired confidence and allayed the unrest. Once counted, and finding that no evil resulted, the superstitious Santal was content, and the census passed in his mind among the things known and understood, and consequently no longer to be feared. The first census then taken proved a great surprise in the number of Santals returned. Fifty years before there had been no Santal in the Daman-i-koh and comparatively few within the larger area now known as the Santal Parganas. With the first great rush that followed their admission in 1832 something like thirty thousand are supposed to have arrived, while the census of 1872 gave the enormous and unexpected total of 455,513. Each succeeding census has shown a steady increase of the race within the district, that of 1901 returning the number as 663,471. Outside the district the increase has been even more marked, the 346,392 of 1881 reaching the total of 1,164,121 in 1901, most of them being found in the neighbouring districts of Manbhum, Birbhum, and Midnapore. These figures show the Santals a strenuous and prolific race, excluding as they do the large numbers who have emigrated beyond the limits of Bengal.

It was a striking proof of the inherently peaceful nature of the Santals and of their belief in the sincerity of Government's endeavours to redress their grievances that they took no advantage of the Sepoy Mutiny which followed so closely on their own rebellion of 1855. The disaffection of the native regiments, which had been stationed at Rohini, Bausi, Deoghar, and Dumka to assist the civil authorities in settling the Parganas, gave the Santals every opportunity, had they so desired, to let loose once more the spirit of revolt. Yet, far from this, they had so quickly proved their loyalty that in the dark days of 1857 the Commissioner of Bhagalpur recommended the enlistment of a body of Santals for police purposes—a recommendation that was at once approved by Government and successfully carried through.

Those were anxious days for the recently appointed officials in the Santal Parganas. From all sides, from Patna and Jalpaiguri, from Chittagong and Dacca, came wild rumours of mutiny that shook the already wavering loyalty of the local troops. On August 14 the 5th Irregulars at Bhagalpur, carried away by the news of their comrades' revolt at Patna, finally broke out into open mutiny, and marching off to Rohini in the Santal Parganas joined the detachment of their regiment stationed there. Among the latter disaffection, culminating in the treacherous murder of

Sir Norman Leslie, had already been at work, and after extorting twelve thousand rupees from the local inhabitants the united force marched on to Bausi, the headquarters of the 32nd Native Infantry. But here they had been forestalled. A loyal zemindar, learning their designs, had hastily despatched a messenger to give warning of their approach. So fast, however, did the mutineers travel that the messenger only reached Bausi half an hour ahead of them. But that was time sufficient to enable Colonel Burney, who was in command of the regiment, to undertake some hasty measures of defence, and his men proving loyal the rebel Sepoys were forced to march on, continuing south-west towards Deoghar. Here, too, however, the officials had been warned, the messenger who brought the news having covered eighty miles in thirty hours. Lieutenant Cooper, who was in command of a detachment of the 32nd quartered there, was an officer exceedingly popular with his men, and his firmness and tact held them in check as the mutineers approached. The latter, thus a second time disappointed of recruits, marched off westward to join the Patna mutineers, making no attempt to reach the other detachment of their regiment at Dumka. There much anxiety was felt owing to the very doubtful loyalty of the troops, and had the main body of the 5th Irregulars advanced they would in all probability have thrown in their lot with them. The local officials, however, by acting promptly in sending off the treasure and the prisoners to Suri in Birbhum, averted further danger.

During all this time the 32nd Native Infantry had remained loyal, resisting the repeated efforts of the 5th Irregulars to draw it into revolt. The main body, indeed, stationed at Bausi, remained loyal to the end, quietly and of their own free will later on laying down their arms when called upon to do so. But suddenly, on October 9, seized by one of those wild inexplicable impulses that swept through all ranks of the native troops in 1857, the detachment of the regiment at Deoghar broke into open mutiny. It was nearly two months since the 5th Irregulars had halted within sight of the famous city, calling upon their comrades in arms to join the revolt. Yet then the detachment had well proved its loyalty, and no outward sign of disaffection had been apparent since. There was every reason to believe that the storm had passed by, and that no further danger need be anticipated. But suddenly, on the night of October 9, without any previous warning, a wild spirit of mutiny and fanaticism seems to have seized the whole detachment. Lieutenant Cooper, in command, with Lieutenant Rannie, of the same regiment, and

Mr. Ronald, the Assistant Commissioner, were spending the evening together in the officers' quarters, absolutely unsuspicious of impending danger. Taken by surprise, they were quickly hemmed in. The Sepoys, transformed from the orderly disciplined troops of but a few hours before into raving fanatics, drunk with passion, pressed round the bungalow, blocking every entrance. Then the strangest incident in this unexpected outbreak occurred. Lieutenant Cooper was an officer particularly devoted to his work and to his men, who in return had always exhibited the greatest devotion towards him; Lieutenant Rannie, a younger officer, was neither as well known nor in any way as popular among them as his senior; while Mr. Ronald was practically an entire stranger to them. Yet the Sepoys, crowding round the bungalow, especially singled out Lieutenant Rannie, calling upon him by name to come out and allowing him to escape untouched. Then, rushing in, they brutally murdered Lieutenant Cooper and Mr. Ronald. Why they should have spared Lieutenant Rannie, for whom they had no particular affection, and murdered the officer, to whom they had appeared sincerely devoted, and the civilian, against whom they could have had no grievance, must always remain one of the many unsolved mysteries that fill the annals of the Sepoy mutiny.

Dumka, the headquarters of the district since the Santal rebellion, is a pleasant station, healthy and well situated, surrounded with a glorious wealth of trees; but, altogether of recent growth, it has little of special interest to present. Nearly forty miles distant from the railway at Rampur Hât, it still has to be reached in *ticca gharis*, not of the most comfortable description. Woe be to him who attempts to reach it from the other direction on the west! The distance is little more from Deoghar, but mode of conveyance there is none save two of the most rickety *ticca gharis* conceivable, drawn the whole way without a change by the smallest of country tats. Wheels have been known to come off halfway in the middle of the night—a misfortune, indeed, on the Dumka-Deoghar road, where anything faster than a bullock cart rarely passes, and where there is little hope of help in time of need.

Rajmahal on the Ganges, the town of greatest historical interest in the Santal Parganas, is now the headquarters of a subdivision; but time has dealt hardly with the splendours of Musulman power that once adorned the river's bank. Selected as the site of the new capital of Bengal by Man Singh, the Rajput general of Akbar the Great, on his return from the conquest of Orissa in 1592, it quickly grew into a magnificent city, with all the rapidity and cunning deftness of workmanship characteristic of the Musulman at the height of his power. Commanding the Ganges not far from its sudden turn from east to south as it sweeps round the foot of the hills, and close by the famous Teliagarhia Pass, the gateway of Bengal, its position was unrivalled. Man Singh, intent upon building a palace for himself, did not forget, even in the midst of the enemies of his faith, to build a temple to the god of Hinduism whom he worshipped. But Fatih Khan, governor of the neighbouring province of Behar, jealous of his rival's power and recent victories, caught at this defiance of the Musulman faith, and sent off alarmist reports to Akbar that Man Singh was meditating revolt from imperial control. But Man Singh was even with his rival. Hastily finishing what he had begun as a Hindu temple, he opened it with great pomp as a Musulman mosque, and in compliment to Akbar renamed the city Akbarnagar. Deserted for a few years, 1607 to 1639, it was restored by Sultan Suja after the Portuguese power had been crushed in the storming and sack of Hughli Fort in 1632. Of the palace built by Sultan Suja but little remains, save a terrace right on the bank of the Ganges, and the site of the well, still pointed out, down which the ladies of the household threw themselves when, basely deserting them, he fled before Aurungzeeb's general, Mir Jumla. All around Rajmahal are the ruins of temples and palaces, long since fallen on evil days, lichen-covered and overgrown with foliage, serving only to recall the memory of the greatness of Musulman power in the days of its strength. Six miles south of the city is the battle-field of Udhanulla, where the English troops, under Major Adams, defeated the army of Nawab Mir Kassim in 1763, and it was in the near neighbourhood that Suraja Dowlah, fresh from his final enormity of the Black Hole, was captured by a fakir, to meet with the fate that he deserved shortly afterwards at the hands of Miran, the son of the Nawab Mir Jafar of Rajmahal.

Godda, Pakur, and Jamtara, the other sub-divisional headquarters, are of recent growth, and have nothing of special interest, while Deoghar, the Divine City, has been thought worthy of a chapter to itself. But the subdivision of which it is the headquarters is one of the most interesting parts of the Santal Parganas. Set apart from the rest of the district it is the home neither of Santal nor Paharia in any large numbers, all its northern side belonging ethnically and linguistically to Hindustan. In the old days it was occupied by the Katauri, a Hinduised section of the Mals, who were driven out by the Bhuiya invasion from the south in the sixteenth century. The Bhuiya themselves were a Dravidian tribe, affecting

Hinduism and claiming to be classed as Rajputs; but their triumph was short, and they in turn quickly fell under the sway of the Pathans of Birbhum from the south. They proved themselves, however, to be turbulent and rebellious subjects, and the Rajas of Birbhum, anxious to preserve their hold, conciliated them by granting them back their lands on Ghatwali tenures. They were to hold on condition of rendering military service and keeping the peace each within his own estate, while paying only the lowest of quit-rents or in many cases nothing at all for the lands themselves. This was the position of affairs when the British Government took over the Birbhum territory. Finding that the Ghatwals were still unruly and not fulfilling the condition of their tenure by providing police and maintaining law and order, while continually engaged in quarrels with the Raja of Birbhum, Government in 1813 deputed a civilian, Mr. David Scott, to make a settlement of the Ghatwali estates. The whole of Deoghar, with the exception of a few acres round the town of Deoghar itself, was allotted out into Ghatwali holdings. Government declared that the Ghatwals and their descendants in perpetuity 'shall be maintained in possession of the lands so long as they shall respectively pay the revenue at present assessed upon them, and that they shall not be liable to any enhancement of rent so long as they shall punctually discharge the same and fulfil the other obligation of the tenure.' This permanent settlement on a small scale was confirmed by Regulation XXIX. of 1814, Deoghar being the only part of India to which it applies.

Many of the Ghatwals are Bhuiyas, that race of doubtful origin and history arrogantly claiming Rajput descent, yet bearing in their nigritic features disproof sufficient of their claim. But the variety of races and castes found among the Ghatwals is characteristic of this common meeting-ground of Bengal and Hindustan. One Ghatwali at least was held by a Brahmin, that of Kuron, bestowed by the Raja of Birbhum in return for good offices done him at the court of the viceroy at Murshedabad. Another, the Ghatwal of Rohini, is an offshoot of the proud Rajput house of Khaira. The Ghatwal of Sarath is a Hindu Kaist, while a Bhuinhar and a Bengali Sunri hold tenures side by side. Two other Ghatwalis are held, the one by an Englishman, the other by a Scotchman, the creations of Sir George Yule when Commissioner of Bhagalpur in 1858.

CHAPTER IX

THE YEARLY ROUND IN SAGARBHANGA

In the very heart of the Daman-i-koh, far from the noise and stress of life, lies the most picturesque and typical of Santal villages. It is here that the Santal after many days has found a home, and free from outside interference, in his jealous seclusion he has preserved intact his ancient customs and beliefs even as they have been handed down to him through many generations of his race. Save for the change that a permanent abode and the knowledge that his wandering days are over have inevitably brought, the Santal of to-day is even as his fathers were, rejoicing in his strength and independence and fearful only of the unseen powers of evil and of interference from the world without.

The Santal, though he loves the vicinity of the hills, is content to place his dwelling on the plains at their foot. To him, with his passion for cultivation, the steep slopes of the hills where the Paharia loves to place his home make no appeal. His work lies on the fertile plains below. That intense love of the soil which lies deep down among the primitive instincts in the heart of man has always held the Santal in its grip. To grapple hard with Nature, fighting against her rampant wastefulness and ceaseless efforts to obliterate man's labour, has been the lifework of the Santal race. Time and again, the victory won once and for all, he has grown restless, unused to the unaccustomed ease of toil where Nature was subdued. The joy of the intake has called him, and little outside influence has been needed to induce him to leave his new-made homestead and his fertile fields to face once more that invigorating struggle against a foe, stern and relentless to the weakling, but once subdued a prodigal and generous ally.

It was thus that this primitive village of Sagarbhanga, and countless others like it in and around the Daman-i-koh, first had their beginning. The land, untouched as yet by the hand of man and rejected of the Paharias, lay waiting for the coming of the race that should tame its wild luxuriance into an ordered and life-giving fertility. The Santal, recognising here at the end of his wanderings a land that Nature had fitted for his own, forced his way through the pathless jungle, and, clearing the undergrowth where his choice fell, made for himself a home. Unlike the Paharia, he has proved himself no great respecter of the monarchs of the forest. They, like all else, have been sacrificed to his one absorbing passion for the cultivation of the soil. Only here and there on the plains, where too huge for the primitive implements in use or left to form the sacred grove of the gods, do any of the mighty trees that once covered the land survive. Banyan and pepul, tamarind and nim, have been ruthlessly levelled with the ground, and those that remain are but a tithe of the forest that stood untouched before the Santal came. Yet where they have weathered the storm their grandeur and antiquity win for them respect and worship from the superstitious Santal. A stone's-throw from the confines of the village stands the Sacred Grove, a patch of primæval forest, a hundred feet square, preserved intact as in the days when as yet the destroyer was not in the land. Here banyan and pepul, tamarind and sal, palas and kend, flourish together, overtopped by the giant palm, round whose trunk the many-stemmed banyan is slowly winding, serpent-like, its close death-giving embrace. Beneath their shade the Santal worships, desiring no symbol of the gods in this their home, but careful only to mark with *sindur* the branching roots and the rough slabs of stone beside them as a sign of his veneration and respect.

Sagarbhanga, trim with all the Santal neatness

—not even the Paharia is a better housewife than the Santal—is nothing but a jumble of huts clustering on either side of the winding sagar track. Fifty houses all told, their very irregularity and seeming irresponsibility attract. The one dividing road, just wide enough to let bullock cart or sagar pass, fully retains its reputation that long since must have given the village its name. Sagarbhanga means the 'breaking of a sagar,' and a road that is a danger to this most primitive and hardy of native carts must be bad indeed. To the sagar, nothing but bamboos lashed together and placed upon two wheels cut out of solid blocks of sal wood, the worst of roads as a rule can do little damage. But deep in ruts, cut clear in the hard-baked earth, with rough boulders imbedded in the soil or scattered loosely here and there along the path, the road through Sagarbhanga attests much strength in the cart that passes safely along it. On either side the houses, mud-built and thatched with straw or more pretentiously roofed with bright red tiles, have each its courtyard attached surrounded by wall or hedge to secure that privacy the Santal loves to maintain in his domestic life. The first house one reaches on approaching the village exhibits all the characteristic traces of the pride and care bestowed upon it by its owner. Facing the road stands the house itself, but there is no entry from the front save the door in the wall that runs all round the spacious courtyard on to which the house opens from within. Outside all is trim and neat, the mud walls plastered to a perfect smoothness and the tiles newly laid on house and wall adding their touch of colour brick-red. Running the full length of the house is a low projection, also of solid mud but freshly white-washed, in dazzling contrast to the dull drab of the wall above whereon the inmates sit and gossip with their friends when the day's work is done.

Within the promise of cleanliness and order gained from the outside is well fulfilled. The house itself is of but two rooms—one open to the deep verandah that runs along one side, the other closed to view by a rough made door of matting. All is of the same hard-baked mud save the wooden posts that support the roof and the rafters of bamboo whereon first the thatch and then the tiles are laid. Furniture there is none save the crazy *parkom*—a rough wooden framework crossed and recrossed with stout string—that serves as the most primitive of beds. The family is large, outnumbering even the usual prolific Santal household, father and mother, sons and daughters, and daughters-in-law with a small swarm of children of varying ages of the third generation; but the one *parkom* suffices for the old

A SAGAR

man—a venerable patriarch—and the rest of the family know no more comfortable resting-place when night comes than the bare ground covered only with a strip of cloth or, by great good luck, a blanket. But the brass plates, lotas, and *chelangs* —the Santal's cooking and household utensils—are the pride of the housewife's heart. Polished with ashes until the brass shines like gold, they stand in a row against the wall, and no cottager in an English village takes greater pride in the display of her kitchen shelves than the Santal matron takes in these her sole possessions. Above them against the wall hangs a drum, bowl-shaped, ingeniously made of iron thinly beaten out and covered on the top with hide black with age and much use. This and the flutes fashioned out of hollow bamboos are the glory of the men and boys, and their possession gains for them much dignity and a sure welcome at every feast and festival. There is little else in the first open room save the fireplace, which is nothing but a hollow space enclosed by neat walls of hard-baked mud whereon to rest the pots and pans. Here it is right in the centre of the room, and the walls once white-washed are blackened to the roof by the smoke that has no outlet of its own and fills the room in clouds. But the Santal finds this no inconvenience. Indeed he prefers it, thus adding, as it does, to the warmth during the winter days and nights and supplying the place of clothing that he lacks and loathes to be encumbered with. In the inner room, closed by the thick mat door, it is even worse. Here there is no escape for the dense clouds of smoke that rise from the wood fire, and the atmosphere inside would quickly drive out any but a Santal.

The courtyard, larger than most in the village, has the same baked mud floor swept clean, one corner only close against the house being occupied by the structure like a dog-kennel of a larger growth wherein the pigs and fowls herd at night. Outside a larger shed, trimly made of sal-wood saplings, affords shelter to the cows and goats, packed tight, a motley herd wherein what comfort there is to be obtained is to the strong, and the weak and small fare ill. Over and around it in rampant luxuriance grows the thick bean creeper with its flowers a mass of blossom purple and white. Beside the shed, scarce equal in size to the courtyard within, is the tiny patch of garden filled chiefly with the large-leaved tobacco plant, chillies with their brilliant red against the pale green, and brinjals with their purple-green fruit occupying the small portion of space that remains.

Passing on down the winding village street—if the rough uneven track can be dignified by the name—there is infinite variety. No two houses are alike. Each, built at the whim and fancy of its owner, has its own individuality, limited though the Santal's ideas of architecture and the variety of material to hand must necessarily be. Here a house, the poorest in the village, of but one room, exposes all its interior to the public gaze save a corner screened by a wall of matting; there a more pretentious dwelling with its wide verandah set back from the road reveals nothing of what lies beyond; while further on the most primitive of shops displays its meagre contents—flat open baskets of rice and pulse with a jar of ghee or a tray of bright red chillies.

Right at the end of the village stands the Manjhi Than. Though a place that figures so largely in the village life, it is nothing but a raised mud platform some two feet high, square, with wooden posts at the corners, supporting a roof of dilapidated thatch. Yet here the elders of the village meet in solemn conclave to decide important affairs that affect its interests, or to pass judgment on any who have offended and broken the tribal law. Here, too, reside the spirits of departed Manjhis, and public acts of worship are performed in their honour and at many of the annual festivals besides. Knowing the fear and respect that the Santal entertains for the spirits of his ancestors, its tumble-down uncared-for look cannot fail to attract the attention of the passer-by after the trim and neat appearance of all the other houses in the village. Inquiry from the Manjhi himself, who has strolled up with a quaint mixture of curiosity and indifference, elicits a somewhat unexpected reply. Raising his stick he points with a casual smile to a wisp of new straw tied carelessly on the top of the roof. No one in the village could afford to thatch the Manjhi Than afresh after the expense of repairing his own house before last rains, he explains. So that knot of straw was tied on the roof to deceive the spirits into the belief that the thatching had been properly done. The Manjhi smiles complacently as if taking to himself the credit of a good joke. But one cannot refrain from asking how it comes that the spirits of whom the Santal goes so continually in fear can be so easily deceived. The Manjhi shrugs his shoulders expressively. Of course the Manjhi Than should have been completely thatched and repaired, but still—his smile broadens—that wisp of straw may have deceived the spirits, and, if so, the village has been saved much labour and expense. He points again to the earthen *ghura* hanging to one of the posts that support the roof. It is half full of water, rank and long unchanged, but it is the only drink supplied by the Santal to the shades of his ancestors who so much loved the good rice beer during the time of their stay upon earth. But the Manjhi waves aside with a smile the suggestion that the *ghura* should be filled with a liberal drink of that much-loved beverage. Were that done the spirits would hover about the Manjhi Than too closely to be pleasant, he says, showing at the same time his disbelief in his own superstition by asking cynically why, under pretence of supplying the spirits, they should supply the village drunkards, who would not scruple to imbibe what their departed ancestors could no longer enjoy.

Such is Sagarbhanga, the most primitive of village communities, and one, the casual passer-by might think, where monotony reigns supreme from year's end to year's end. But behind, to one who is content to watch, there is infinite variety and change of scene. To see the village in its ordinary sleepy workaday mood is but to gain the faintest idea of its possibilities in the way of life and interest. The recurring seasons, each bringing its special need for special labour, keep the Santal ever busy, while the innumerable feasts and festivals, each with its own appropriate and symbolic meaning, afford a constant round of merry-making to fill his leisure hours.

The Santal year begins with the Sohrae. In all the calendar no festival is celebrated with a greater will and enthusiasm than this. As it falls in January, when the hard work of the last few months in the fields is over, the Santal, complacently viewing his well-stocked granaries against the year to come, can seek his relaxation with an easy mind. After his long spell of strenuous labour, he feels in his own words 'full of devilry' and ready to throw himself without restraint into the fitting celebration of the Sohrae—the Feast of Harvest. What that means a glimpse of Sagarbhanga during its progress reveals. In the old days, the Santal was careful not to celebrate it at one and the same time in every village. That would have curtailed the possibilities of neighbourly visits and failed to satisfy his craving for a long-continued spell of licence and debauch. So arrangements were carefully made for its celebration in different villages at different times, thus enabling the Santal, insatiable where festivals are concerned, to pass from one scene of revelry to another, prolonging the round of orgies until even he had had his fill and could do no more. But such prolonged merry-making has now been prevented, and the Santal perforce celebrates the Sohrae on the same days throughout the Parganas.

It is the night before the festival proper is timed to begin in Sagarbhanga, and the last household duty done, the whole village wends its way towards the Manjhi Than. There the Manjhi, the Paranik, the Naeke, and the Jogmanjhi have already met, supported by a group of officials from a neighbouring village, who have arrived early so as to miss nothing of the beginning of the festival on the morrow. Round them presses an eager crowd assembled there to hear the deliberations that it can so well foretell, but which at each annual recurrence never fail to excite the keenest interest and enthusiasm. As the sun that is to rise to-morrow upon the opening scene of the Sohrae sets behind the line of hills that overlooks the village from the west, the words forming the essential part of the proceedings are spoken. Custom and tradition, stern and invariable, prescribe the formula: 'Now let us put earth upon our eyes,' say the wise men in unison, 'so that each may not see what the other does, and let us put cotton in our ears, so that none may hear what his neighbour saith until what time the Sohrae has passed.' Such a beginning augurs well for the fitting celebration of the festival. Each man is free to follow his own desires secure from the reproach of his neighbours. The wildest excesses of licence and debauch are sanctioned, and the worst that the Santal can do is easily atoned for by a libation with the prescribed formula when the Sohrae is at an end.

A murmur of satisfaction as the time-honoured proceedings draw to a close passes through the waiting crowd, which, tense and eager during the recital of the momentous words, sways with pent-up excitement let loose now that the words of licence that allow free play to their passions have been spoken. As the drums are sounded and the flutes call a shrill salute, all move off towards the *akhra*, an open space close by beneath the trees, where the ground has been carefully cleared and levelled for the dance. It is a picturesque sight as the crowd moves along, the dancers leading the way and dancing a fantastic measure as they beat their deafening monotonous notes, the pipers adding their wild plaintive music, heard even above the roar of sound as all raise their voices to the highest pitch to sing the song of the Sohrae. Night has fallen, and the rough-made torches, swaying with the movement of the crowd, cast a weird and flickering light upon the darkness, revealing here the group of drummers, there a band of maidens, with their flower-decked hair, linked arm in arm and dancing as they move, or falling further back upon the older men and women, whose chief joy in the festival comes later, when the rice beer is handed round, and imbibings oft repeated and reminiscences oft retold lead gradually to the dazed but happy slumber of oblivion that to them represents the highest joy to which they can ever attain.

The *akhra* reached, the dance begins in earnest. Formed in a semicircle round the drummers, the girls in close array, linked arm in arm, dance to their tune, retreating and advancing with even rhythmical steps that never seem to tire. The solid phalanx, moving as one in perfect unison, keeps time with wonderful precision, presenting a charming picture of unstudied grace and symmetry. Few of the men join the dance save the drummers and pipers, who lead it with grotesque fantastic contortions and wild gyrations. Only occasionally, when the rice beer long imbibed has had its due effect, do some of the gayest spirits join the drummers, outdoing them even in enthusiasm and energy, until from sheer exhaustion they fall out to be revived again by another draught of the much-loved beverage. But upon the Santal maiden the long monotonous progress of the dance has little effect. Continuously without a break the moving phalanx advances and retreats, covering the same small space of ground a thousand times to the same dull throbbing of the drums and the same accompaniment of an oft-repeated, never-ending chorus, unvarying in tune and meaningless to any but a Santal. Hour after hour the dance goes on, and even as the dying torches cast their uncertain light upon the scene they reveal no falling off in the spirit and energy of this tireless people. Only here and there a maiden has laughingly dropped out to readjust the flowers of her headdress that the motion of the dance has disarranged or to bind up more securely the knot of coal-black hair that threatens to unslip its coil. But upon the spectators the rice beer has not failed of its effect, and stupor has at last succeeded hilarity among the older men, many of whom have already staggered off or been led reeling away down the village street towards their homes; while the younger men, beguiling the maidens of their choice from dance and song, have sought for greater seclusion where the light from the flaming torches does not reach. So at last the dance dies down. Even to the Santal in the Sohrae must come a temporary lull in merry-making. Still dancing by the way, the most energetic of the dancers move off towards the village, their attendant swains following close behind and the drummers expending their last efforts in a final burst of sound that seems to throb upon the stillness of the night. A silence falls upon the *akhra*, the last torch leaping spasmodically into flame, revealing it deserted, only the flower-strewn dancing-floor bearing evidence of the scene just passed. The drums, beating with rapidly muffling sound as the distance lengthens, grow fainter, and ceasing at last proclaim the fitting inauguration of the Sohrae an accomplished fact.

But late as the hour was when it retired to rest Sagarbhanga is astir with the dawn. Much *haria* imbibed the night before has little after-effect upon this sturdy energetic people, for whom but a few hours suffice to sleep off the worst debauch. The dawn breaks cold and grey, the mist over the low-lying fields at the foot of the hills hanging low and chill until the sun has fully risen and causing the scantily clothed Santal to go shivering huddled up in his cloth or blanket that affords at best but small protection. Nothing, however, but physical infirmity would keep a Santal abed this morning of all mornings in the year, for one of the most important events of the Sohrae takes place with the dawn. While yet the first faint light is struggling out of the East the whole village is awake, a scene of life and excited interest. Every man is busy driving whatever he possesses in the way of cattle towards the end of the village street, filled with the hope that the good fortune which must fall to one man's lot to-day may by good luck be his. Every animal of the cow kind that Sagarbhanga can produce is brought by its anxious owner to the trysting-place, and when all is ready the struggling noisy crowd is driven off up the village street towards the Manjhi Than.

There, in the midst of the large open space opposite, a layer of rice has been spread in a circle over the ground, and in the centre has been placed a single egg, new laid that same morning. An excited eager crowd of villagers watches with breathless interest the oncoming of the promiscuous herd of cattle, one of whom, blundering along, unconscious of the momentous import of its steps, is safe to break the egg. Fortunate in the estimation of all is the owner of the animal that does so, for to him the coming year shall be one of continuous good fortune: his flocks and his herds shall flourish and multiply, and to all that he sets his hand shall come success. Great is the excitement as the cattle draw near. First a pair of oxen, frightened by the clamour, dart by wide of the mark; then a cow with a ten days' calf, still more frightened, rushes past, frisking and hugging the wall on the further side of the road far from the magic circle. Behind two bullocks, slow and heavy of foot, come labouring along, their meek heads thrust forward, as if in mild supercilious protest. Straight for the rice circle makes the larger and more ungainly of the two, blundering on, with never a glance at the ground in front, and a sudden hush of breathless expectation falls upon the watchers. Its foot is almost on the rice when, perversely lowering its head, it sees the patch of white on the brown earth and swerves uneasily aside. Its owner curses his luck; it is not on him that good fortune is to fall. Behind a miscellaneous crowd is driven on, but though the rice is trodden under foot the egg, by a seeming miracle, long escapes, until at last a calf, the smallest-footed of them all, stumbling upon it, breaks the shell, and makes its herdsman the most envied man in all the village. His neighbours press around him congratulating him on the good fortune that they doubt not will attend his enterprises through the coming year. He is but a youth whose thoughts have already gone forward in anticipation to the marrying season soon to come, and the pleased smile that overspreads his features at this propitious omen is reflected on the face of a buxom maid who hangs back, shy but radiant, from the laughs and jokes of her companions.

Then come the religious ceremonies of the Sohrae. The trial of luck made, the villagers proceed to the Jaher Than, or Sacred Grove, where a patch of primæval forest left untouched forms a fitting home for the vague, invisible, mysterious gods of the Santal. Here each deity has its appointed place, all save Thakur, who is supreme among gods, but who, being too great and too far off to intervene in the petty concerns of this world, delegates his authority to another. Marang

Buru, the Great Spirit, his first lieutenant and vice-ruler of the earth, holds chief place, while beside him, beneath the trees, worshipped in awe and fear, reside Moreko Turuiko, a vague group of Bongas said to consist of two families of five and six brothers, Gosai Era, presiding Goddess of the Grove, and the Paragana Bonga—gods whose attributes are ill-defined, but whose festivals and sacrifices never fail of strict performance.

It is to Marang Buru that the sacrifices are made during the Sohrae, and the priests leading the way, all the villagers follow to the Sacred Grove. There placing *sindur* on the stones at the foot of the trees, and murmuring his time-honoured formulas, the Naeke sacrifices a number of fowls which the worshippers have provided. Custom has ordained the manner of the sacrifice. The sharp Santal axe is held securely on the ground with the blade pointing upwards, and the priest, taking the bird in both hands, presses its neck heavily upon the upturned edge, severing the head from the body. The blood of the victim, which forms an essential part of every sacrifice, is then scattered over the stones that represent the altars of Marang Buru. As a further offering the Kudam Naeke draws a few drops of blood from his left forearm to complete the sacrifice and propitiate the deity.

A SACRIFICE IN THE SACRED GROVE

This short ceremony over, a return is made to the village with much dancing and singing by the way. There, at the Manjhi Than, further sacrifices are made of goats and pigs and fowls, the flesh of which later on towards evening forms the feast that precedes another night of licence and debauch. For the next three days all is given up to merry-making. Ordinary occupations are suspended, and save for the brief hours given to sleep, which even Santal nature must occasionally demand, the same monotonous round of dance and music, feasting and drinking, goes on without a break. It is the highest form of enjoyment that the Santal knows Though the monotony of it never varies, he is content, and his own celebration of the Sohrae over, he is ready, where no official order forbids, to set out for the next village to taste its hospitality and assist once more in the festival of harvest home.

The next festival that wakes the village to life succeeds so quickly that it is almost a continuation of the Sohrae. But there is little work to be done in the fields for many a day to come. His barns are full, and the Santal can afford to celebrate his national festivals with spirit and without a care. The Sakrat lasts two days, and is essentially the festival of the men, filled as it is with bow and arrow shooting competitions, athletic sports, and the dancing of the famous Pak Don, the sword and shield dance, performed in the good old Santal days by the flower of their youth on the eve of battle or on the return from victory. Clad in but the scantiest of garments—a loin-cloth about the waist, perchance a necklace, and anklets of tinkling bells—their fine supple limbs have full play as they spring and leap in the wild measures of the dance. A stout stick has replaced the sword of more warlike days, but the shield of beaten brass and copper remains. Thus equipped, the dancers form a complete circle round the drummers, and with a wild ear-piercing shout the dance begins. The deep throbbing of the drums, with the occasional shrill notes of the pipes, the fierce cries of the dancers, and the jingling of their anklet bells, produce combined the pandemonium of sound that the Santal loves. Brandishing their sticks and shields, the performers crouch low, then with an agile spring and unearthly yells leap high in the air, circling the while slowly round the drummers in the centre. So vigorous a dance demands a constant supply of rice beer, and one of the onlookers passes round from time to time with a jar of liquor, pouring leaf-fuls down the throats of the performers as each in turn pauses for a moment to imbibe the refreshing draught. It is a wild scene, and witnessed in the torchlight, when in full swing after the distribution of much *haria*, one can imagine something of the madness and unbridled passion with which the tribe danced in the old days on the eve of battle or on the return home, drunk with the lust of victory and bearing the spoil with them.

The Jatra Festival, adopted by the Santals from their Hindu neighbours, follows after no long interval in the month of February. It is the time for looking into the future and for the price of a few annas obtaining knowledge from those inspired of the gods of things to come. First a sacrifice is performed in the Sacred Grove. Uncooked rice, mixed with milk, butter, and betel-nut, is the strange offering that the Jatra Bonga demands, to be followed by the sacrifice of a pigeon or a goat, and the sprinkling of the blood upon the sacred stone. During this performance, the oracles of the Bonga, three or four in number, have been preparing themselves to see into the future, and answer the questions that the anxious villagers are but awaiting the conclusion of the sacrifice to propound to them. Rolling from side to side as they sit on the ground, wagging their heads and waving their arms, they work themselves into a frenzy of excitement and prophetic fervour. Then one by one those who have aught to fear or hope of the future come tremblingly to learn their fate. One man has a lawsuit. Will he succeed? Another suspects the presence of a witch, even among the members of his own family. Is he mistaken? A third has lost many of his cattle through disease and others are sickening. What is the cause? A fourth is contemplating marriage with the maiden of his choice. Are the gods favourable to the union? So one by one the villagers pass before the oracles, each with the question on his lips that is of so much moment to himself and to his own peace of mind. It is seldom that the answers are unfavourable, though the gods, through these very mundane oracles, are apt to demand fresh sacrifices as the price of their magnanimity.

Often during the Jatra festival at the larger places of resort a fair is held. It is of the most primitive and unpretentious kind. The booths spread out on the ground display nothing but the cheapest wares, many of them of Birmingham make, or bearing the still more common 'made in Germany' stamp. Looking-glasses of all sizes with tawdry frames, combs, beads, and necklaces, with bracelets and anklets of native make, compose the glittering array, and delight the Santal heart, while the sweetmeat stalls, judging from the continuous stream of customers, appeal no less strongly to another sense in spite of heat and dust and flies innumerable that have long since robbed the wares of their first freshness. The crudest of roundabouts is patronised by young and old alike. Between two posts firmly set in the ground is fixed a rough circular framework to which, at equal distances apart, four swinging seats hang suspended which are made to revolve rapidly one over the other in a circle, to the intense delight of the shouting occupants.

With the month of March begins the marriage season—the most festive of all times in the Santal village after the Sohrae. With no work to be done in the fields and with granaries well stocked the Santal youth has time to let his fancy lightly turn to thoughts of love. There is a certain freedom of choice allowed by custom to the contracting parties unknown among most other races in India. Both the contracting parties are of full age, and a mutual understanding having been arrived at, they leave their parents to make all the preliminary arrangements that custom demands. But the young man's choice must fall on no woman of his own sept. Marriage within the sept is strictly prohibited, though in any sept but his own a man may seek a wife. There is only one exception. In consequence of an ancient feud, the cause long since forgotten but the bitterness remaining, the Hasdak and Murmu septs jealously refuse to intermarry, maintaining with true Santal tenacity a tradition the origin and meaning of which have been altogether lost.

There is much to be settled before the marriage can take place, and over deep potations of rice beer the respected elders of both families are not unwilling to lengthen the negotiations. The most momentous question is that of the bride-price. How much is the bridegroom to pay the father of the bride for giving him his daughter to wife? The bride goes dowerless to her husband, but it is upon her family that the by no means inconsiderable expenses of the marriage fall, and they often exceed the bride-price many times over. The amount of the latter varies according to the social position of the bride's family. If an alliance with it is much desired in the neighbourhood, the price is high, otherwise, as in Sagarbhanga, where none can claim much superiority over his neighbour, a few rupees and a present of cloth are all that custom demands. These preliminaries satisfactorily settled, there remains only to fix a day for the happy event. To secure an auspicious day it is necessary to consult the Ojha, the village soothsayer, who comes at the call of the parties, frail and old and blind, leaning on his wand of office half as high again as himself. Seating himself on the ground outside the bridegroom's house, he surrounds himself with mystery, anxious to prolong the temporary importance that is his while the fixing of the marriage day still remains with him. Muttering his formulas not understood of those who crowd around, and consequently so much the more regarded with respect, he places a sal leaf on the palm of his hand and dropping oil and turmeric upon it rubs it slowly between both hands. This he repeats, sometimes as often as twenty times, knowing full well that the more difficult he makes the fixing of the date and the longer it takes, the greater will be the interest and the deeper the respect he will inspire. Sitting crosslegged in the centre of the crowd, his fervour increases as he throws away each crumpled sal leaf, his muttered formula rising to a shout as he rolls his body from side to side in a paroxysm of enthusiasm. At last, when he has worked the interest to its highest pitch, he stops abruptly, shouting aloud the auspicious date. Thus the preliminaries of the marriage are duly settled, and the parties separate to await the appointed day. There is one difficulty, however. The Santal has no calendar, his ideas of time are vague, and he cannot count beyond the fingers of his hands. So, in order that there may be no mistake as to the day fixed for the wedding, he has invented an ingenious plan. Long pieces of string are produced, and the Ojha ties in each a number of knots corresponding to the number of days that must elapse before the date fixed for the wedding. Every morning one of the knots in the string is undone, and so at length, without fear of mistake, the actual date is arrived at. Similar pieces of knotted string are sent out as invitations to the guests, so that they too may have a calendar to guide them without mishap to the appointed day.

The last knot unloosed, the bridegroom sets out with the dawn, accompanied by his relatives and friends, for the home of the bride. It is a picturesque procession that winds its way across the fields in the cool of the morning towards Sagarbhanga. At the head the bridegroom, decked with flowers, red palas, white sal, and yellow genda, and wearing a saffron cloth, marches proudly between his father and the Manjhi of his village. Behind, each with decorative evidence of the festive occasion, come the younger men, some with drums and flutes that herald their approach to the bride's abode, and that meet with an answering sound from the bridal party, unseen as yet within the village. As they draw near the Jogmanjhi comes out to greet them, attended by the girl friends of the bride decked in gay attire and bearing with typical eastern grace earthen *ghuras* of water on their heads. Just beyond the Manjhi Than beside the *akhra* the two processions meet. Salutations having been exchanged with oft-repeated 'Johars' (salaams), the women, lifting the water-pots from their heads, proceed to wash the feet of the guests. With much laughter and many jokes the ceremony is performed, and both parties, joining together in song and dance, proceed to the bride's house in front of which the ceremony is to take place. All day with much dancing and music the merry-making goes on, only the bridegroom sitting apart and taking no share in it, fasting against the great event of the night to come, the bride the while remaining modestly retired within the house preparing likewise for the evening ceremony. But when night has fallen and fires of sticks and leaves and torches light up the courtyard, the hour for the formal celebration of the marriage has arrived. Carried in a large basket by her friends, amidst the shouts of the guests, the bride is brought out from within the house. All the art that a Santal maiden knows has been expended to make her comely for this most important moment of her life. Bright red palas blossoms deck her coal-black hair, oiled until it shines again, while round her neck and arms, wrists and ankles, are innumerable ornaments of bell metal and beads red, blue, and white, her usual one garment of white with border of red supplemented for the occasion by a saffron cloth, flung lightly from right to left across her shoulders and loosely tied beneath the arm. No priest is necessary to carry through the Santal marriage. Custom and tradition demand but two essentials, and to these all the assembled guests are witnesses. The first, at once proceeded with, is the inevitable marking of the bride by the bridegroom with *sindur* on the forehead—an inseparable accompaniment of every form of marriage among the aborigines. The drums and singing cease suddenly and the whole assembly watches with breathless interest. The firelight playing on the group throws into relief the bride and bridegroom, a fine upstanding couple, he strong and supple of limb, she laughing of face and graceful of carriage, with a charm all her own in her bravery of attire and perfect natural self-possession that many another bride in other lands might envy. The *sindur* plentifully besmeared in a great red patch on the bride's forehead, the crowd of guests bursts out again into song, drums and flutes playing their loudest, the burden of the marriage song being little more than a monotonous variation of the refrain :

> Let us sing! Joy! joy!
> The bride's head is marked
> Repeatedly with the red paint,
> She is signed for ever and ever.

Then, while the song continues, the newly wedded couple proceed to the second essential part of the marriage ceremony. In the full view of all they sit down to partake together of a special feast that has been prepared for them alone. This is the first time that the girl has sat at meat with any man outside her own family, and the act of eating thus from the same plate and drinking from the same cup signifies that they are man and wife, and that henceforth the woman belongs no more to her former sept, but to that of her husband.

These important parts of the ceremony having been duly performed, the dancing and feasting continue throughout the night and the greater part of the next day, when the guests depart leaving nominal presents to show their goodwill, such as rice, chillies, or a few pice for the bride. Later on the married couple set out for their new home, the bride being escorted to the boundary of the village by her father and her train of girl friends and companions. The final leave-taking is of the merriest description. No anxious fears need be entertained on behalf of the bride. In her new home she will have an assured position of authority and respect. The Santal seldom has more than one wife, and domestic quarrels rarely disturb the peace of the household, while such a thing as wife-beating is an almost unknown enormity throughout Santalia.

Right in the middle of the marriage season

comes another of the gayest of Santal festivals. Known as the Baha Purab, it occurs in March when the sal flower is in full blossom. It is the festival held to celebrate the birth of the earth at each recurring spring, when Nature reawakes, and the giants of the forest put forth fresh leaves and buds. Sacrifices are made to all the chief deities in the Sacred Grove, notably to Marang Buru, the Great Spirit, who rules the earth and demands more sacrifices than any other god. The same dancing and feasting that accompany every festival fill the two days of the Baha Purab, only one incident giving it a special character apart from the rest. All the villagers go to the sacrifice in the Jaher, carrying on their heads vessels of all sorts—*ghuras*, lotas, and gourds—full to the brim of water from the tank. The sacrifices duly performed, a wild scene of confusion follows. Each of the worshippers proceeds to douse those nearest to him with the contents of his water-pot, and in the general *mêlée* few escape, all by the time their vessels are empty being thoroughly drenched to the skin. Few Santals to-day stop to think of the origin or meaning of this strange custom, but the oldest men among them say that it is symbolical of the rain watering the earth, without which its annual reawakening could not be.

Following close on the Baha Purab comes the

Pota Festival. It is equivalent to the Churuk Puga of the Hindus, but modern days have robbed it of its chief interest and excitement to the native mind. Outside the village close by the *akhra* and the Manjhi Than stands a stout wooden post some fifteen or twenty feet high, and round it in the old days at the Pota Festival gathered a dense crowd from far and near. Across the top of the post swung horizontally a long bamboo, worked from the ground by means of ropes like the wooden pulley of a native well. Attached to one end of the bamboo were two large hooks, and these lowered to the ground were thrust into the flesh of the back of the devotee beneath the shoulder-blades. A cord having been fixed under his arms, to prevent the strain tearing through the flesh, he was swung up into the air to the accompaniment of the hoarse cries and enthusiastic shouts of the crowd. It was the same spirit in another race that stirred the vast multitude of onlookers as the victims fell beneath the car of Jaganath. Such self-inflicted torture roused to enthusiam the wild race in whom the primitive lusts of blood and passion had but slowly died, while the religious mysticism that surrounded the ceremony appealed no less strongly to their superstitious minds.

There is yet another festival to take place while the hot weather remains, the last of the long idle period that precedes renewed labour in the fields with the coming of the rains. It is the greatest gathering of the whole year, partaking partly of the nature of a vast hunting party, partly of a religious ceremony, and partly of a solemn assembly of the clan. But the chief *raison d'être* of the meeting is shikar. It is the national hunt of the Santals, reminiscent of the old days when they banded together to clear the jungle that each man might work his intake in peace, unmolested by the beasts that had till then maintained undisputed sway. Formerly held everywhere late in the hot season just before the rains broke, the time of meeting was in recent years, in some parts of Santalia, changed to an earlier date. Violent thunderstorms for some years in succession broke up the meet, the lightning killing several of the beaters, and this repeated misfortune struck fear into the superstitious mind of the Santal. It was evidently the will of the Great Spirit that the date of the meet should be changed, and it was consequently advanced some weeks and fixed during the month of May. The actual date, however, now varies in different parts of Santalia, and the fear caused by the succession of storms is being already forgotten in the immunity they have lately enjoyed. An official known as the Dihri is the master of the hunt—an office hereditary in one family—and he appoints the place of meeting and the rendezvous towards which all are to make their way when the hunt is over at the close of the day. Religious ceremonies are prescribed by custom to form the preliminaries of the hunt. Before the Dihri leaves home he has a duty to perform. Binding his wife lightly hand and foot, he lays her on a *charpoy*, her face towards the centre of the room. Then placing a bowl of water on the ground easily within her view his duty is performed, and he leaves her thus, starting himself direct to the place of meeting. Upon the wife a strict injunction is laid. She must remain exactly as her husband left her, and continue to gaze into the bowl of water until she sees its contents turn to blood. That she always does see it so turn to blood speaks much for her imagination, or the hypnotic effect of concentration of thought and vision coupled with desire. Once the miracle accomplished to her satisfaction, she may seek release and go about her household duties, knowing that all is well with the hunt. Should she prove untrustworthy and move before the appointed time, the whole success of the gathering would be jeopardised. So the huntsman's spouse needs to be endowed with something of the qualities demanded of Cæsar's wife.

Arrived at the place of meeting, generally some spot at the foot of the hills where the vast tree jungle stretches away over the slopes for miles, the master of the hunt finds a huge concourse assembled. All who are not suffering from bodily disablement and who can carry bow and arrow, axe or stout bamboo, have come from the whole countryside to join in the national hunt. Youths who have but just now learned to follow the plough, young men in the first flush of strength and manhood, men in the prime of life in the unadorned glory of well-knit frame and splendid athletic limbs and muscle, old men who have followed the hunt for thirty years and more, and who are loth to admit that the time is fast coming when they must desist and remain at home with the women and children, to live over again their former experiences only in reminiscence —all these make up the great throng that impatiently awaits the word to show its prowess in the chase. But sacrifices must first be performed. It is now the turn of the hunt master himself to be bound, and he is tied with his back against a sal tree, only his hands left free to officiate at the sacrifice for the success of the expedition.

Then, all the traditional preliminaries complete, the hunt begins. Forming into a long straggling line on the outskirts of the jungle, the beaters move forward, the tomtoms sounding, and the clear liquid notes of the reed flutes echoing far over the hillside. The wild shrill cries of the huntsmen

A SANTAL SHOOTING

and the crash of the undergrowth, made brittle by the long drought, as the beaters force their way through, startle the denizens of the jungle, and woe be to the chital, barking deer, pig, or jungle fowl that lags behind or runs terrified along the line, for the Santal with his bow and arrow is an unerring shot. Only very occasionally nowadays a leopard or bear swells the bag—a sufficiently varied one when the day's beat is over. Little comes amiss to the Santal, who, bow and arrow in hand, cannot resist the temptation to bring down every living thing that comes within range—deer, pigs, hyænas, doves, pigeons, squirrels, and even fox and jackal, all are to him legitimate prey.

Arrived at the rendezvous, near stream or tank where water is available, some of the game is cooked and the beaters refresh themselves after the arduous toils of the day. Then, the evening meal done, the national hunt takes on a different character. Seated there far from the haunts of men in a clearing of the forest with the jungle-clad hills on every side, the vast assembly holds solemn conclave. Row on row, with a strange order and regularity, the members sit facing the master of the hunt, who, with the Parganait and the Manjhis, occupies the place of honour beneath a wide-spreading banyan tree that crowns a slight eminence on the outskirts of the forest and commands the whole gathering. It is an impressive sight, this most primitive of supreme courts of justice. Illuminated only by the light of the moon and the circle of fires, lit all along the edge of the jungle, the men who are to decide the great questions of state that agitate the tribe sit close-packed, stolid, silent, immovable, like some vast horde of inanimate beings—so still they sit—who await the word to wake them into life. Each man has a voice in the decision, but it is beneath the banyan tree, among the elders of the tribe, that the chief discussion takes place. The Manjhis represent the villagers, and the voice of the hunt master bears great weight; but in case of need the matter is referred to the whole assembly, whose verdict is the Santal's highest court of appeal. Varied and difficult are the questions that come up for discussion. The Manjhi and wise men in a certain village may have given a judgment that does not meet with general approval, and an appeal is preferred. Or a member of the tribe may have violated the strict rules of the Santal table of consanguinity, or there may be charges of witch-craft, or a man may have done that for which there is but one punishment, the greatest and last of all and which can only be pronounced by the Supreme Court—outcasting from the tribe.

At last, far on in the night, all business being

MUSICIANS BEING REFRESHED WITH LIQUOR DURING THE PROGRESS OF A FESTIVAL

transacted, the assembly breaks up. But none think of sleep during the national hunt. Untired by the long beat, they are ready at once for song and dance, and all through the night the surrounding hills re-echo to the sound of drums and pipes and song. On through the few remaining hours of the short summer night the revelry continues—a scene of striking contrast to the great gathering sitting there but now in solemn conclave, immovable, earnest, intent as still and dignified as nature in these same jungles on a breathless summer night. The motionless silent crowd has suddenly awoke to life. Slowly the fires, unreplenished now that the dawn is near, die down, and the waning moon slips behind the crest of the hills, leaving the revellers in the first faint half light half shadow of the coming day. On few stranger scenes assuredly will the rising sun look in the course of this day's run. The wide open clearing in the jungle is a seething mass of dancing, shouting, black-skinned humanity, bare but for a cloth about the waist and shining with moisture from the heat, the violent exercise, and much rice beer. The rising sun is greeted with a final burst of energy, and the now hoarse and raucous voices are raised in a pæan of praise to the great Sing Bonga. The cool fresh breeze, that comes but with the dawn in the month before the rains, plays gently through the forest, bringing its grateful breath to the panting revellers, while the stars pale one by one before the spreading crimson gold of the all-conquering Sun God as he rises in majestic splendour over the distant hills. Small wonder is it that the ignorant Santal worships him, the joy of the whole world and the author of so much mystery, in whom is the power to make darkness light, to create warmth, and whom no mortal hand can stay.

The sun fully risen, the chase is resumed, this time on the homeward way. The bag is smaller on the second day, for the passing of the Santal host and the noise of the night's revelry have scared all living things from their accustomed haunts near by. Scattering towards the end, each man makes his way towards his own house, carrying proudly home the trophies that have fallen to his skill and eager to relate over the evening meal the story of the hunt and all that befell him by the way.

The hot weather passes at last, and with the first falling of the rain the Santal throws off the sloth engendered by long months of ease, preparing again to take up the battle of existence and force from Nature supplies for the year to come. But no step may be taken without an offering of propitiation to the gods. So at seed time there is the Erok Sim Festival, and the blessing of the goddess who presides over the crops is invoked by the sacrifice of chickens in the Sacred Grove. Then having done all that he can to ensure its fertility the Santal sows his seed. When the fresh young shoots of the early rice appear above the ground fresh sacrifices must be offered. It is the birth of the harvest, and the gods, having been so beneficent as to allow the seed to sprout, need further propitiation to allow it to grow to maturity. So once more chickens are sacrificed in the Jaher, and the Hariar Sim Festival is duly celebrated.

The days that follow are full of anxiety to the Santal. Numberless misfortunes may befall to destroy the early promise of the harvest. The enemy who comes by night may wantonly uproot the seedlings or carry them off to transplant them in his own land. And who, once the thief has got clean away, can identify paddy that groweth alike for the just and for the unjust? Or the pig may come out of the jungle at dusk and trample it under foot; or his neighbour's cattle may stray and eat up the young shoots, even as they break into the ear; or, most fatal calamity of all, the gods may withhold the rain, and the paddy wither and die as it stands in the fields for lack of moisture. A thousand dangers surround the young crop. Yet to the Santal its preservation is a matter of life and death, for on these fields of sprouting corn depends the existence of himself and of his family for the coming year. Constantly he watches them, building for himself a *machan*—a small platform of bamboo raised some ten feet high on four upright posts and covered with a rough straw thatch to afford some shelter from the sun and rain. There he sits guarding his fields, his long low melancholy cry ringing out with weird effect through the darkness of the night to scare away the beasts of the forest and let the night prowler know that he is ever on the watch.

The transplanting of the rice is a time of much anxiety, and the Rain God needs constant propitiation, for if he stay his hand at this critical moment it will go hard with the harvest. But, given a sufficiency of rain, the cultivator pursues his labour with hope renewed. It is a busy scene in the fields. Undeterred by the heaviest downpour the workers stand ankle deep in the rain-soaked earth pressing down the young shoots with their hands into the fertile soil that is eager to give them root and bring them to fruition. The women no less than the men take their full share of the labour, as unmindful of the drenching showers as they.

The transplanting at length finished, there is time for one more festival before the all-absorbing season of the harvest. The Chhata Purab, the special festival of the Hasdak sept, is celebrated at different times in different villages, generally in the month of August. It is the festival of the umbrella, the meaning of which one asks in vain. A long lithe sal tree shorn of its branches supports the smallest of umbrellas roughly made of gaudy tinsel, and together, amidst the excited shouts of the celebrants, they are raised aloft until standing perpendicularly the sal trunk is fixed firmly in the ground. As it slowly settles into place the people, gathering up handfuls of dust and earth, pelt the umbrella with wild cries and much laughter, dancing round it the while as round a maypole, while the men turn somersaults and perform wonders of athletic and acrobatic skill. Much feasting and drinking of rice beer prolong the celebration of the Chhata Purab far on into the night.

When at length, having escaped all the dangers that beset it, the paddy is in the ear, and the season of harvest approaches, it is time for the Janthar Festival—the offering of the first fruits. Tiny sheaves of the half-ripe corn are placed in the Sacred Grove upon the sacrificial stones and prayer is made that the gods who have brought the grain to such maturity will graciously allow it to be safely reaped and garnered. A pig, which is afterwards cooked and eaten in the Grove by the men of the village, is always included in the sacrifices of the Janthar Purab.

But the end of the long round of festivals has come at last, and the Santal has no time to spare now from the gathering in of the crops that gods and malignant spirits have allowed to come to maturity. All day long the village is deserted, and the fields are alive with workers. Ridge on ridge, one above the other, right back to the foot of the tree-clad hills, the fields lie spread like a giant's staircase, a mass of waving corn in every shade of yellow and green and gold, the grass-grown *ails*, zigzag and irregular, running through and across them like a trellis-work of brilliant green. The busy groups of workers dotted here and there on almost every plot look from a distance like a swarm of busy ants harvesting their stock of grain against the days of scarcity to come. Everywhere men, women, and children, each family combining all its strength to make the labour light, reaping and binding and stacking the golden corn, move quickly and silently about their work. Armed only with the short semicircular sickle that compels them to stoop low, they yet prove themselves tireless at their toil, pausing but now and again to stand upright and snatch a moment's breathing space. On the best and most fertile fields, the moisture left over from the rains carefully banked in and tenaciously preserved remains, and the reapers as at transplanting time stand ankle deep in the pools and sodden earth. Down in the hollow at the foot of the lowest ridge, whence the ground rises on both sides terrace on terrace, lies the best and most coveted land. There the rain, sweeping down off the higher ridges, stays long after those same higher fields have parted with their last drop of moisture, and the seed here sown returns a hundredfold. Each field in the ascending scale, lacking moisture in proportion, is less fertile than its neighbour just below, the scanty crops on the highest of them all at the foot of the hills ripening quickly in the hard-baked earth, but with a none too generous return.

While cutting his paddy, the Santal has been busily employed besides in the preparation of his threshing-floor. If the courtyard of his house be large enough it will suffice; if not, the *kamar* (threshing-floor) must be made ready on some convenient open spot near by. Levelling the ground for a space some ten to twenty feet square and plentifully besmearing it with wet mud, the Santal leaves it to harden firm and flat in the sun. Then, his paddy gathered in from the fields, he spreads it layer by layer on the threshing-floor, driving his bullocks, three or four abreast, round and round in a circle over it to tread out the grain. With slow unvarying steps the cattle move, sinking knee deep in the piled-up straw until their progress is wellnigh stopped. Then a brief respite is theirs, and the straw, well shaken out, is removed and the grain beneath carefully gathered up. This done fresh paddy is laid down, and the bullocks, their mild eyes uttering a seeming protest at the shortness of their rest, renew their weary round of labour. The winnowing is done in large flat baskets by the women, who, throwing the contents in the air again and again, separate the grain from the chaff with neat-handed skill.

There is only one last stage before the Santal's work is at an end. First there are payments in kind to be made—so much to the blacksmith who has repaired his ploughshares free throughout the year awaiting this moment for his dues; so much to the moneylender if perchance he was forced to borrow grain for the sowing of his crop; or so much to the landlord should his rent be payable in kind. Then at last, all dues fully settled, there but remains for him to store his grain with care against the multitude of dangers that may yet beset it. Rats and insects are the chief enemies that threaten, and to ward off these he has invented a primitive but effective storehouse of his own. Plaiting the straw into long ropes, he binds them tightly together, barrel-shaped, carefully twisting them close across the ends so that nothing may get within. Inside the grain is securely guarded. Protected by the thick tight-bound straw ropes it can come to little harm. These *bandis*, as the Santal calls them, standing on small stone pillars to keep them from the white ants, are placed against the wall in the courtyard against the day when the grain is needed for his household use. The long months of anxiety and toil are finished, and the Santal, regarding with complacency the wherewithal to keep himself and family during the coming year, is ready to turn to thoughts of relaxation and the coming delights of the Sohrae.

To anything beyond this yearly round of festival and labour the Santal gives but little thought. Death must come to all, and, true to his fatalistic creed, he awaits it with resignation and without fear. He is confident that his relatives will faithfully perform the funeral ceremonies imposed upon the race by custom and tradition, and that, his body having been burned, the ashes reverently gathered will be at the last committed to the sacred river, the Damuda, to be borne on its swift current into the bosom of the mighty ocean, whence the race first had its being, and where returning it fittingly seeks its final rest. That there is some future state beyond, the Santal vaguely believes. On his left forearm every member of the race bears the *sika*, round marks burnt into the flesh with a red-hot coal or stick. Unless these marks are fully visible when he comes to die, a terrible fate will befall him. As soon as the breath leaves his body a large worm will burrow into his breast and slowly devour his body, protracting the agony to show the displeasure of the gods. The spirits of all those who bear the *sika*, however, fly after death to the region where Jom Raja and Hudul Raja reign. But, though they have left the cares of earth behind and entered the kingdom of the gods, there is little respite from their worldly labour. All the spirits are employed in grinding the bones of past generations with a pestle made of the wood of the castor-oil tree in order to provide the gods with a good supply of material to produce the children yet unborn. Only to those men who have chewed tobacco during their lives, and to those women who have borne children, is any respite given. If any one ceases from his labour, the taskmaster among the gods at once demands the reason. If a man replies that he has stopped to prepare the tobacco leaf, or a woman that she has paused to nourish the child at her breast, the taskmaster passes on. But for no other reason is a brief spell of rest allowed in this hard-working paradise. It is typical of his limited scope of vision that the Santal can imagine nothing better for the world beyond than this ceaseless round of labour, varied only, like his life on earth, by the constant recurrence of the festivals he so much loves.

CHAPTER X

LIFE IN A PAHARIA VILLAGE

HIGH up on a ledge of the steep hillside lies the Paharia village. Perched there as if in a cleft of the rock designed by Nature for its home, it nestles close beneath the luxuriant foliage, protected by the sheltering boulders against the storms that sweep the upland heights. It is the most primitive of villages, scare an acre in extent, yet complete within itself and independent of the world beneath, of which its habitants know little and care still less.

Here live the Sauria Maler, as they love to call themselves in their euphonious tongue, the wildest and furthest back from civilisation of all the Paharia race. These are the Malli or Sauri of the ancient Greek geographers, who chronicled their presence around Mount Maleus which threw a shadow so miraculous. Here in its vicinity from that day to this, they have remained as primitive and untouched as when they first made this land their own. Their only movement during all the centuries that have intervened has been to retreat still further into the inaccessible places of their hills, looking ever askance at the foreigner and all his ways. Safe from intrusion from the outer world, their tribal life and customs have been preserved through countless generations unaffected by the lapse of time.

No spot could well be more isolated than that chosen by the Maler for his home. Unapproached save by a steep and narrow path winding over rough-hewn rock and boulder zigzag up the slopes of the hill, the Paharia village rests secure from the life and stir of the world at its feet. Here the spirit of the twentieth century has found no place and nothing has entered in to mar the pristine simplicity of this jealous and exclusive people. Away, seemingly out of reach, it is a long climb up not to be undertaken lightly by the plainsman, untrained to the rough life that has given the hillman his well-knit frame and his powers of marvellous endurance. Shaded by the magnificent monarchs of the forest that reign here in all their glory unmolested by the vandal hand of man, the road is one long avenue from foot to summit, an ever-changing panorama of perfect beauty. Further and further below the plains recede revealed only in a glimpse like a picture in miniature where the foliage breaks its tangled network of luxuriant green. Here a mighty pepul seemingly implanted in a mass of black basaltic rock stands athwart the narrow path, its struggling roots creeping along the hillside as if seeking for some kinder soil where they may find greater sustenance for the parent stem. Close beside it, still greater in its girth and wider in its reach, a banyan with its multiplicity of roots forms a perfect arch across the way, a slender downward-going tendril from a branch overhead having forced itself a home among the smaller boulders at its feet. The sal, ubiquitous but compelling admiration by reason of its strength and indomitable persistence, forcing its roots into the barren sun-baked soil where other trees make no attempt to thrive; the palas, waiting for the warm west winds to break forth into the glorious salmon-pink mass of blossom that hides for a brief season its ragged unkempt form; the tamarind, with its delicate leaves of tender green, each one a marvel of Nature's perfect workmanship—all these and more are to be met with as the path winds upwards. While high above them all—if it be when the rains are done—creeping from tree to tree and encircling each in its delicate brief embrace, runs the exquisite *pongo nari* clothing the whole hillside in a mantle of purest white like snow.

There is something surprisingly trim and neat about the Paharia village when at last one comes upon it suddenly high up near the summit of the hill.

Here for the first time, save for the track beaten by the feet of many generations, since the climb up began and the plains were left behind, the work of man becomes apparent. Uncivilised as its builders are, the village has yet an air of regularity and cleanliness lacking in many a more advanced community. Sun-baked mud such as the Santal loves to prepare to build his house is not so easily obtainable on the bare hillside, and the Paharia is content to construct his dwelling solely of wattled bamboos, filling the interstices with the long coarse grass that makes so excellent a thatch, proof alike against sun and rain. Neatly made and finished with the greatest care, half buried beneath the shade of tamarind and pepul, mango and nim, the cluster of Paharia huts fits with perfect harmony into its picturesque setting, composed as they are of nothing save what the jungle in the immediate vicinity provides. Almost every house has its tiny garden, sometimes wellnigh perpendicular on the steep hillside, surrounded by a hurdle fence as neat as the house itself, or covered completely by the luxuriant bean creeper with its white and purple blossoms. Within the enclosure in the patch of garden flourish—not too well, for the soil is rocky and dry—a few country vegetables—brinjal, patal, and shag, with the never-absent tobacco—while the taller plantain, papita, and castor-oil trees fill the little space that remains. Adjoining are the outhouses, built like the main dwelling itself but smaller, where the cattle and goats, pigs and fowls, reside together in close proximity to the rest of the family. Fixed in the ground in front of the house is a long bamboo, placed there to ward off the evil and malignant spirits that in the imagination of the Paharia always seek to find admittance. The last picturesque touch is given to the outward aspect of the village by the granaries, quaint rectangular Malayan-like structures well thatched and supported on posts wherein the Paharia hoards his winter store of grain.

To keep the courtyard and the little space in front of the house brushed clean as broom of twigs can make it, is the Paharia housewife's pride. Though she moves with lazy grace, and haste is foreign to her nature, hers is a busy round of daily life, beginning with the dawn and ending only with nightfall, save for a space in the heat of the day when even Nature herself seems to pause and sleep, awaiting the passing of the great Sun God. There are the children, numerous and innocent of clothing, ever ready to play on the most precipitous edge of the cliff, to be watched, and the cattle to be tended, the patch of garden to be looked to, and the corn to be ground, and, above all, the evening meal prepared against her lord's return. All these, varied by occasional journeys to the *hât* (market) in the plains below, fill the Paharia housewife's day, and whatever time remains she spends, broom in hand, making neatness still more neat. On personal adornment she spends but little time. The bracelet, chain and armlet, anklet and necklace, that the Santal maiden loves make less appeal to her still simpler neighbour on the upland slopes, where luxury in any form has not yet found its way, and where actual coin of the realm for the purchase of the manufactured produce of the plains below is scarce. But not even the most primitive of maidens is wholly indifferent to personal adornment, and the bright coral necklaces worn row on row, a most effective contrast to their dusky skins, are the especial weakness of Paharia womankind. In her dress itself she is singularly neat and graceful. A long strip of white cloth wound round the waist forms a skirt reaching just below the knees, while a square of coloured tussur silk or cotton thrown gracefully across the right shoulder and fastened high up underneath the left arm completes the costume. It is the simplest of garments, without cut or seam, but put on with the artistic skill and worn with the touch of grace that seems inherent in the women of the East.

The Paharia himself, though short of stature—

he rarely overtops five feet four—is well knit and strong of limb. The hardy frame of the hillman built up through many generations has come down to him as a priceless inheritance, equipping him with much strength, the one thing needful for the man who, standing face to face with Nature, has no reserve to fall back upon in time of need. Erect of carriage and muscular of limb, he has all the freedom of gait and independence of mien that come of long immunity from outside control and the untrammeled life of his native hills and jungles. About the Paharia features there is an openness and frankness that is singularly attractive. Good humour and a happy content with life as it is are self-evident, and though these shrink behind a blank wall of suspicion at the approach of the stranger they are soon restored when once confidence has been inspired. Described in detail their features sound anything but desirable, yet overspread by this superabundant good humour and content they cannot fail to please. Of the mild Tamulian type, their faces are oval with lips full but well formed and not approaching the nigritic as closely as the nose, which is broad at the end and inclined to lie flat, with wide-spread nostrils. The eyes are well set straight in the head, not imbedded in the face obliquely like the Mongolian. The forehead is fairly broad and high, and well back from it, crowning the head, is a wealth of coarse black hair, the Paharia's greatest pride, on which he lavishes all his attempts at personal adornment. Worn long and well oiled until no further gloss is to be obtained, it is gathered in a knot and fastened at the back of the head, kept in place, if need be, by a slip of wood or twig. His costume consists of little more than a loin cloth round the waist with a second cloth occasionally thrown lightly over the shoulder, but little used as a real covering save on the cold nights of the Indian winter when the temperature falls low on the Rajmahal Hills.

At the end of the village street stands the most primitive of temples, nothing but an open shed built for the residence of the tutelary deity, the Gosain. The Paharia, unlike the Santal, delights to make rough representations of his gods, save of the Great Sun deity, Bedo Gosain, whose majesty is visible to all and needs no counterfeit made by the hand of man. But in representing his gods the Paharia makes no attempt to impart to them beauty of form or indeed even to fashion them in human shape. A rough stone placed in the rude shed temple suffices for the tutelary Gosain, as vague and as unformed in outline as the idea of the deity itself in the mind of the worshipper.

If it be at the beginning of the harvest season

the shed temple is astir with life and the scene of a curious ceremony. Every member of the small village community is gathered there, seated round on the open space without, each with his offering to propitiate the gods in whose hands the fate of the harvest lies. One family more prosperous than the rest has brought a goat, another a fowl, and a third rice, while the poorer or those less dependent on the favour of the God of Harvest bring only *sindur* and oil with which to anoint the rough-hewn stone. There is no priest, but the village headman acts in that capacity, thereby gaining for himself at such times as these increased respect in his neighbours' eyes. Taking an egg in his hand when all is ready, he passes among the group of worshippers, waving the egg in the air and reciting the names of every known evil spirit at the top of his voice. When the last name has been spoken he throws the egg with all his strength as far as he can in the direction away from the village as a propitiatory offering to appease the evil spirits and avert their malign influence from the approaching sacrifices. This done the offerings are made, the *sindur* smeared on the stone god, and the oil poured out. Then the feast inseparably connected with Eastern ritual begins. But of those things sacrificed to the gods in this harvest festival no woman may eat; only the male worshippers may partake of the food thus consecrated. The prohibition is typical of the small part allotted to women in the family worship among all the aboriginal tribes.

Formerly the Paharias had priests called Naiyas, but their duties now fall partly upon the village headman and partly upon the Demanos, who correspond somewhat to the Ojhas among the Santals. It is the former who performs the active duties of the priest, but by far the greater power lies with the Demano. He it is who holds communion with the spirits of the other world, and in his hands consequently the fate of every individual in the village lies. Alone holding converse with the unseen powers he has the ordinary mortal at his mercy. Does a man fall sick, or his crops die, or a mysterious disease take off his cattle, the Demano alone can assign the cause. It may be that it is due to the evil eye of a hitherto honest and unsuspected villager, and once such an accusation made it fares ill with the unfortunate victim of the Demano's divination. His neighbours, superstitious and afraid, at once shun his society, passing him by with averted look, while even the children flee at his approach as from one endowed with malignant power. For such a one there is little left in his native village unless he can break the spell, and he is fortunate if he escape without actual physical molestation. Though the days have gone by when one suspected of the evil eye could be done to death with impunity by his terrified fellow villagers, there are other and safer means left of harassing a man without fear of punishment. His house may be burned down mysteriously in the night or his cattle stolen or killed; and for such things as these the unfortunate man has no redress, for not one of the villagers will give evidence on his side. So it is to the interest of all to be on good terms with the Demano, who can cause such calamity to befall. Even though he may not go so far as to accuse one of the evil eye, there are a host of petty exactions in his power to inflict upon the helpless villager, such as the sacrifice of a cock or a goat to avert threatened disaster to his crops or a smaller offering of rice and ghee to propitiate an angry spirit. Whatever the Demano with his intimate communication with the nether world may order, it would need a bold and free-thinking Paharia to refuse.

There are a large number of deities in the Paharia pantheon. After Dharmer or Bedo Gosain, the Sun God who rules the world, dividing it at his will into day and night, comes the tutelary deity of each village, Bara Dwari, deriving his name from the temple with the twelve doors in which he is supposed to reside. He is worshipped with much ceremony in the month of Magh, that season of especial festivity among all the neighbouring aboriginal tribes. Raksi is the deity of strong drink and the most popular of gods. Before the brewing of liquor when the mahua crop is ripe it is necessary to propitiate him with an offering, so that the outturn may be good. The deity is sometimes represented by a black stone set up under a mukmum tree hedged round with euphorbia plants, but Raksi is a god in much request, and deigns to be present without visible sign or symbol wherever the brewing of the much-loved liquor takes place.

Ancestor worship is performed at the shrine of Gumo Gosain, who is represented by nothing more godlike than the pillars that support the rafters of the roof of the shed-temple. Upon these wooden pillars the blood of goats is sprinkled to propitiate the spirits of the dead and long-forgotten ancestors of all the generations of the race. Chalnad is a powerful god, presiding over the destinies of groups of ten villages, and in the old days of Paharia prosperity and independence, when raids and forays brought much wealth in cattle, he demanded the sacrifice of an ox. Now, however, those palmy days having long since passed, he has perforce to be content with the sacrifice of goats and pigs, not even disdaining fowls and humbler offerings usually reserved for lesser gods. Almost equally exacting in former times was Pau Gosain, the god of highways, who lurks beneath every mukmum, bel, and kurare tree beside the roads, demanding constant propitiation from the traveller lest evil befall him by the way. No true Paharia ventures on a journey without first invoking Pau Gosain. Here, again, the offering required has changed with the times; but whereas formerly the god of the highways was content with a white cock, custom now decrees a white goat—a far more exacting demand. And, in addition to the goat, much rice beer is offered to Pau Gosain, though the sincerity of this offering at least is open to question, since the assembled worshippers proceed to drink it themselves directly it has been formally placed before the god.

But more exacting even than Chalnad and Pau Gosain is Chanida Gosain. Of all the gods he demands the largest offerings, and the village that can afford to worship him with the tale of sacrifices complete ranks high in the estimation of its neighbours for many a day to come. Carried out on so large a scale it is an affair of great ceremony, and the fame of the preparations it entails spreads among the Paharia villages far and near along the countryside. Eager to see the spectacle crowds of spectators make their way towards the shrine of Chanida Gosain as the day approaches. For a sacrifice such as this of twelve goats and twelve pigs, with maunds of rice, ghee, and oil, enough to feed the whole village for days together, is a spectacle but rarely to be seen. Such a sacrifice must needs be a strain on the resources of the richest Paharia community, but with typical improvidence the villagers forget all save the excitement of the moment and the temporary importance in the eyes of their neighbours that so great an outlay gives. Then, too, there is a pleasing reminder of this great sacrifice that remains as a permanent witness to the fact that it has been duly performed. In a conspicuous place in the village, to represent for the time being the god Chanida Gosain, are set up three of the tallest bamboos that the neighbouring jungle can provide. To the first of these are attached ninety streamers of tiny strips of bark painted black and red at the ends, with the centre left untouched. On the second bamboo are sixty streamers, and on the third thirty, with peacocks' feathers interspersed among them, adding their brilliant touch of colour to the black and brown and red. Round these the dancing takes place, continued for hour after hour through the moonlight night—for the Paharia is partial to the moon, and fixes his festival for the time when it shines with its brightest light. With the first glimpse of the dawn, far away across the plains, sacrifices are offered, first in front of the bamboos, then outside the village in the fields, so that a blessing may come upon the village and upon the land, upon the family and upon the crops, and upon all that they possess. Then, the great feast over, and the last of the admiring worshippers gone back again to his daily avocation, the three bamboos are taken down and hung from the roof of the temple as a long-abiding memorial of the great day of the sacrifice to Chanida Gosain.

Like all the neighbouring aboriginal tribes in Chota Nagpore, the Paharia includes dancing and the imbibing of much rice beer as a prominent and essential part of all his festivals and worship. The gayest time of all the year is when the birth of Bhuindeo, the Earth God, is celebrated, a proceeding that takes three days of constant merriment. Two branches of the sal tree are planted in the middle of the dancing ground, and round these the men, with their hair especially oiled and decked with flowers for the occasion, and the women, with every available necklace of bright red coral, dance the picturesque steps of the *jhumar*. Facing each other, the men and women form into long separate lines, the musicians occupying the space between. The women, standing shoulder to shoulder, join hands, the left and right forearms touching, and held straight out in front of them as they move. The men in similar array opposite grasp each other above the elbows, the left hand of one holding the right elbow of the other, whose right hand in turn grasps the other's left elbow, the forearms thus touching and swinging with the measures of the dance. The drums and flutes playing, the two lines advance, move sideways and retire, sometimes stooping low, sometimes erect with slow even motion, their steps in pure rhythm and accord. In none of their dances do the women and the men join hands and dance together Western fashion, though many a jest and laughing compliment is flung from line to line, and flirtation, though perforce a trifle public, by no means languishes.

A marriage is a source of unfailing delight to the pleasure-loving Paharia. The hot weather is the favourite season for its celebration. Then there is little doing in the fields, the labour of the past year is over, and the earth sleeps awaiting the reawakening touch of the coming rains. The Paharia, never overworked at any time, has nothing then to interfere with his unrestrained enjoyment, and over the preliminaries of the marriage contract and the actual wedding itself he loves to linger, prolonging both over many a bowl of the good rice beer. Infant marriage is unknown among them, though under Hinduising influences it is being gradually adopted among the outlying sections of the race. But, as a rule, bride and bridegroom are of full age, and their union is the result of mutual consent, perfect freedom of choice within the tribe being allowed, always excepting the persons mentioned in the Paharia table of consanguinity, which, however, is nothing like so elaborate as that in vogue among the Santals. The all-important choice having been made, the bridegroom employs an intermediary known as Sibhu to arrange the preliminary negotiations and to settle the delicate question of the bride-price. To lessen the difficulty of fixing the latter, however, custom has imposed a limit. The bride-price must be an odd number of rupees not less than five, nor more than twenty, and they must be paid either in a lump sum or in instalments before the marriage can take place. All preliminaries settled and an auspicious day for the wedding fixed, the bridegroom, accompanied by the Sibhu and his friends, starts for the bride's house, taking with him a goat as his contribution to the wedding feast. At daybreak next morning the ceremony begins, dragging its monotonous length with a minimum of incidents throughout the day. Face to face, surrounded by a crowd of rejoicing friends and villagers from far and near, sit the bride and bridegroom, the former facing east and the latter west. Behind the bride stands a group of girl companions busily engaged in combing out her hair and showing off her dusky tresses to the best advantage by a plentiful application of oil. Constant singing and dancing and much beating of tomtoms supply the place of incident in the marriage ceremony, until at last the father of the bride advances, and taking her by the hand leads her before the bridegroom, reciting her virtues and good qualities, as well as pointing out that she is neither blind, nor deaf, nor dumb, nor halt. Enjoining him to treat her with kindness and consideration, he places her hand in his. Then the Sibhu, who acts as priest, takes the bridegroom's right hand, and dipping his little finger in *sindur* makes five marks with it on the girl's forehead. This done, he takes the bride's finger and performs the same office for the bridegroom, so that both of the contracting parties have the five *sindur* marks on the forehead that constitute the essential part of the marriage ceremony. The noise and clamour that are hushed for the moment as this most important rite is being performed break out again with renewed vigour. Bombs are exploded, and guns of the most antique pattern, wondrously made, are fired to mark the final union of the happy pair. Now at length they are lawful man and wife, and to symbolise their union they partake in public of their first meal together from the same dish. This is the sign for the feasting to become general. It is on a liberal scale, bullock's or goat's flesh forming the substantial portion, with an abundance of rice and ghee and oil and turmeric, with such vegetables as the hot dry season will allow. But a good supply of rice beer is the most essential element of the feast. Standing in large earthenware pots against the wall, it is always at hand to refresh the exhausted dancers, or to wash down the good things of the feast that the Paharia never fails to take advantage of to the utmost of his capacity, which to the ordinary observer appears wellnigh limitless. Only absolute exhaustion or somnolence, produced by much food and liquor, puts an end to the feast. Yet give him but an hour or two hours' sleep, and the Paharia is fit and ready for the long tramp home across the hills, as if such things as revel and debauch had never come within his ken.

From the union thus festively cemented the Paharia law allows escape under certain circumstances should the couple find their condition insupportable. But there are many formalities to be observed, and divorce is not lightly sanctioned. All the facts of the case must be publicly stated before the Manjhi and the wise men of the village, and on their decision rests the fate of the unhappy couple. It is a weighty matter for more than the parties actually concerned, since the bride-price that was paid at the time of the marriage has to be considered. In certain cases the law allows the bridegroom to claim it back. Should there be no children of the marriage, should the wife's moral character be in doubt, or even should she have been found to be incorrigibly lazy, a divorce may be obtained and the bridegroom allowed to recover from her father the price which he paid for his bride. But if after mature deliberation the villagers assembled decide that the bridegroom's grounds for claiming the divorce, though valid, do not throw such blame upon the bride, he may get his divorce, though he is not allowed to claim the bride-price. But here the wife is at a disadvantage. Should she claim a divorce, on whatever grounds it may be, her family must restore the bride-price. The divorce, if sanctioned, takes place immediately in the presence of all the village elders. Man and wife stand up together, holding a sal leaf in their hands. This, at a sign from the headman, they tear across as a symbol of their separation, while over the woman's head is poured a vessel of water, symbolising the washing off of the *sindur* marks that had made her a wife. Henceforward she is free and may marry again at will.

But to each and all comes at last the end of the gay round of festivals and worship, of marrying and giving in marriage. Longer lived than most of his fellows by reason of his hardy life and freedom from care and anxiety, the Paharia often reaches a good old age. According to the length of his life so is the measure of respect paid to his remains when at last his hour comes. Laid out on a bed of *bhelak* leaves spread over a newly made *charpoy* with his face looking towards the north, his body is carried to a spot on the hillside just beyond the village to await interment. It is no easy task to dig a grave on the rocky slope, but it is necessary to fashion one not only to contain the body but also the *charpoy* on which it lies, for no Paharia with a curious mixture of consideration for the departed and a selfish desire to be untroubled by his spirit in the future would bury his relative without a bed on which to rest. His long sleep must needs be easier, he thinks, if the cot is left than if he is thrown upon the bare hard ground, and his spirit being thus comfortably provided for is less likely to return to haunt those it has left behind. For the Paharia, like the Santal, firmly believes in the existence of the spirits of those who have passed into the great unknown, holding that though invisible they are ever present in his midst. All spirits are naturally to be feared, but the spirit of the Demano more than all. As he was supposed to have been in close communication with the nether world during his life, so when his spirit departs thither it is believed to take high rank and attain much influence. For this reason the Paharias do not bury their Demanos as they do ordinary men. Resting the body on the layer of leaves spread upon the cot, they carry it away to the jungle, and placing it under the shade of a wide-spreading banyan tree cover it reverently with leaves and branches. There with many incantations they leave it to disappear in time from exposure to the changing seasons. The spirit of the Demano is thus left free, untrammeled by the things of the grave, to join the company of those spirits with whom in life he had held such close communion. But only to the Demano is this special honour done. The layman resting on his cot is placed in the grave, and over and above him are piled rough-hewn blocks of stone forming a cairn, its height being determined according to the rank of the man who lies beneath. But over the grave of the headman, as a special distinction, a hut is erected wherein his spirit may dwell for a time before it takes its final flight to the invisible world. The fence all round is designed to keep the spirit from losing its way into the neighbouring village instead of speeding its way aloft to realms unknown. For to keep away the spirits from his house is the Paharia's chiefest care, since most spirits in his imagination are evil and malign, seeking what deeds of mischief they may perform.

During the five days that succeed the interment of a chief, the villagers from all the countryside are feasted royally, and as the last day arrives and many potations of liquor have had their due effect there is little to mark the fact that they have met to celebrate a funeral rite. Exactly a year later there is another feast, and by a curious rule of unwritten Paharia law no distribution of the deceased's property can take place until this second feast has been partaken of. Consequently this later feast is punctually observed, and the eldest son is then at liberty to take his half share of his father's property and divide the other half among his kinsmen.

For the spirits of the suicide and the murderer there is no hope. Shunned by the other spirits, they are condemned to wander homeless up and down the nether world seeking rest and finding none. But with regard to the other spirits there is hope of things to come. Though they must remain to people the invisible world for a time, those that have done good in this life may hope to be born again in due time in a higher and more comfortable position than in their former incarnation. Those who have misused their opportunities or abused their position in former days will be born again in a lower grade. This process of reincarnation may be repeated again and again until the good man reaches the highest position, and the wicked man ceases to be born of a woman, and joins the ranks of the inferior animals. 'God is just,' says the Paharia, 'and every man sooner or later will get his deserts.' So, with a dawning knowledge of good and evil before him and a great contentment with things as they are, he pursues the selfsame path of life that many generations of his race have trod, asking nothing more of this world, and only a speedy return to it, blessed of the gods, from the world to come.

CHAPTER XI

DEOGHAR, THE HOLY CITY

WITHIN sight of the sacred groves and primitive worship of Santal and Paharia stands the Holy City of the Hindus, proudly raising to heaven its multitude of pinnacles and domes, as if in lofty contempt for the vague invisible gods of the aborigines who own no temple upon earth wherein to rest. Only the accident of geographical position joins Deoghar, the House of God, to the wild rocky tree-clad range of the Rajmahal Hills. Between them in sympathy and interest there is a great gulf fixed. Even in the land of sharp contrasts and conflicting elements there are few instances more striking than this. Towards the divine city flows from far and near a countless throng of pilgrims, ever moving ceaselessly in one continuous stream like some river of the plains forging its restless way towards the sea. Instinct with vitality and steeped in the civilisation of the India of to-day they bring with them a breath from the outer world making the Holy City a constant scene of life and interest. Siva the Omnipotent, supremest among many deities, reigns over the Holy City—his shrine from year's end to year's end the goal of many reverent feet. Across the plains towards the steep hillside where Dwara Gosain demands the sacrifices of the Paharia or the forest-bound village where none dispute the sway of Marang Buru, the foot of the stranger but seldom comes, and no breath from the outside world disturbs the repose and seclusion, so religiously guarded through the centuries that have passed. Between them and the proud city that rears its head within their sight there is no communion. The one is typical of the India of to-day, the other still reminiscent of the prehistoric past unheeding the lapse of time, as unchanged now as it was in the beginning before the memory of man.

Yet it may be that in the beginning the proud god of the Divine City and the vague invisible spirit of the Santals were one. Centuries before the domes and pinnacles of the temples of Deoghar had raised their heads, while as yet the Hindu had not made his presence felt in this remote corner of the land, the aboriginal tribes had worshipped their gods with dark mysterious rites and human sacrifices in all the surrounding hills and jungles. How it came to pass that the Holy City of the Hindu god rose in their midst no man can tell. Yet to this day the temples of Siva are known by the name of a Santal, thus strangely forming an inexplicable connection between the widely different religions of two antagonistic peoples after the lapse of many centuries. The Hindus, scornful of the aboriginal tribes, throw contempt upon the implied connection, and to account for the name Baijnath they have invented a legend to supply the place of the true explanation which has been long since lost in the myths of antiquity.

The Holy City—so runs the Hindu legend—owes its origin to Raban, king of Lonka. On his way with the image of the great god Siva which he carried to bless his undertaking against Ram, the king of Oudh, he stopped to purify himself where Deoghar now stands. But finding no water he dashed his fist in anger on the ground, and straightway in the huge depression made by the force of the blow a lake—the Sivagunga—appeared. But the image of Siva being set down upon the banks of the lake saw that it was a fair land and good to look upon, and refused to move further in company with Raban. So, making for the god a suitable dwelling-place beside the lake and receiving his blessing in return, Raban set out on his travels, leaving a company of Brahmins to perform the worship of the shrine. Thus were the foundations of the Holy City laid, and as the fame of the temple where Siva dwelt spread over the land the stream of pilgrims which has never since ceased began to wend its way towards it from all along the plains of Northern India.

But the aborigines who dwelt in the vicinity refused to bow the knee to Siva, still clinging to the worship afar off of those mysterious spirits in whom they believed, and of whom they went perpetually in fear. Upon the newcomers, with their arrogant pretensions and strange images of unknown gods, the Santal looked with a great suspicion and distrust. The Brahmin priests, proud and contemptuous, inspired them with no respect, but only with a great loathing and contempt. For the guardians of Siva's temple proved exacting neighbours, demanding from the ignorant Santal gifts and labour, causing him thereby, against his will, to contribute to the worship of their temple. So the great bitterness of the Santal towards the Brahmin which has continued to this day first took its rise.

But the Santal patiently bided his time to take his revenge for the forced service he had been made to render at the shrine of this strange god. For with success and the offerings of pilgrims and the produce of the fertile fields that they had made the Santal plough and sow, the Brahmins grew fat and slothful, neglectful even of the worship of their temple. The priests took unto

Before him his wife quickly spread the evening meal, and having gone fasting all day, he had sat down to it hungrily before remembering his vow. The temptation to eat was great, but tearing himself away, even as he was raising the food to his mouth, he set out for the temple and beat the idol with his club according to the vow that he had made. Then even as he gave the last blow, and was turning to leave the temple, a voice came from the image of Siva. 'Lo! here is a man who, though hungry, footsore, and weary, remembers to perform his vows,' said the god, 'while my priests, fat and glutted with the good things of life, sleep the sleep of the slothful, forgetful of their solemn vows and obligations.' Then addressing Baiju he said, 'I forgive thee the insults thou hast offered me in consideration of thy fidelity to thy vows. Ask of me whatsoever thou wilt, and it shall be thine.' Then Baiju answered, 'What is there that I need ask of thee? I am rich in land and cattle and a leader among mine own people. What more needs any man? Yet, so that punishment may fall upon these slothful Brahmin priests, let me be called Nath (Lord), even as thou, and let thy temple be known henceforth by my name.' 'So let it be,' replied Siva. 'From this day thou shalt be called no more Baiju, but Baijnath, and my temple shall be known by thy name for all time.' Thus runs the legend that the Hindus tell to account for the name of their temple, which left to itself would suggest an aboriginal origin—a suggestion they reject with scorn.

The early days of the shrine of Baijnath, like all else in this land of vague traditions and unwritten history, is shrouded in obscurity. The first of the twenty-two temples that now form the glory of Deoghar is said to have been built by one Raghanandan Jha under the auspices of Raja Poornu Mul, ancestor of the Maharajas of Gidhour. In the hands of the latter the famous shrine remained until it was usurped by the Raja of Birbhum, who conquered the whole of the territory belonging to the Gidhour family in the neighbourhood of Baijnath. To the Rajas of Birbhum it was a source of no inconsiderable profit. Making an arrangement with the chief priest by which they left him a six-anna share of all the offerings at the shrine, they appropriated the rest after defraying the expenses of certain of the great festivals. In the days when the English Government first began to make its presence felt in the land the fame of the temple was at its height. No less than from fifty to a hundred thousand pilgrims were estimated to visit it every year, and impelled by religious fervour their offerings were large and generous. Mr. Keating, the first English

Collector of Birbhum, taking over the temple tax with the rest of the fiscal administration, thought to improve returns still further by more direct control. It was a strange part for the newly installed British Government to play—that of tax gatherer at a Hindu shrine—but it was only one of many unexpected rôles that circumstances in those early days forced upon it. In 1788, under Mr. Keating's order, Mr. Hesilrigge, his assistant, who was probably the first Englishman to visit the Holy City, set out to supervise personally the collection of the pilgrims' offerings and dues. He found peculation and dishonesty rife, the priests secreting what they could and defrauding the Government of its fixed share. Before leaving the Holy City he established a more complete system of tax gathering whereby he hoped that the pilgrims might not escape payment of their dues, and the priests render a full and true account of all that passed into their hands. But the zeal of the officials received a check when it was found that these arrangements, so far from increasing the revenue, had surprisingly diminished it. In 1789 fifty thousand pilgrims found their way to the shrine, yet the amount of the offerings was returned at only 430*l.* Resenting the direct interference of the unbeliever in orthodox affairs, the priests set themselves to bribe the men of their own race who had been left in charge and secure the pilgrims' offerings before they reached the temple itself, where the taxgatherers waited. Receipts fell to an alarming extent, and Mr. Keating determined to visit the Holy City himself to exert his personal influence to secure better returns. Attended by a guard of sepoys, necessary in travelling the eighty miles of wild forest country that lay between Suri and Deoghar, he reached the city in February 1791. His official letters on the subject give a vivid picture of the conditions of the pilgrimage a hundred years ago. It was one beset with dangers from the outset, and the constant flow of pilgrims that no amount of hardships and perils by the way could daunt speaks volumes for the sincerity of belief and the hold that Hinduism then had over its votaries. Through wild unprotected country, without roads, across hilly ranges and by narrow passes where dacoits awaited them, the timid pilgrim from the plains had perforce to make his way before his eyes might rest upon the City of God. But even as he finally surmounted the perils of the way and approached his goal troubles of another kind beset him. The servants of the unbeliever guarded the gates to see that none escaped the toll, and that each made offering according to his rank, and so it behoved the priests, if they would gather in a rich harvest of their own, to send emissaries along the road to meet the pilgrims while as yet the hard-earned savings that they carried in their waist-cloths remained untouched. Thus it often happened that the unfortunate pilgrim, even after escaping from the perils of the way, found himself fleeced at the very approach to the Holy City itself, arriving there penniless and destitute, without even the fee to gain admission to the court of the temple where Siva dwelt—the end and goal of all his journey. Mr. Keating, camping just outside the city, could not fail to perceive the reason of the falling off in the receipts. Only the richest among the pilgrims—and the rich were few—could come through the dangers that beset the way with anything of value to offer at the shrine. There was but one small door that gave admittance to the temples, and none without the necessary offering might pass within. Thousands who had successfully overcome the hardships of the road failed at the last when they stood before the inflexible door-keeper, who sternly demanded what was due, and upon whose ears the most piteous tales of distress fell all unheeded. Truly, rough was the path and narrow the way that led to the City of God. It was a pathetic sight; even to the stern unbending official mind of the Collector, who had come with the express object of increasing the offerings, it made a strong appeal. For more than a mile all round the city lay a vast encampment of pilgrims, unsheltered from the elements save for the flimsiest of coverings—a blanket supported by four sticks or a rough roof of bamboos and dried grass. Everywhere the signs of direst poverty were evident. The priests owned all the surrounding cultivated lands, and prices ruled high. They were fortunate who had the wherewithal to buy the bare necessaries of life and secure as well admittance to the temple. That they should go back into the world of everyday life penniless and empty of all the worldly goods with which they had set out could be endured with fortitude, if so be that they had been allowed to worship Siva in the holy place.

But hopeless as Mr. Keating recognised it to be to expect further offerings from the pilgrims, who were already leaving all that they had behind them at the shrine, it was possible to increase Government's share of the profits by preventing the obvious sharp practices of the priests. The Collector had come out to increase the revenue, and he was not the man to retire without having made every effort. Before he left the Holy City he had practically surrounded it with an armed band of men whose business it was to see that the offerings of the pilgrims were openly made, and not secreted by the priests. One hundred and twenty policemen with fifteen officers were placed in charge of the temple, and thus a new danger was added to those that already beset the worshippers of Baijnath. Soon something like a state of terror reigned in the Holy City. Difficulties by the way and exactions on the part of the priests had not affected the enthusiasm of the pilgrims; but when they found an armed band surrounding the temple, not always without suspicion of peculation itself, demanding from them all that they possessed, even to the last pice, the constant stream of worshippers began at length to waver. Only fifteen thousand braved the troubles of the way in 1791; and though no less than 860*l*. was extorted from them, it was only too evident that nothing but a further decrease in the number of pilgrims could be expected in succeeding years. Even Mr. Keating was at last convinced and forced to abandon his policy of direct interference. John Shore, then Senior Member of the Board of Revenue, and Lord Cornwallis both disapproved of trading on Hindu superstition and of the apparent sanction the collection of the tax at the door gave to the worship of the temple. Consequently, in 1791, an arrangement was arrived at with the priests whereby they farmed out the revenue of the temple, paying a fixed sum in return. In the immediate neighbourhood they owned no less than thirty-two villages, and the tax which was assessed

PRIEST ABOUT TO SACRIFICE TO MAHADEO

upon them was nominally a tax for these lands, though in reality for the shrine itself. Thus Government retired from its anomalous position as a co-sharer with a Hindu god and his priests in the offerings of the faithful among his worshippers.

When handing over the full control of the temple to the high priest, Ramdut Jha, Government showed itself strangely solicitous for the proper performance of its worship and for the protection of the worshippers whom it had so lately helped to plunder. The high priest was enjoined to see that worship was duly performed according to the Shastras; that the temples were kept in order and repair; that neither the Dwaries and Musrifs nor any of his subordinates should at any time make demands or levy duty upon the pilgrims as formerly; that nothing whatever in the shape of a tax should be exacted from them save what they should offer of their own free will; that he should keep an account of the receipts and disbursements of the temple and file the same whenever called upon to do so by Government; that the poor, the lame, and the blind and persons afflicted with disease should be fed daily at the expense of the temple; and finally that disobedience to any of these conditions should render the high priest liable to any order that Government might think fit to pass against him.

But though Government had given up direct control of the temple there were continual disputes to occupy the attention of the local authorities. The office of Ojha, or high priest, had practically become hereditary in one family, but there was a strict rule that no leper and no man under forty years of age could occupy that high position. Poornanund, the son of Ramdut Ojha, was a leper, and he being of necessity passed over a struggle ensued between his younger brother and his eldest son. For many years a bitter dispute raged between the claimants and among the priests their partisans, and though Isserinund Dut Jha, the grandson of Poornanund, the leper, finally succeeded, a large and influential party refused to acknowledge his headship of the temple. In 1860 Mr. Braddon, Assistant Commissioner,[1] was inquiring into the quarrel which threatened to destroy the prestige of the shrine. He found that to such a pass had things come that the temple itself had been attached for debt, and fourteen villages had been sold in execution of a decree. Only one bright spot occurs in his report: 'As regards the lame, halt, blind, and indigent receiving supplies,' he writes, 'I must give the present Ojha all credit for the manner in which he has acted in this matter, he having agreed that the distribution

[1] Afterwards Sir Edward Braddon, K.C.M.G., Premier of Tasmania.

of this dole shall be made in my presence and under my superintendence. The daily allowance to all such deserving objects is now given out, and the enemies of the Ojha are at least disarmed in this one of their allegations.'

The list of attendants who were needed for the service of the temple is a long one, and their offices doubtless gave unlimited opportunities for petty exactions and extortions. At the head of them were the Musrifs, who worshipped the idol in the absence of the Ojha and collected the presents offered at the shrine. The Dwaries performed the duties of porters, and their pay, like that of the Musrifs, was one rupee a day. The Daroga was a private servant of the Ojha supervising generally the affairs of the temple. The Punbhuras prepared the food for the idol and the priests; the Phooldareas supplied flowers for the worship and garlands for the worshippers; the Chandanwalas prepared perfumes and sweet-smelling spices. The four Ghareewalas kept the time and struck the gongs every hour day and night. The Dewan kept the accounts of all the receipts and expenses of the temple, while the Bhandary kept the keys of the Tosakhana. Besides these, to complete the list, were the four Shikdars, who sacrificed the goats that the pilgrims offered, and the two Napits, who shaved the heads of those who thus performed their vows. The Koondoopras, who cleaned the drains, and the Jharoowalas, who swept the courtyard, occupied a position apart, the lowest in the temple household.

Changed as it is from the scene depicted in these old records of the past, the divine city is still worthy of a pilgrimage to-day. Everywhere the twentieth century has laid its desecrating hand. Much of the glamour of romance that once surrounded the temples of Baijnath is gone, and the fervent belief that raised them has passed away. Yet even time and change have failed to obliterate entirely the memories of their glorious early days when the fervour of religious zeal filled the courts with a throng of eager worshippers, in whom the true spirit of devotion burned, loading the shrine of the great god Siva with a wealth of offerings of the best that India could boast. To-day a throng of pilgrims still wends its way towards the Holy City, but it is not the same throng as of old. No longer dangers by the way, miles of rugged country to be traversed on foot, dacoits in the mountain passes, or wild beasts lurking in the dense jungle by the wayside beset the pilgrim who ventures forth to worship at the shrine of Siva. Now the railway lands the worshipper at the very gates of the Holy City. The one thing needful is a sufficiency of cash to purchase a third-class return ticket, and that obtained the pilgrim need fear no danger by the way. Train after train lands its freight load of pilgrims at the shrine, bearing them away again with a minimum of trouble and fatigue when their brief spell of worship in the holy place has been performed. It is this facility of coming and going that has revolutionised the whole character of the pilgrimage. To-day no fervent religious enthusiasm is needed to bring the worshipper from some far-off city of Upper India to the sacred shrine as in days gone by. Then it was a pilgrimage in stern reality that nothing but a spirit of true belief or deep-rooted superstition could induce a man to undertake. Now it has degenerated into something of a holiday affair easily and quickly undertaken with the smallest amount of trouble and expense. The new spirit is everywhere apparent. The fervour and enthusiasm that scorned personal ease and comfort and the faith that overcame the perils of the way are gone. They are unnecessary adjuncts of the pilgrimage of to-day. A third-class return ticket has supplied their place and carries them with greater security and much less trouble to the goal of their desire.

But once within the Holy City and wending one's way along the narrow streets towards the temple something of the old glamour of the pilgrimage returns. Outwardly here at least the passing years have left but little in the way of change. The same huge pillars of rock that have frowned gallows-like for centuries upon the ceaseless stream of pilgrims at the entrance to the city still confront the pilgrim of to-day, mystic, inscrutable, the origin and meaning whereof no man knows. A solid masonry platform, six feet high and twenty feet square, supports two huge monoliths of gneiss rock, they in turn supporting a third horizontal beam similar in form and size. Quadrilateral, each face two feet six, giving a circumference of ten feet and standing twelve feet high, they form a striking monument, the mystery that surrounds their origin and the manner in which such huge blocks of solid stone could have been raised into position in those far-off days adding their touch of awe and interest, though to-day their effect is sadly marred by the growth of houses all round that hem them in on every side save one. Known to the present generation as the Dole Manch, the pilgrim to Baijnath offers a prayer before them in passing as he hurries on to the more famous shrine beyond.

Up along the narrowing street the pilgrim passes to the small temple by the roadside where Siva is supposed to have first found a home, and where Baiju Bhil, coming to desecrate his shrine, found favour in the eyes of the deity and gave to the temple his name. But the glory and importance of this earliest of the temples of Baijnath have waned and the worshipper passes on to the famous group of temples in which all interest now resides. The approach that leads to them is nowise impressive or inspiring. Through all the dust and heat of the bazaar with its intensely worldly associations and busy life, distracting the attention from higher things, the pilgrim must needs force his way jostled by the buyer, the seller, and the money-changer, each keenly intent upon mundane affairs and sharp set to best his neighbour. It is a thriving mart, for the flow of worshippers never ceases, bringing much custom to the shops innumerable that line the route. The merchants display their wares, each like his neighbour, with uncompromising sameness in open baskets level with the ground or raised on rough-made stalls. Grain of all kinds, a heap of bright-red chillies, and a large earthen jar of curds, for which the town is famous, make up the sum total of each one's stock in trade, with perchance a tray of sweetmeats, rolled betel-nut, or cheap cigarettes (ten a penny) in coloured cardboard packets, looking strangely modern and out of place, to tempt the casual passer-by. All is stir and life—the life of a thousand other eastern bazaars with no outward sign that this is the Holy City made sacred through long centuries as the dwelling-place of Siva.

Suddenly in the midst of the busy mart, in one of the narrowest, dirtiest streets, one comes upon the low archway that gives access to the temples. Narrow in truth is the way that leadeth into the holy place. Yet through that door only on this side is access to be gained by the worshipper, and beneath the archway has passed the countless throng of pilgrims who have visited the temples through all the centuries of their existence, the rough stoneway beneath worn smooth by the passing of a myriad bare and reverent feet.

Inside, facing the entrance, stands the chief temple of Siva himself, joined to the temple of Gouri Sankar his wife across the courtyard by long festoons of gaudy coloured cloth typifying the union of the god and goddess. It is somewhat disappointing—this temple of the great god whose fame has gone so far abroad. There is little in its outward aspect, first glimpse as it is of the inner place of the Holy City that catches the eye on entering the courtyard, to inspire the worshipper. Its imposing front is marred by its very solidity, giving it a touch of sombreness and gloom, while its narrow door affords but the faintest glimpse within the darkened holy of holies, where Siva the seven-headed reigns, dimly discernible a vague black shape, raised on a huge stone slab whereon the flickering earthen lamps at his feet, replenished night and day by his attendant priests and burning perpetually before him, throw their uncertain light. From within come the droning voices of the priests, chanting their *mantras* of praise and worship to the deity, the pilgrims passing continually within to place their offerings before the shrine. Gouri Sankar across the courtyard opposite, though the wife of Siva, meets with less respect, for her temple is one of the latest of all, and the imagination turns from her to the god himself installed in the ancient temple, the building of which has long since passed out of the memory of man.

But it is at the back of the temple of Siva that the centre of human interest lies for the visitor to Baijnath. Here is the especial place of prayer where gather those among the pilgrims who greatly and fervently desire some gift of the gods. Every part of the long verandah is covered by the prostrate forms of worshippers, each full length on the ground wrapped from head to foot in a linen cloth, as in a winding-sheet, motionless like mummies, dead for a space to all the life and interest of the outside world. Hour after hour they lie deep in prayer and meditation, rousing themselves but once in the day to drink the water from the sacred river Ganges, and the sparest of fare brought them by the priests. Stretched there, packed close together row on row, they unite a marvellous diversity of aims and interests, of hopes and aspirations. Here, each hidden from sight by the linen shroud, lie the leper, the halt, the maimed, and the blind, and those afflicted with disease—a piteous crowd remaining on from day to day in the hope that the gods may yet have pity and grant the boon so earnestly desired. And to those who stay long, brooding day after day on the greatness of the gods and their own passionate desires, it may be that the healing of faith comes, for many are said and believed to have gone forth cured from this threshold of the gods.

Others there are who have come, not on account of sickness or disease, but simply to lay the burden of a great desire before the gods. Just coming away, her time of vigil ended, is a woman already past her first youth, and a wife of many years who, for long days and nights, prostrate on the temple floor, has wrestled in prayer for the son so long desired, and so long withheld. Her face is alight with the expectation of joy fulfilled, for even that very hour on the twentieth day of her prayer and fasting, as she lay asleep on the stone-paved verandah, she had seen a vision, and the great god Siva himself had placed a male child in her outstretched supplicating hands. With a cry of joy she had awoke and risen up from the still praying crowd, for her prayer had been answered by the gods. And as she moves off gladly to take her place again in the life of every day, one can but hope that disillusion may not follow, and that a Greater than the god in whom she trusted may fulfil the vision and give to her her heart's desire. Still others there are among the recumbent worshippers who have come, not to pray for themselves, but for those whom they hold dear. Chief among them is a wealthy raja, shorn now of his purple and fine linen, and clothed in a common white *dhoti*, praying in anguish of soul for the one son of his house so long desired, and now when granted so grievously afflicted—for the child has been blind from its birth. The son of another suppliant is a leper, claimed by that most terrible of all diseases; while yet another prays for the son, sick unto death of a sickness that has baffled many physicians, and which a weary round of pilgrimages has failed to cure. With such as these is the place of prayer filled continually even to its utmost limits, for the world of Hinduism is very full of the desires of the sick and sorrowful.

Round the huge courtyard in an irregular square lie the remaining temples. First on the right of Gouri Sankar stands Manik Chuk with its diamond-shaped ornamentation, large and massive, the temple of Anand Koirab, another name for Siva, adjoining it and completing the first of the four sides of the square. Next to it, commencing the second side, is the temple of Ram and Lachman, finer than the rest, with pillared verandah and shining black gods dimly visible in the dark recess beyond. This is one of the most popular of shrines where the worshipper goes to the god of joy to crave the special blessing that he can bestow. Opposite, apart by itself, stands the small octagonal temple sacred to the Ganges wherein a tiny stream of water welling up from beneath the stones never fails of its supply. Close by is the temple of Bujla Debi, the militant goddess, who gives victory to such as call upon her; while beyond, completing the second side of the square, are the temples of Surj Narain and Sarsati, the goddess of learning, much frequented in these latter days of many examinations, over which she presides, awarding success or failure according to her will.

On the third side lie the temples of Matsa, goddess of snakes, small, narrow, iron-barred with nought but fear and the desire of propitiation to attract the worshipper; of Hunuman, bedaubed with red and surrounded by a heap of shapeless black stones, reminiscent of the days when the priests demanded an offering for each god, and a new stone was added as the need for offerings grew with their rapacity; of Kuber, god of wealth, most popular of shrines, where earnest supplications from sharp-faced keen-witted men of the world never fail; and of Kal Boreat, the god of destruction, much to be feared and zealously propitiated, represented only by a black stone beneath pillared arches, crowned with red garlands by the worshippers. Beyond is the huge bell presented by the Maharaja of Nepal fifty years ago, its deep tones reverberating across the courtyard through the temples every hour of the day and night. Then in order come the temples of Gaȝatri, mother of the Vedas, of Siva again under the name of Nilkunt, and of Lachman Narain, the god and goddess of wealth, with its square-cut towers surmounted by wheels and tripods. Further on again is the temple of Anopȧrna, the goddess who bestows rice upon the worshippers by deigning to protect their crops, and her shrine never fails of prayers and offerings from among the poorest of the pilgrims, with whom almost everything in life depends upon the success or failure of the harvest. Last of all the temple of Kali, goddess of destruction, completes the square, bringing one again to the shrine of Gouri Sankar opposite the temple of Siva.

It is an interesting round, guided by the high priest's son and attended by a crowd of Brahmins, priests and pilgrims, each putting in his word of comment, boast, or explanation. But one is loth to leave without a sight of the high priest himself who rules with undisputed sway over Baijnath and all who come and go within its sacred precincts. The son pleads his father's age and illness in excuse, but with many a complimentary turn of phrase offers to go and see if he is well enough to come and receive the visitor as he would most assuredly wish to do. Taking a survey of the busy courtyard as one waits for his return, one cannot but fail to be struck by the general air of neglect and sloth that has settled over all. Truly 'Ichabod' is writ large over the temples of Baijnath. The brilliant afternoon sun shining aslant across the courtyard and gradually lengthening the shadows of dome and minaret on its white stone pavement but serves to reveal the dreariness that has fallen like a pall over the Holy City. Unswept, ungarnished, each temple shows by its very uncared-for look that the enthusiasm of its worshippers has waned. The flowers that careless hands have dropped before the shrine are but swept aside in a rotting decaying heap close by to make room for others, as carelessly thrown, withered and shrivelled already from the touch of hot hands and the midday heat. The gaudy tinsel trappings wound about the shapeless stones or crude presentments of gods have

THE HIGH PRIEST OF DEOGHAR

long since lost their freshness, exhibiting all the piteousness of tawdry finery soiled. The strings of coloured flags that join the temples of Baijnath and Parbati, draggled and faded from long exposure to sun and wind and rain, hang drooping and dejected with all the depressing air of once festive decorations that have survived their day. The cattle stray at will about the courtyard, unmolested in and out among the crowd; the goats, less fortunate and immune, awaiting their turn to furnish forth the sacrifice, tied to a row of posts at the side of Siva's temple. But to the Eastern mind there is nothing of desecration in these things, and here at least cleanliness has not yet attained a place in close proximity to godliness.

But the high priest's son returns bringing his father's message. It is with great regret that he is unable to come himself as he would desire, but if the visitor would come to him, then, in the courtly Persian phrase, will he and his father's house be honoured indeed. Across the courtyard through a maze of narrow passages and corridors one passes, still escorted by a group of interested spectators, until at last with an unexpected turn of the way one comes upon the smallest of rooms where the high priest spends his days. At one end sit cross-legged on the floor the usual attendants, some writing, some reading from the sacred books, others silently engaged in the contemplation to which their religion and their inclination alike exhort. Facing the door and waiting to receive his guest sits the high priest himself cross-legged but raised from the ground on the lowest and broadest of modern footstools. Smiling with gracious courtly gesture, he welcomes the visitor, and the first glimpse of this venerable priest, with the unmistakable look of dignity, refinement, and intelligence in his face, comes with sudden contrast and relief after the sadness that the departure of its old-time glory from Baijnath has impressed upon the mind. Here in this tiny room, at the back of the temples, one finds at last something higher and above the sordidness, the carelessness, and the worldliness that are the prevailing features of the Holy City of to-day. There is a charm of old-world courtliness about the high priest Shree Sailajananda Ojha that contrasts strangely with the bustling, eager, worldly spirit of twentieth-century Deoghar. The look of sympathy and understanding, the refinement and culture, the soul that has made some escape from things of the earth and finds expression in dignity of countenance—these sought for through all the temples of Baijnath have been found to-day only in their high priest, himself but a survival of a day that is past. Weighted by years and crippled with rheumatism, the ills of the flesh have not dimmed in his eyes the light of other things: they have perchance but deepened the spirituality and kindliness and sympathy that illuminate his face. It is small wonder that even the most ignorant of worshippers admitted to his presence feels that this is holy ground, and reverently takes the shoes from off his feet. He is the embodiment of the old religion in its strength, its fulness, and its enthusiasm; but one looks around in vain to-day among the younger generation for even one to carry on as faithfully the old traditions. The spirit of a great faith is burning low and the old beliefs are fast losing their grasp in the light of modern knowledge. Only the forms and symbols and the worship perfunctorily performed remain. For the revival of the Hindu faith the twentieth century offers but little hope. Yet rapidly the light is failing and the darkness of scepticism and unbelief is falling round the temples of Baijnath and such as they throughout the land. Changes such as Hinduism has not experienced for ages cannot fail to come with the succeeding years. But whither the period of doubt and darkness will lead the countless throng of pilgrims that still by force of custom wends its way towards the Holy City, no man can foretell. The gods of stone sit helpless, ignorant that the enthusiasm of their worshippers is waning fast, and powerless to recall them from their backsliding.

Their day of greatness has for ever passed, and for them the future holds no prospect. But for the worshippers it may be that the darkness that is falling is but the darkness that precedes the dawn, and that from the ruins of the old religion may arise another and more perfect faith that shall accomplish yet greater things than those once in days gone by inspired by the gods who have so long ruled over the Holy City.

APPENDICES

I

AUGUSTUS CLEVELAND

Singularly little information is to be obtained concerning Augustus Cleveland apart from his work in India. I am indebted for many of the following facts to Mr. William Foster, of the India Office.

Cleveland was the son of John and Sarah Cleveland, and was born on September 19, 1754, being baptised at St. Martin-in-the-Fields on October 16 of the same year. In the baptismal certificate the name is spelt Clevland, and the same spelling is observed in his petition to the East India Company, but he was generally known throughout his Indian career as Cleveland. He was appointed a Writer for Bengal on November 16, 1770, upon the nomination of a director named Frederick Pigou. His securities were John Cleveland, of Savile Row, and Lewis Ginguer, of Fulham, Esquires, the former probably being his father. He is said to have been a cousin of Sir John Shore, afterwards Lord Teignmouth, which might account for his choosing the Company's service as a career. My efforts to obtain a portrait of Cleveland have been unsuccessful, and have led me to believe that none exists. When the India Office, Whitehall, was built, the list of persons to be commemorated by relief portraits included his name, but another was finally substituted for his on the ground, I believe, that no likeness could be obtained to work from.

With the help of a manuscript list of services of Bengal civilians in the India Office, the following brief summary of Cleveland's Indian career has been compiled :—

1771. July 22, arrived in India as Writer.
1772. Assistant in Select Committee Office.
1773. Assistant to the Collector at Rajmahal.
1776. Factor and Assistant at Bhagalpur.
1779. Collector of Bhagalpur.
1782. Also Judge of the Adawlat.
Died January 13, 1784.

II

THE SANTAL SEPTS AND SUBSEPTS

The Santals were originally, according to popular tradition, divided into twelve septs, of which eleven only remain, one having entirely disappeared. Each sept, again, is divided into subsepts, of which the number is supposed to be twelve, though a glance at the following list, for many of the names of subsepts in which I am indebted to the Rev. Dr. Campbell, of Pokhuria, will show that the number varies considerably.

Sept Kisku. Subsepts Nij Kisku, Gaṛh Kisku, Ok' Kisku, Obor Kisku, Manjhi khil Kisku, Naeke khil Kisku, Son Kisku, Aḍ Kisku, Badaṛ Kisku, Biṭol Kisku, Sada Kisku, Paṭi Kisku, Jabe Kisku, Ṭika Kisku, and Katwa Kisku.

Sept Hȧsdak'. Subsepts Nij Hȧsdak', Cil Bindha Hȧsdak', Boḍoar or Bonḍwar Hȧsdak', Keḍwar Hȧsdak', Jihu Hȧsdak', Kuhi Hȧsdak', Sada Hȧsdak', Obor Hȧsdak', Kȧṛȧ gujia Hȧsdak', Kahu Hȧsdak', Sȧk Hȧsdak', Naeke khil Hȧsdak', Rok' lutur Hȧsdak', Bedwar Hȧsdak', and Kunda Hȧsdak'.

Sept Murmu. Subsepts Nij Murmu, Sada Murmu, Obor Murmu, Manjhi khil Murmu, Naeke khil Murmu, Bitol Murmu, Garh Murmu, Badaṛ Murmu, Ok' Murmu, Lat' Murmu, Jihu Murmu, Ṭika or Tilok Murmu, Kuḍam Murmu, Gajar Murmu, Copiar Murmu, Ponḍ Murmu,

Boara Murmu, Handi Murmu, Kolha Murmu, Ṭuṭi Sarjom Murmu, Samak' San Murmu, Oara Murmu, Munḍa Murmu, Jugi Murmu, Kaḍa Murmu, Turku lumam Murmu, Sau Murmu, and Powar Murmu.

Sept Hembrom. Subsepts Nij Hembrom, Manjhi khil Hembrom, Naeke khil Hembrom, Sada Hembrom, Biṭol Hembrom, Gua Hembrom, Gua soren Hembrom, Obor Hembrom, Badaṛ Hembrom, Gaṛh Hembrom, Hanḍi Hembrom, Sole Hembrom, Ṭhakur Hembrom, Lat' Hembrom, Datela Hembrom, and Kuâri Hembrom.

Sept Marnḍi. Subsepts Nij Marnḍi, Goda Marnḍi, Manjhi khil Marnḍi, Naeke khil Marnḍi, Rot Marnḍi, Rok' lutur Marnḍi, Obor Marnḍi, Biṭol Marnḍi, Sidup' Marnḍi, Jugi Marnḍi, Kaḍa Marnḍi, Khara Marnḍi, Garh Marnḍi, Kulkhi Marnḍi, Turku lumam Marnḍi, Sada Marnḍi, Khanḍa jogao Marnḍi, Ṭika Marnḍi, Ponḍ Marnḍi, Keḍwar Marnḍi, Buru beret' Marnḍi, Khanḍa Marnḍi, Babṛê Marnḍi, Rupa Marnḍi, Jonok' Marnḍi, Miru Marnḍi, and Bhoso Marnḍi.

Sept Soren. Subsepts Nij Soren, Sidup' Soren, Sada Soren, Jugi Soren, Manjhi khil Soren, Naeke khil Soren, Biṭol Soren, Ok' Soren, Manḍa or Badaṛ Soren, Mal Soren, Jihu Soren, Sâk Soren, Baṛchi Soren, Sada Sidup' Soren, Ponḍ Soren, Khanḍa Soren, Obor Soren, Mâṛ Soren, Cehel Soren, Datela Soren, Rok' lutur Soren, Gua Soren, and Turku lumam Soren.

Sept Ṭuḍu. Subsepts Nij Ṭuḍu, Cigi Ṭuḍu, Lat' Ṭuḍu, Manjhi khil Ṭuḍu, Naeke khil Ṭuḍu, Sada Ṭuḍu, Gaṛh Ṭuḍu, Jugi Ṭuḍu, Dâtela Ṭuḍu, Ok' Ṭuḍu, Biṭol Ṭuḍu, Obor Ṭuḍu, Baske Ṭuḍu, Tilok Ṭuḍu, Babṛê Ṭuḍu, Curuc' Ṭuḍu, Kuḍam Ṭuḍu, Bhokta Ṭuḍu, and Kharhara Ṭuḍu.

Sept Baske. Subsepts Nij Baske, Manjhi khil

Baske, Naeke khil Baske, Biṭol Baske, Lat' Baske, Kuhi Baske, Ok' Baske, Munḍu Baske, Obor Baske, Bindaṛ Baske, Sada Baske, Keḍwar Baske, Jihu Baske, Saru gaḍa Baske, Bhiḍi Baske, Suṛe Baske, and Hende Baske.

Sept Besra. Subsepts Nij Besra, Manjhi khil Besra, Naeke khil Besra, Kuhi Besra, Son Besra, Bindaṛ Besra, Gaṛh Besra, Tilok Besra, Biṭol Besra, Lat' Besra, Baske Besra, Ok' Besra, Obor Besra, and Kahu Besra.

INDEX

Abdul Rasul Khan, Cleveland's Sazawal and successor, 114; his conduct suspected by Government, 116; his thirty-four years' rule, and death, 117

Adams, Major, his victory at Udhanala, 48, 287

Agmahal, another name of Rajmahal, 46

Akbar the Great, 42

Ali Verdi Khan, last great Nawab of Bengal, 52

Ambar, Pargana, claims to be included in Daman-i-koh, 108–9; a Brahmin temporality, 129–130; included in Santal Parganas, 212

Anoparna, temple of, 335

Assam, Santal emigration to, 218

Bagdi caste, 20

Baha Purab, a Santal Festival, 270

Baijnath, temples of, Chap. XI.

Baiju Bhil, legend of, at Deoghar, 315–7

Bara Dwari, Paharia deity, 297–8

Barhait, 4; Santal rebellion at, 188; execution of rebel leaders at, 206

Barkop, a *tappa* of Mainhari, 59

Bausi, headquarters of 32nd N.I., 232; loyalty of troops there during Mutiny, 233

Bedo Gosain, Sun God of the Paharias, 297

Behar, adjoining Santal Parganas, 2, 6, 12, 47; Company becomes Dewan of, 55; Fateh Khan, Governor of, 286

Belpâtta, included in Daman-i-koh, 108–9, 124–5; restored to Birbhum, 126–7; included in Santal Parganas, 212

Bengal, 2, 6, 12; under Hindu kings, 35–7; conquest of, by Musulman invaders, 37–8; independent Musulman kingdom of, 38–42; reconquest of, by Akbar's generals, 42–8; condition of, at the coming of the British, 53–4

Bhagalpur, Collector of, 17; Cleveland Collector of, 78–80; dacoity on Ganges near, 85; Daman-i-koh transferred to, 86; Commander-in-Chief visits, 93; Hill archers commanded by Collector of, 95–7; memorials of Cleveland at, 110–2

Bhagalpur Hill Rangers, raised by Cleveland, 94–5; Lieut. Shaw appointed Adjutant, 97; their duties, 98; self-government by means of their own Court, 99–100; constitution of the Hill Assembly, 101–2; military activity of, 102–3; during the Rebellion, 197; their victory at Sangrampur, 204–5; disbanded after the Mutiny, 98

Bhuinhar Ghatwals of Deoghar, 239

Bhuiyas, a Dravidian tribe, 12;

calling themselves Hindus, 20; found sovereignties of Lachmipur and Passi, 41; invasion of, 237; as Ghatwals under Rajas of Birbhum, and subsequently under British Government, 238-9

Bidji of Titoria, Sardar, 104; hanged by order of the first Hill Assembly, 107-8

Birbhum, adjoining Santal Parganas, 6; magistrate's report of, 202; portion of, included in Santal Paganas, 211; Pathan Raj of, 212; Santals in, 230; creation of Ghatwals by Rajas of, 238-9; temples of Deoghar under Rajas of, 317; Mr. Keating first Collector of, 317; action of Collector with regard to Deoghar temples, 318-23

Bird, Brigadier-General, engaged in subduing Santal rebellion, 206

Black Hole of Calcutta sealed the fate of Musulman rule in Bengal, 48

Braddon, Mr. Edward, Assistant Commissioner in Santal Parganas, 213, 324

Brahmini River, forms portion of boundary of Daman-i-koh, 129-30

Brahmins, hostility of Santals to, 20; Pargana Ambar a Brahmin temporality, 129-30; Brahmin Ghatwali, 239; priests of Deoghar, the Holy City, Chap. XI.

British Government, relations with Paharias, 9-10; first representatives of, 15-8; firmly established in Bengal, 50-7; in the Rajmahal Hills, 59-77; demarcates the Daman-i-koh, 119-32; admits Santals within the Daman-i-koh, 158; surprised by Santal rebellion, 193; adopts measure of reform, 207-9; forms Santal Parganas, 211; administration of revenues of Deoghar temples, 317-323

Brooke, Capt., raised corps of Light Infantry, 72-4

Browne, Capt., in command of Light Infantry corps, 74; his scheme for reducing the Paharias to order, 75-7

Burmese War, occupies Government's attention, 119

Burney, Colonel, in command at Bausi during the Mutiny, 232

CAMPBELL, Sir George, Lieut.-Governor of Bengal, passes Act XXIX. of 1871, 122; redresses Santals' grievances, 226-7

Census of 1872, disquiet among the Santals during, 228-9; number of Santals returned in, 230

Chae Champa, where Santals enjoyed their greatest prosperity, 146-9

Chalnad, a Paharia deity, 298-9

Chamar, a semi-Hinduised caste, 20

Chandra of Pupat, hanged by order of the first Hill Assembly, 107

Chanida Gosain, a Paharia deity, 299-301

Chhata Purab, a Santal festival, 280-1

'Chilmili,' the Paharias' name for Cleveland, 28

Chota Nagpore, adjoins Santal Parganas, 1, 2; in many ways resembles them, 6, 12; the home of many aboriginal tribes, 41; Santals in, 161

Chowkidar, his duties, 215

Christianity, progress of, 20-1; educational work of missionaries, 219-220; rumours concerning, during census of 1872, 229

Church Missionary Society, its work in Santal Parganas, 219-20

Churuk Puja, a Hindu festival, 271

Cleveland, Augustus, his work, 9,

16, 28, 78–112; Appendix I., 341–2
Clive, Lord, his victory at Plassy, 55
Colgong Hills, 123–4
Collector of Bhagalpur, 17; duties of, 78–80, 86, 117, 128; of Birbhum, 318–23
Commissionership of Bhagalpur, Santal Parganas under, 212–3
Cooper, Lieut., in command at Deoghar, 232; murdered by mutineers, 233–4
Cornwallis, Lord, his disapproval of temple tax, 322
Corps of Light Infantry raised by Capt. Brooke, 72–3; Capt. Browne in command, 74–7

DACCA, capital of Bengal, 47
Daman-i-koh, the 'Skirts of the Hills,' 9–11; transferred to Bhagalpur, 86; Cleveland's pacific measures with regard to, 87–100; withdrawn from ordinary jurisdiction, 101; under Abdul Rasul Khan, 114–8; Mr. Ward appointed to demarcate, 119–29; change made by Resumption Commissioner, 130; Mr. James Pontet superintendent of, 158; settlement of Santals in, 159, 164
Damuda, the sacred river of the Santals, 157, 285
Dasahara Festival, 64
Daud Khan, last Afghan ruler in Bengal, 42
Demano, duties of, 296–7; funeral ceremonies of, 307–9
Deoghar, its similarity to Behar, 6, 12; Bhuiya invasion of, 41; sub-division of Santal Parganas, 237; the Holy City of, 311–40
Deputy Commissioner of Santal Parganas, Hon. Ashley Eden first to hold office, 212–3; pacifies the Santals, 225
Des Manjhi, assistant to the Jogmanjhi, 221
Dihri, the master of the hunt, 272–4
Divorce among the Paharias, 305–6
Dravidian race, Paharias belong to, 7, 25; Bhuiyas, 12; Oraons, 28–31
Dumka, headquarters of the Santal Parganas, 235; during the Mutiny, 231–3
Durga Puja Festival, celebrated by Santals during rebellion, 202

EDEN, Hon. Ashley, first deputy Commissioner of Santal Parganas, 212–3
Erok Sim Festival, 278–9

FAGAN, Capt., in command of Hill Rangers during Santal rebellion, 197; his victory of Sangrampur, 204–5
Fakiruddin, Musulman viceroy, 88
Famine, the, of 1770, 65–9
Funeral ceremonies of Santals, 265; of Paharias, 307–9

GANGES, north-east boundary of Santal Parganas, 1–2, 7, 24; great highway of trade, 31–3; dacoities upon, by the Paharias, 83–4; sacred river of Hindus, 331
Gaur, 2; its rise, 35–6; decline, 37–8; last days, 39-45
Gazatri, temple of, 335
Ghatwals, 41; their position in Deoghar, 238–9
Gidhour, Maharajas of, 317
Girideh, coal-fields of, 218
Godda, loyal zemindars of, 85; C.M.S. Missions in, 219; subdivisional headquarters, 237
Gosai Era, Santal goddess, 258
Gouri Sankar, temple of, 330–2
Greek geographers, 23–4
Gumo Gosain, Paharia deity, 298

Haradata, the Santal legend, 144
Hariar Sim Festival, 279
Harwood, Mr. William, first supervisor of Rajmahal, 56
Hasdak sept, special festival of, 281; its subsepts, 342
Hendue, dependent *tappa* of Manihari, 59
Hihiri in Santal legend, 144
Hill archers, the. *See under* Bhagalpur Hill Rangers
Hill Assembly, the, formed by Cleveland, 100; its functions, 101-2; its first sitting, 104-8; its meetings regulated by Reg. I. of 1796, 114; its falling away after Cleveland's death, 115-6; Reg. I. of 1796 repealed by Reg. I. of 1827, 121-2
Hindus, their influence upon aboriginal tribes, 11-22, 20-1; their place in Paharia legend, 26; their supremacy in Bengal under the kings, 35-6; fall of their power, 37; hostility of Santals towards, 161-2; their oppression of the Santals, 164-85; their Holy City of Deoghar, 311-40
Hiranpur, C.M.S. Mission at, 219
Home Mission, Santal, 219
Hughli Fort, storming of, 236

Irregulars, 5th, Mutiny of, 231-3
Isserinund Dut Jha, Ojha of Deoghar temples, 324

Jagannath, temple of, 37
Jagir or service tenures, 61
Jaher Than, Sacred Grove of Santals, 257-8, 279
Jarvis, Major Vincent, in command of first troops sent to quell Santal rebellion, 193-4
Jatra Festival, 261-3
Jaura, Manjhi, of Tatakpara, 107
Jherria coal-fields, 218
Jogmanjhi, duties of, 221; at marriage festivals, 266

Kaist, Hindu caste, 289
Katauri, semi-Hinduised tribe, 11; Chieftainship of Manihari, 211-2; in Deoghar, 287-8
Keating, Mr., Collector of Birbhum, takes over control of Deoghar temples, 317; endeavours to raise revenue from them, 318-9; visits Deoghar, 320-1; finally settles temple question, 322-3
Khaira, Rajput house of, 289
Kharakpur, overrun by Bhuiya invasion, 41; Pathan Raj of, 212
Kharwars, their place in Paharia legend, 26
Khojkaman, 144
Kiratis figure in Paharia legend, 27
Kolarian race, the, 27; Santals, the advance guard of the, 41
Kudam Naeke, Santal priest, 221, 258
Kuron, Ghatwal of, 289

Lachman, temple of, 334
Lachmipur, Bhuiya sovereignty of, 41
Lakshman Sen, King of Bengal, 37
Lloyd, General, in command during Santal rebellion, 195-206

Madho Singh figures in Santal legends, 150-5
Mahananda River, 38
Mahrattas, the, advance of, 52
Mahua crop, importance of, 225
Malin Budhi, 134-6
Mals. *See under* Paharias
Manbhum, settlement of Santals in, 157; present large number of Santals in, 230
Mandar, the Mount Maleus of the Greek geographers, 23-4
Manihari, nominal supremacy of, 59; demarcation of Daman-i-

koh begun in, 123; Katauri chieftainship of, 211–2
Man-im-Khan, Akbar's general, victorious invasion of Bengal, 42; succumbs to pestilence in Gaur, 43–5
Manjhi, the position of among Paharias, 59–60; their annual agreement with zemindars of the plains, 60–3; massacre of, by zemindars, 64; their revenge, 69–71; Cleveland's measures with regard to, 86–93; enrolled among Hill Archers, 94–9; compose Hill Assembly, 100–8; Regulation I. of 1827, 121–2; duties of, among the Santals, 220–2; grievances of, 225–6; engaged in census, 229; their part in the Sohrae, 251; in the National Hunt, 275–6
Manjhi Than, the Santal village meeting-place, 184–5, 247–9
Man Singh succeeds Man-im-Khan, 45; transfers capital to Rajmahal, 46, 286
Marang Buru, the Great Spirit of the Santals, 134; the first two human beings placed under his care, 139–44; worshipped in the Sacred Grove, 258
Marriage customs among Santals, 263–9; among Paharias, 302–5
Midnapore, Santal migration to, 156; present large numbers settled in, 230
Miran, son of Nawab Mir Jafar, 287
Mir Jumla, Aurungzeeb's general, 286
Mir Kissim, Nawab, defeat of, 48, 287
Moraroi, seat of discontent in 1871, 225
Moreko Turuiko, Santal deities, 258
Murshedabad, Musulman capital, 2–3; adjoins Santal Parganas, 6; death of Surajah Dowlah at, 48; corrupt Court of, 54
Musulman Empire, rise of, in Bengal, 37–8; its independence of central authority, 38–42; reconquest of Akbar's general, 42–6; fall of, 47–9
Musulmans, still numerous in Rajmahal, 12–3; their place in Paharia legend, 26; their annual agreement with the Paharias, 60–3; their massacre of Paharia headmen, 64; Paharias' revenge, 69–71; their oppression of the Santals, 168–78
Mutiny, the Sepoy, in the Santal Parganas, 231–4

Naeke, Santal village priest, 221; his part in the Sohrae, 258
Nageswarbagh, Mir Kasim's palace in Rajmahal, 48
Naiyas formerly Paharia priests, 296
Narainpur, zemindar of, 198
National hunt of the Santals, 272–8

Ojha, the, Village Witchfinder, 222; consulted at time of marriage, 264–6; the High Priest of the Deoghar temples, 324–6
Oraons, cognates of the Paharias, 28–31
Orissa, conquest of, by Man Singh, 285

Paharias, the, early settlement in Rajmahal Hills, 7–8; future of, 18–20; first mention of, by Greek geographers, 23–4; their legend of the origin of the race, 25–8; their independence maintained against Hindu and Musulman conqueror, 31–49; their relations with Musulmans, 57–71; their first meeting with the British, 72–3; Capt. Browne's scheme for reducing them to order, 74–7; Cleve-

land's efforts at conciliation, 86–93; enrolment of Hill Archers, 94–8; the Hill Assembly, 100–8; their veneration for Cleveland, 110–2; lapse into their old habits after his death, 118–6; Mr. Sutherland's report, 116–9; Mr. Ward appointed to demarcate the Daman-i-koh, 119–29; Paharias refuse to settle in the newly demarcated lands, 130–2
Pahn, the, Santal official, 168
Pak Don, the, a Santal dance, 260–1
Pakur, Brahmin house of, 212; sub-divisional headquarters, 237
Panchayat, village council, duties, of, 221–3
Pandua, former splendour of, 2; made seat of government of Fakiruddin, 38–9
Paramanik, the, duties of, 221
Pargana Bonga, Santal deity, 258
Parganait, the, 221–2; his part in the National Hunt, 275–6
Passi, Bhuiya sovereignty of, 41, 212
Pathan Raj of Birbhum, 212
Patna, the Prasii of, 24; Surajah Dowlah attempts to escape to, 48; news of Mutiny received from, 231
Patsanda, dependent *tappa* of Manihari, 59; included in Santal Parganas, 212
Pau Gosain, Paharia deity, 298–9
Pilchu Budhi, wife of Pilchu Haram, 139–44
Pilchu Haram, figures in Santal legend, 139–44
Pipihri, 144
Pirpainti, demarcation of Daman-i-koh begun near, 123
Pontet, Mr. James, appointed to settle the Daman-i-koh, 158; the difficulty of his task, 163–6; affection of Santals for, 192–3; metes out justice to Sidhu Manghi, 206; made scapegoat for official blunders after the rebellion, 208–9; his death, 210
Poornanund, son of Ramdut Ojha, a leper, 324
Poornu Mul, Raja, 317
Portuguese power, rise of, 47; decay of, 236
Pota Festival, Churuk Puja of the Hindus, 271
Prasii, the, of Patna, 24
Puri, temple of Jagannath at, 37

RABAN, King of Lonka, traditional founder of Deoghar, 318
Raghanandan Jha, said to have built first of Deoghar temples, 317
Rajmahal, Musulmans remain in, 13; seat of Government transferred there, 47–8; description of, 235–7
Rajmahal Hills, 3–4; the home of the Paharias, 7–8; early history of, 23–49; conditions in, on arrival of British, 59–71; first attached to Birbhum, 81–2; transferred to Bhagalpur, 86
Rajputs, Bhuiyas claim to be, 12, 239; rulers in Sultanabad, 34–5
Raksi, Paharia deity, 298
Ramdut Jha, high priest, given control of Deoghar temples, 323
Rampur Hat, railway station for Dumka, 235
Ranchi, Kherrias of, 29
Ranigunj, coal fields of, 218
Rannie, Lieut., extraordinary escape of, 233–4
Regulation, I. of 1796, 114–5; I. of 1827, 121–2; XXXVII. of 1855, 211; XXIX. of 1814, 238–9
Rohini, detachment of 5th Irregulars mutiny there, 231-2; Ghatwal of, 239
Rohtas, legendary home of the Oraons, 30
Ronald, Mr., Assistant-Commissioner, murdered by Sepoy mutineers, 234
Roshan Bakt, a Hindu Teli, 211
Rup Marayan Deo, zemindar of Chandwa, 34–5; 103

SACRED GROVE of the Santals, 257, 279
Sagarbhanga, a typical Santal village, 240-86
Sahebgunj, on the Ganges, 21
Sakrat Festival, 259-61
Sangrampur, Santals defeated at, 204-5
Sankara, petty state ruled by Tribhuban Singh included in Daman-i-koh, 108-9; and his son Sumar Singh, 124-6; cut off from the Daman-i-koh by Mr. Ward, 126-7; death of Sumar Singh, Raja of, 198
Santal Parganas, description of, 1-13; early history of the district, 23-49; settlement of Santals in, 157-68; formed as separate district, 211-4
Santals, their legendary origin and early wanderings, 133-56; admitted to the Daman-i-koh, 157-63; their grievances, 166-86; rebellion of, 187-206; grievances finally redressed, 207-16; emigration of, 217-8; Christianity among, 219-20; their village system, 220-3; later grievances redressed, 223-30; yearly round of festival and labour among, 240-86; legend of Baiju Bhil at Deoghar, 314-7
Santuk Manjhi, 215-6
Saont in Santal traditions, 156, 161
Sarath, Ghatwal of, 239
Sarbeswari, Rani of Sultanabad, 84-5; joins Paharias in raid and foray, 103
Sardars, divisional headmen among the Paharias, 59; their agreement with the zemindars, 60-3; treacherous murder of by zemindars, 64; their revenge, 65-71; attempts at conciliation of, by Capt. Browne, 74-7; by Cleveland, 87-92; form corps of Hill Archers, 94-9; and the Hill Assembly, 100-8
Sauria Maler, most primitive of all the Paharias, 287-8
Scott, Mr. David, settles Ghatwali estates in Deoghar, 238-9
Seru Monjhi, a leader in Santal rebellion, 202
Shaw, Lieut., first adjutant of Bhagalpur Hill Rangers, 97; leads them to their first victory, 102-4
Shore, Mr. John (Lord Teignmouth), his views on temple tax, 322
Sidhu Manjhi, a leader in Santal rebellion, 185-92; hanged at Barhait, 206
Siva, presiding deity of Deoghar temples, 311-40
'Skirts of the Hills,' the. *See* Daman-i-koh
Skrefsrud, Rev. Mr., his Santal Mission, 219-20
Sohrae, the, great Santal festival, 249-59
Somija Paharia tried by the Hill Assembly, 118
Sultan Suja restored Rajmahal, 236
Sultanabad, claims to be included in Daman-i-koh, 108-9; ruled by Rajput chiefs, 212; Sarbeswari Rani of, 84, 85, joins Paharia raid, 103
Sumar Singh, self-styled Raja of Sankara, 124-6; Sankara cut off from Daman-i-koh, 126-7; his death, 198
Sumarpul, a hill *tappa*, cut off from Daman-i-koh, 130
Surajah Dowlah attacks the English, 47-8, 63
Suri, headquarters station of Birbhum, 33-4; panic in, during Santal rebellion, 194-6; threatened by rebel Santals, 202-4
Sutherland, Mr. James, deputed to inquire into condition of affairs in Daman-i-koh, 116-7; his report, 117-9; contains first mention of Santals, 157

TALJHARI, C.M.S. Mission station, 219

Teliagharia Pass, Moghul invaders pass though, 37; its strategic importance, 46; the northern limit of the Santal Parganas, 211
Thakur, the supreme god of the Santals, 184–9; delegates his authority to Marang Buru, 257–8
Trial of luck, the, during the Sohrae, 255–7

UDHANALA, battle of, 48, 287
Usila, dependent *tappa* of Manihari, 59

VINDHYAN Hills, 8

WARD, the Hon. John Petty, appointed to demarcate the Daman-i-koh, 119; opposed to Cleveland's system, 120–2; arbitrarily demarcates Daman-i-koh, 128–9
Warren Hastings, his report on the state of Bengal, 53–4; Company stand forth as direct rulers of Bengal under his guidance, 55–7; his difficulties prevent any adoption of Cleveland's schemes, 91–2

YULE, Sir George, Commissioner of Bhagalpur, 218; creates Ghatwals in Deoghar, 239